The Warrior's Way – A Treatise on Military Ethics

Other Books By Richard A. Gabriel

Scipio Africanus: Rome's Greatest General (2007)

Muhammad: Islam's First Great General (2007)

Soldiers' Lives: Military Life in Antiquity (2006)

Jesus the Egyptian: The Origins of Christianity and the Psychology of Christ (2005)

Ancient Empires at War, 3 vols. (2005)

Subotai the Valiant: Genghis Khan's Greatest General (2004)

Lion of the Sun (2003)

The Military History of Ancient Israel (2003)

Great Armies of Antiquity (2002)

Sebastian's Cross (2002)

Gods of our Fathers: The Memory of Egypt in Judaism and Christianity (2001)

Warrior Pharaoh (2001)

Great Captains of Antiquity (2000)

Great Battles of Antiquity (1994)

A Short History of War: Evolution of Warfare and Weapons (1994)

History of Military Medicine: Ancient Times to the Middle Ages (1992)

History of Military Medicine: Renaissance to the Present (1992)

From Sumer to Rome: The Military Capabilities of Ancient Armies (1991)

The Culture of War: Invention and Early Development (1990)

The Painful Field: Psychiatric Dimensions of Modern War (1988)

No More Heroes: Madness and Psychiatry in War (1987)

The Last Centurion (French, 1987)

Military Psychiatry: A Comparative Perspective (1986)

Soviet Military Psychiatry (1986)

Military Incompetence: Why the US Military Doesn't Win (1985)

Operation Peace for Galilee: The Israeli-PLO War in Lebanon (1985)

The Antagonists: An Assessment of the Soviet and American Soldier (1984)

The Mind of the Soviet Fighting Man (1984)

Fighting Armies: NATO and the Warsaw Pact (1983)

Fighting Armies: Antagonists of the Middle East (1983)

Fighting Armies: Armies of the Third World (1983)

To Serve With Honor: A Treatise on Military Ethics (1982)

The New Red Legions: An Attitudinal Portrait of the Soviet Soldier (1980)

The New Red Legions: A Survey Data Sourcebook (1980)

Managers and Gladiators: Directions of Change in the Army (1978)

Crisis in Command: Mismanagement in the Army (1978)

Ethnic Groups in America (1978)

Program Evaluation: A Social Science Approach (1978)

The Ethnic Factor in the Urban Polity (1973)

The Environment: Critical Factors in Strategy Development (1973)

The Warrior's Way – A Treatise on Military Ethics

By

Richard A. Gabriel

Canadian Defence Academy Press
PO Box 17000 Stn Forces
Kingston, Ontario   K7K 7B4

Produced for the Canadian Defence Academy Press
by 17 Wing Winnipeg Publishing Office.
WPO30280

Library and Archives Canada Cataloguing in Publication

Gabriel, Richard A.
The warrior's way : a treatise on military ethics / Richard A. Gabriel.

Issued by Canadian Defence Academy.
Includes bibliographical references: p.
ISBN 978-0-662-46114-2 (bound).--ISBN 978-0-662-46115-9 (pbk.)
Cat. no.: D2-206/1-2007E (bound). -- Cat. no.: D2-206/2-2007E (pbk.)

1. Military ethics. 2. Soldiers--Professional ethics. I. Canadian
Defence Academy II. Title.

U22.G32 2007   174'.9355   C2007-980246-X

Printed in Canada.

1 3 5 7 9 10 8 6 4 2

In Memoriam

James Markham Lufkin
1919-2007

combat veteran, fighter pilot, intelligence officer, son, brother, father,
grandfather, great-grandfather, teacher, photographer, and writer

Here is your servant, Jim
Take him, Lord
But do not take him lightly

"'To be or not to be' is not the question. 'How to be and how not to be,' that is the essential question."

Rabbi Heschel

As Robert F. Kennedy lay dying on the floor with a bullet in his brain, he opened his eyes and spoke his last words. "Is everyone safe," he asked. "Does everyone have a place to hide.".......The answer is No!

R. Gabriel

"Honour is that natural and inherent standard of distinction of proper conduct in dealing with one's fellow-man, and is that quality which is essential to him who is, or intends to be, a leader of men in the profession of arms."

2nd Lt. James M. Lufkin
U.S. Army Air Corps
September, 1941

CONTENTS

FOREWORD

I am delighted to introduce *The Warrior's Way – A Treatise on Military Ethics*. This book represents yet another addition to the seminal Strategic Leadership Writing Project created by the Canadian Forces Leadership Institute (CFLI) and the Canadian Defence Academy (CDA) Press. This volume demonstrates our continuing commitment to capturing key themes and operational topics of importance for military personnel serving in the complex security environment of today.

With this in mind, no topic could be more germane than military ethics. The ambiguous, chaotic and complex operational missions of today demand the highest order of discipline and ethics. As such, *The Warrior's Way* provides an excellent treatise on military ethics to assist individuals in ensuring that they are, and remain, ethical soldiers, sailors and airmen/air women, particularly in the demanding asymmetrical and savage battlespace in which they often find themselves.

In closing, I wish to reiterate the importance of this book, as well as all others in the Strategic Leadership Writing Project series. They are produced to provide you with theoretical knowledge, as well as vicarious experience. They are designed to assist you to better prepare to lead and command in the demanding environment you will assuredly find yourself in. Our publications are also designed to allow military professionals to fill their own knowledge gap on their own time, as well as at their own speed. After all, professional development is both an institutional and personal responsibility.

At the Canadian Defence Academy we hope that our efforts at providing well-researched, relevant and authoritative books on key operational topics both enlightens and empowers those who serve in, and for those who interact with, the profession of arms in Canada.

Major-General J.P.Y.D. Gosselin
Commander, Canadian Defence Academy

PREFACE

The Canadian Forces Leadership Institute (CFLI) is proud to release another publication in its Strategic Leadership Writing Project under the auspices of the Canadian Defence Academy (CDA) Press. Our intention has always been to create a distinct Canadian body of operational leadership knowledge so that professional development centres, military personnel, civilian members of defence, scholars and the public at large could study the military profession, particularly within the Canadian context. However, frequently, we have attempted to solicit foreign viewpoints to provide the largest breadth of experience, knowledge and perspective. This volume, *The Warrior's Way – A Treatise on Military Ethics*, by renowned American scholar, and former infantry officer, Richard A. Gabriel, is one such example.

The Warrior's Way is a significant addition to CDA Press collection. It is an updated and revised version of the author's seminal 1982 work, *To Serve with Honor*. It is a powerful book that focuses on ethics within the military profession with the goal of identifying and clarifying those precepts, values and obligations that a military professional must recognize, understand, accept and observe, if they wish to be an ethical soldier. Although originally inspired by challenges the U.S. military faced in Vietnam, this updated and revised volume remains a seminal work on military ethics.

I believe you will find this book of great interest and value whether you are a military professional, a scholar or simply interested in the study of war and conflict. As always, we at CFLI and the CDA Press invite your comment and discussion.

Colonel Bernd Horn
Chairman
Canadian Defence Academy Press

AN IMPORTANT PURPOSE

To attempt a treatise* on military ethics and to suggest ways in which it may be understood and applied within the context of the profession of arms is the primary purpose of this book. One of its goals is to identify and clarify those precepts, values, and obligations that the military professional must recognize, understand, accept, and observe if he or she is to be an ethical soldier. The book attempts to provide a clear philosophical and practical basis for these precepts, values, and obligations. It is not sufficient that a soldier only observe the ethical values of the profession. To be an ethical soldier, to act ethically, and to exercise ethical judgment, the soldier must know *why* certain things are right and wrong, *why* he or she clings to certain values, and *why* he or she chooses to do one thing over another. In the complex societies that modern military professionals serve, the soldier must have firm ethical moorings. If not, the soldier risks being overwhelmed by the strong social, cultural, and organizational forces of the society that restrict the soldier's intellect and freedom, reducing the warrior to an instrumentality of another's will. Under these conditions, the soldier may seek to escape from ethical responsibility because it is too difficult to deal with, seeking safety in the command to follow orders, and will become a danger to himself/herself and to his/her profession. To prevent this, the military professional must be an ethical soldier.

A central challenge of military ethics is to identify those ethical precepts that constitute the central values of the military profession in a democratic society. We might reasonably call these central values the ethical code of the profession since all true professions have ethical codes. For reasons that will be clear later, the profession of arms is a profession unique among others. Suffice it to say here that an understanding of the military's ethics begins with the realization that the profession of arms is different from other social institutions. Its primary function requires organized social violence in which the sacrifice of its members in pursuit of the community's right to self-protection is often demanded. Moreover, it requires the deliberate taking of the lives of other human beings, and sometimes results in the deaths of completely innocent others, in the conduct of legitimate military operations. These activities involve grave questions of right and wrong that the soldier cannot legitimately escape merely by following

---

* A treatise is defined as a conceptually comprehensive and systematic treatment of an important subject.

orders. The soldier must understand that what he or she is asked to do is far more ethically burdensome than what any other social institution asks its members to do. Not surprisingly, then, the values that govern the actions of the soldier are different from those of other social institutions.

Some of the critical questions that need to be answered by a military profession within a democratic society include: Should the military, like all other true professions, possess a code of ethics? Can military ethics be taught or is it rather, as some would have it, that the ethics of the soldier is so thoroughly absorbed from the larger society that when a recruit enters the profession he or she brings ethical baggage from which there is no escape and which the profession must accept? If this is true, what are the implications for sustaining military professionalism and ethical behaviour within the profession itself? Are some Western democratic civilian values antithetical to those required for an effective military profession and, if so, what are the implications for the profession? To what degree can a military profession be separate from the society it serves without becoming a threat to it? Is there a set of values appropriate to military service that is inappropriate to civilian society and vice versa? What are the limits of the soldier's loyalty to the profession and to the state? When may or must the soldier refuse to obey one or the other? Have we confused loyalty with obedience, and then disguised this obedience and made it a virtue on the assumption that an unquestioning military that executes *all* orders of civilian authorities simply because they are civilians is less of a threat to the democratic state?

While the answers to these questions are always less than ideal in the pragmatic context in which they are likely to arise, the soldier can only attempt to answer them when they are understood within the context of those ethical values and obligations appropriate to the profession itself. The search for moral bearings must first be directed at the identification, definition, and clarification of those ethical precepts that ethically orient the soldier to the profession and the profession itself in the exercise of its critical functions in service to the democratic state. Of course, members of the military are no more or less ethical than those in other professions. It may be, however, that the task of the profession of arms is so different and the ethical responsibilities attendant to it are so burdensome that ethical standards that are acceptable by the larger democratic society, and even those of other professions, are simply insufficient to govern the behaviour of the military professional. Other, more exacting, and relevant standards may be needed, and they may only be able to arise from within the profession itself. Soldiers may be no more or less ethical than anyone else, but they often confront difficulties in dealing with ethical problems within the military environment that the members of other professions do not.

First, the soldier is likely to have received little training in recognizing ethical dilemmas. Many times a soldier simply does not perceive a problem in ethical terms or recognize the obvious ethical dimensions associated with it. In contrast, the medical and legal professions spend considerable time training their novices in the ethical responsibilities required of their professions, at the same time providing their practitioners with a clear code of values and conduct relative to the activities in which the profession is engaged.

Second, few soldiers are likely to have had any training in moral reasoning. It is often assumed in a democratic society that the ethics of the military are essentially the ethics of the larger society. If so, the means by which citizens recognize and resolve ethical difficulties are no different from those of the soldier. It is assumed further that the ethical values of the solider are forged within the civil society long before he or she enters the military and are virtually unchangeable. If this is so, then it makes little sense to speak of special training in moral reasoning for the soldier. The difficulty is that both assumptions are false. What the soldier is asked to do and the ethical problems he or she is likely to confront as a member of the profession of arms are likely to be starkly different from what is encountered by civilians, with the result that the soldier will require instruction in how to recognize and deal with these difficult ethical situations. Without training in ethical reasoning, a soldier will find it difficult to develop ethically acceptable solutions to ethical problems because he or she is not accustomed to reasoning in moral terms.

Third, the highly structured environment of the military profession can create soldiers with a propensity to resolve ethical dilemmas always in favour of the organization's imperatives. The soldier may adopt a tendency to carry out *all* orders, even if he or she has serious ethical reservations about them. But it is unrealistic to expect soldiers who have not been exposed to recognizing ethical problems and trained in ethical reasoning to do anything else but to resolve the ethical dilemmas in terms of the imperatives of the organization. Any other course based on ethical grounds but which runs contrary to the organization's norms forces the soldier into the solitude of being an ethical minority, perhaps even a minority of one, at odds with the profession in which he/she claims special membership. Unequipped to deal with ethical ambiguity, the soldier naturally does what is safest and most familiar.

In their attempts to produce an ethical soldier, the military professions of both old and new democracies, have not had an easy time of it. A number of larger socio-economic forces that have influenced the profession have made the task difficult. The shift in the standards of morality and permissiveness evident in democratic societies over the last fifty years, coupled with liberalization campaigns for greater individual rights, privileges, and cultural recognition within military establishments have created a number of challenges at all levels of command and leadership that make ethical instruction and training, to say nothing of enforcement of professional values, problematic. The rise of all-volunteer military establishments throughout the West has encouraged many to regard the military as but another occupation owed no more loyalty or sacrifice than one would expect to owe in a business corporation. There is often a general societal denial of any sort of higher expectation of discipline, hardship, and sacrifice that have historically been attendant to military service. If the military is not different, why, then, should its values or ethical challenges be any different? One important consequence of this civilianization of military service has been the introduction of managerial values and corporate entrepreneurialism into the profession, the adoption of values and practices drawn largely from the business corporation. Such values and practices tend to erode the values and practices that are at the root of the military profession, forcing many to choose between their roles as military professionals and managers.

Forces within the profession itself have sometimes worked against ethical clarity. The emphasis military institutions place on effectiveness, on getting things done, can lead to a perverse utilitarianism in which results eclipse all other considerations, including ethical ones. A "loyalty syndrome" emerges in which subordinates come to regard loyalty to superiors as an imperative to the point that unquestioning obedience to a superior's judgment or even carrying out unethical orders becomes perceived as one's duty. An excessive concern for the profession's public image can lead to a tendency to conceal embarrassing information which an informed public and elected representatives have a genuine right to know. Finally, it is hardly surprising that as military organizations began to imitate the values and practices of business organizations, the inordinate drive for success so characteristic of the successful business executive also became the model for the "successful" officer. All these are institutional conditions that serve to substitute bureaucratic procedures for ethical judgment and responsibility, undercutting the soldier's opportunity and ability to exercise ethical judgment. Choice is at the centre of ethics, and the only way to make a soldier ethical is to give him the opportunity to act ethically, and this involves the opportunity to act unethically as well.

It ought to go without saying that if military service is a profession, then, like all other professions, it has the primary obligation to set forth the values and obligations that are the conditions of membership and the obligations that govern the behaviour of its members. *The profession of arms must be the keeper of its own flame.* This has not been and will not be easy. Most military establishments have done little to foster a corps of teachers of ethics that can be called upon to design and teach courses in ethics. Teaching ethics must be done correctly and well. A badly taught ethics course can degenerate into "war stories" whose unfocused discussion will tend to confirm the persistent (but fundamentally wrong!) notion that ethical reasoning in military matters is both impractical and inconclusive. The lack of an established required curriculum in ethics in most military establishments has also made it difficult for the military to identify a coherent core of subjects importantly related to ethics.

For these reasons, officers and soldiers often have scant opportunity to be exposed to ethical debate and to acquire the skills necessary to ethical reasoning. Most soldiers lack a basic understanding of the fundamental terms, definitions, and concepts that are vital to making sense of an ethical universe. Fewer still have any knowledge of how to work through an ethical problem. The purpose of this book is to acquaint the soldier with some of the basic concepts, terms, and definitions of ethics and the rules of ethical thinking in the hope of providing the soldier with the knowledge required to make ethical choices in the harsh and the stressful circumstances in which we expect our officers and soldiers to do what is right.

UNDERSTANDING MILITARY ETHICS

I f soldiers are to be held responsible for conducting themselves in an ethical manner, they must understand the nature of military ethics as part of the general discipline of ethics. Since most members of the profession have little or no training in ethical reasoning, they are often unclear about what ethics is, the obligations it entails, and how to think their way through to solving ethical dilemmas. Even the requirement that soldiers observe the precepts of a code of professional ethics will have little meaning if they do not understand *why* certain values and precepts must be followed and others rejected. *It is sometimes thought that philosophy is the antithesis of pragmatic action, but no soldier can be expected to make pragmatic ethical decisions without an understanding of the philosophical foundations of those decisions.* Acting ethically within the profession of arms presupposes and requires that officers and soldiers grasp at least the rudimentary elements of what ethics is all about. This chapter attempts to provide an understanding of the nature of ethics *per se* and some of its more important elements as they apply to the military profession.

A Military Perspective

Military ethics forms the core values for a profession engaged in a very special task that sometimes requires the sacrifice of human life as well as the deliberate killing of other human beings. Given this role of the soldier, it is clear that some set of values is necessary to give a human and humane dimension to the soldier's onerous tasks and burdensome responsibilities. Without ethics, the soldier can easily slip into the moral morass of the value-free technician who applies his or her skills within an ethical vacuum simply because he or she is ordered to do so by a superior or the dictate of the state. The soldier can also lose sight of his or her special ethical obligations and come to regard their personal goals and needs as the sole determinants of right and wrong. In this case, the soldier falls into the trap of ethical egoism and becomes an entrepreneur who uses the position of special trust and confidence primarily to enhance his or her own career. Either road leads ultimately to ethical ruin, to say nothing of military ineffectiveness. Without a strong ethical compass, the soldier not only can become an indifferent destroyer of human life, but, under the stress of battle he or she may also collapse psychologically and lose sight of the reasons for doing what he or she is asked.

The military must operate within the context of the larger society it serves. However, members of the profession of arms must carve from that society an ethical space where the values of the profession itself are the predominant ethical influence on the actions of its members. The ethical precepts of a profession, which are expected to govern the actions of its members, are different from and even, in some instances, antithetical to some larger societal values. Democratic societies are highly role-differentiated. A soldier may be at the same time also a father or mother, a husband or a wife, a parent, a grandparent, a member of a church, a citizen, taxpayer, property-owner, or play a number of other roles, each with its own demands and responsibilities. The soldier must act within the context of several roles in different social settings. It would be foolish, then, to expect ethical precepts, even those central to the military profession, to operate successfully without taking cognizance of this social role differentiation. This differentiation, especially in modern, post-industrial societies, tends to be complex, fragmented, and compartmentalized, and it affects ethics in that standards of ethical behaviour apply differently to different roles and demand different ethical actions.

This is not to suggest that different social roles may ever condone or require unethical behaviour. Although members of a given profession may be expected to behave differently in their roles as professionals than they do in their other roles, it is clear that no professional ethic can ever condone evil. No ethical proposition can ever recommend an act that is evil in itself. *Professional ethics, then, means that soldiers are expected to observe the particular set of ethical precepts that are most relevant to the expected behaviour of members of the profession.* When ethics is regarded as a set of statements of obligation that one ought to observe in certain circumstances, then the circumstances in which one has to decide how to act and what constitutes ethical behaviour have very much to do with what those obligations are in the first place.

It is also clear that different professions require different precepts to guide ethical behaviour. *A list of precepts delineating what one ought to do as a military professional would differ significantly from a list of precepts of what one ought to do as a member of the medical or legal profession.* This implies that what one "ought to do" is strongly influenced by the profession in which one claims special membership. One of the primary characteristics of a profession is that it requires the observance of special values and behaviour not generally shared by the larger society or even by other professions. That is why the ethics of the soldier addresses the question of killing and that of the lawyer does not.

Ethics is, therefore, a *social* enterprise more concerned with what a soldier does (actions) than what he or she is (character), and inevitably concerns what one does or fails to do to another person or group or persons. Ethics always involves considerations of the *consequences* or effects of one's actions *upon other human beings as well as upon oneself.* One's *intentions* are also part of the ethical equation. But neither consequences nor intentions are, by themselves, sufficient to make an action ethical or unethical. Thus, a soldier may resort to torture in order to obtain information that he/she believes might save lives. In doing so, the soldier's intentions may be good, but the *means* chosen and the *consequences* of his/her action are not. *Ethics always involves a relationship between ends intended and means employed.* Both must be ethical for an act to be ethically acceptable.

Professional ethics is forged in and applies to social settings, and is not the invention of the individual but exists prior to the soldier's entry into the profession in much the same way as language exists prior to our learning it. The soldier acquires knowledge of the profession's ethics upon gaining membership in the profession. The soldier's continued membership and participation in the profession is predicated upon his or her continued observance of the profession's values and ethics. The profession itself has an obligation to preserve its values whenever its members fail to live up to them. Thus, ethics has social origins and functions, to guide individual and group behaviour according to the profession's stated values. Ethics always requires social sanctions, the most obvious being the expulsion from the profession of individuals who fail to observe its values. *Thus, ethics constitutes promises made in a social setting to observe certain values and behaviour in certain circumstances.*

None of this implies that ethics is comprised of purely relative standards or that ethics is purely "situational." It means rather that professional ethics is a human application of ethical standards to actions that are required by a profession so that these standards so applied come to define proper behaviour within a profession. The standards of ethical behaviour are rooted essentially in the social enterprise and specific dynamics of the profession itself. *Thus, different professions require different ethical obligations from their members, and the affirmation of ethical obligations by a profession represents an attempt to carve out a definite ethical space within which members of the profession must act in certain ways.* Military ethics, then, deals specifically with those values and rules of expected behaviour that are appropriate to actions taken within the military environment. Military ethics addresses the problem of living an ethical life within the context of the demands and obligations levied upon the membership of the profession by the profession itself.

It is important to understand that *military ethics is only one part of the soldier's larger ethical life, and that to be an ethical soldier is not equivalent to living an ethical life. The soldier is also subject to the ethical claims made upon him or her by the other social roles that he or she occupies.* When these different sets of obligations conflict, the soldier must choose between them. The manner in which the individual must decide which obligations to observe and which to ignore is the process of *ethical reasoning* and will be addressed later. Suffice it so say that the ability to make reasoned ethical judgments is vital to the soldier's ability to conduct himself or herself ethically within the military environment.

Ethics specifies obligations relative to the conditions under which they are expected to be observed, so that one cannot have an ethical obligation when the ability to observe it is not present. Thus, "ought implies can." Such obligations *may* have some absolute value, but this is not necessarily the case. What is clear is that an ethical precept can never condone what is intrinsically evil as such. Therefore that which is absolutely wrong in a larger ethical context, such as murdering children or intentionally shooting civilians, cannot be made ethically right simply because it occurs within the context of professional values. That is why a soldier may not ethically execute a wounded enemy soldier, even if ordered by a superior to do so.

Ethics and Human Nature

The ultimate source of ethics and morals in humans is our very nature expressed in terms of two innate capacities that make it possible for humans to develop and utilize ethical standards and judgments. These two capacities are our *social nature* and our *imagination*. Because human beings have an innate capacity for ethical and moral feeling and thinking, all human societies develop moral and ethical codes to govern and judge the behaviour of their members. The forms these take vary widely, however.

Humans are social creatures by nature, what Aristotle called "social animals," that live in complex social groups. Living in groups requires limits on individual behaviour in order to prevent harm to other individuals or to the group's survival. These limits tend, in humans anyway, to make themselves evident in codes of acceptable and unacceptable behaviour, with the latter normally punished by the group in some way. Even simple herd animals will drive a misbehaving individual from the group. Our very physiology as social creatures creates hard wiring in the brain allowing humans to make distinctions between individual desires (what we want to do) and group norms (what we cannot do if we wish to remain in the social group). Moreover, humans are a special kind of social animal. We are the only social primate carnivore on the planet, a combination of the social primate biology of apes and chimps and the more complex social behaviour of social carnivores like wolves and other pack animals. The social relations of social carnivores are characterized by highly complex restrictive social rules governing bonding, sexual access, the protection of the young, food sharing, territoriality, etc. that are mostly missing from social primates, a hint that our own ability to develop complex norms of behaviour is similarly innate to our human nature.

The roots of morality are found, therefore, in our social nature. Morality, from the Latin *mores* meaning custom or culture, is distinct from ethics, and can be defined as a code of culturally and historically conditioned norms that govern behaviour in a social group. Having evolved through culture and history, codes of social morality are more or less arbitrary statements of functional rules that a society has worked out for itself over time as a way of insuring its survival. *As such, the moral codes of a society have validity only within the society itself, and make no claim to any wider application beyond the society.* So, for example, in some societies women must cover their faces as a sign of modesty, while in others the uncovered face has no moral significance at all. This does not mean that moral codes are unimportant, only that they are limited in their application. It is clear that what is regarded as moral in one society can even be regarded as immoral in another as, for example, is the case with capital punishment. *This is why the morality of the soldier's society is, by itself, insufficient to govern his actions against soldiers of other societies in war.* Something else of a broader application is required. That something else is ethics.

Ethics is rooted in that unique capacity of human nature that is the imagination. The proper term for humans is *homo sapiens sapiensis* or "the man who knows and knows he knows." Two points are instructive. First, humans possess self-awareness and the ability to reason. But not only humans know things. Animals, too, know things, as when a lion "knows" that a certain scent is that of a gazelle. *But humans know that they know, and that is a crucial difference.* It is this knowledge that affords humans the ability to reflect upon and judge what we do as being right or wrong. But why would we want to do that? The answer is that we are social animals and live in complex social groups so that complete freedom to act on individual desires would be harmful to other members or to the group itself.

The ability to reflect and judge would not necessarily produce ethics or conscious norms unless there was some human ability to create standards against which the norms themselves could be measured. This capacity is found in the imagination. *The human imagination permits us to create visions of circumstances that do not yet exist. We call these mental constructions "oughts" or normative statements. An "ought" is really an "alternative moral vision" of circumstances that are preferable to circumstances that do exist.* Thus, if a soldier witnesses the execution of a civilian, he or she might say that one "ought" not to do that, that is, that one can imagine a circumstance in which the civilian was not executed and this would be preferable to the existing circumstances where the civilian is executed. Without the ability to create "oughts" in the human consciousness, there would be no means to assess the validity of moral codes as they vary widely and no means to create standards that apply beyond the various codes. The human imagination is infinite in the sense that it seems capable of imagining almost anything. *Accordingly, the ethical imagination can create ethical norms that transcend specific social norms (morality) and produce norms that are seen to apply to all humans (ethics), even those not members of a specific society.* In this way, ethics can be used to criticize morals. In short, without imagination, humans would not be much different from higher animals that can "know" what to do but cannot know "why" they do it and, therefore, are incapable of ethical reasoning. It is man's imagination that makes ethics possible.

Why do morals and ethics seem to often conflict? The answer is that they are different entities designed to address different situations. Moral social codes are designed to regulate individual behaviour within the social group which itself has been shaped by culture and historical experience. There is no claim that the morality of the group has value or applies beyond the group itself. Morals are a consequence of man's innate social tendencies. Ethics, on the other hand, *is a consequence of human imagination, which is by its nature universal in its capacities.* Accordingly, the norms or "oughts" or moral visions which it produces can transcend the experience of specific societies to consider norms which apply to *all* humans, to man as man not just to man as a member of this or that culture. The results are norms with a much broader scope of application. Only humans have the capacity for ethical behaviour, for only humans have an ethical imagination that can create "oughts" that transcend culture, history, and even themselves. (How does one explain the existence of religions if not in this way?) The signature activities of humanity, then, are ethical thinking, behaviour, and judgment. To deny the requirement for the soldier to consider ethics in determining his or her actions is, therefore, to deny the soldier's very humanity. To paraphrase Aristotle, a person who cannot think or act ethically is either a god or beast.

Basic Distinctions

Before turning to a consideration of military ethics, it is worthwhile to examine the subject of ethics in general because much of what can be said of ethics *per se* also applies to military ethics. And if one is going to think about ethics, there is no better guide to the subject than the thoughts of Socrates. In the *Crito*, Socrates lays down some basic distinctions which constitute points of departure for the discussion of ethics throughout this book. These are basic assumptions about the nature of ethics and clarify some of the difficulties attendant to understanding how ethics operates in a military environment.

In the *Crito*, Socrates says that ethical questions and decisions are best approached through the use of reason. Ethics applies only to humans, and what distinguishes humans from other creatures according to Socrates is the possession of an intellect. However one defines intellect, it is clear that humans commonly attribute to other humans a quality called reason, the ability to explain *why humans do what they do* as well as the *capability to make judgments* as to whether what they do is good or bad, right or wrong, ethical or unethical. When one is dealing with ethics, then, one is involved in the process of ethical reasoning. Ethics has to do with the power of humans to reason, and, as such, ethical questions are best approached through the use of reason and not emotions. We can, then, safely dismiss the claims of some modern psychologists that one can know what is ethical because "it feels right" or because "I know in my gut" what is right, or because one is "comfortable with" something.

Another important Socratic distinction is that one cannot find answers to ethical questions by simple reference to what others think. *The ethical person must remain the agent of his or her own fate, the master of their own ethical autonomy, and responsible for what they choose to do or fail to do in given circumstances.* The idea that a soldier was "only following orders" or that the soldier acted in a certain way because others did is *never* an acceptable mode of ethical reasoning. The soldiers at Abu Ghraib prison who tortured Iraqi prisoners cannot escape ethical responsibility because they were following orders or because everyone else was acting in the same way. Ethics requires that there be reasons why one ought to do some things and reasons why one ought not to do others. A soldier who acts without knowing these reasons and without understanding them cannot be said to be acting ethically even if he or she does the right thing. Such a soldier can only be said to be obeying a set of rules whose value and purpose he or she does not understand.

A fundamental principle that runs through virtually all treatments of ethics is that one ought to do what one ought to do and one ought never to do what one ought not to do. Put another way, ethical "oughts" take precedence over "oughts" that arise from social, prudential, aesthetic, and cultural considerations. While it appears that these two propositions are different sides of the same coin, they actually are not. Often, it is much easier to know what one ought *not* to do than to know what one ought to do. In complex ethical situations, one may not even be able to know if one has done the right thing until well after the fact. Moreover, doing the right thing is not always a comfort. One can easily imagine that the decision to terminate life support for a loved one, even if urged and supported by sound medical, legal, and religious counsel, is not likely to bring the person making the decision much comfort. It is the constant tension between having to do what is right and having not to do what is wrong that constitutes a central dynamic of ethical decision-making. The same tension drives home the fact that *ethical precepts are by nature prescriptive and proscriptive*, that they require some things and prohibit others. It is the task of the human being as moral agent, as it is the task of the soldier as a member of his profession, through the use of reason and ethical principles to decide and to understand why under a given set of circumstances he or she must do something or not do something.

Socrates identifies something called working ethics, which he defines as a pattern of ethical reasoning that helps the individual determine what he or she ought to do. This reasoning occurs with reference to certain general ethical precepts. One "concretizes" these general precepts by attempting to apply them in the specific circumstances in which one finds oneself. This almost always requires the individual to make choices about which obligations take precedence over others. *It is a fundamental fact of ethical life that any given ethical code may confront the individual with a choice among conflicting obligations.* Thus, a religiously observant soldier may find himself having to choose whether to fight in a war that his or her church has publically condemned as unjust. Socrates' point is that ethics has to do with using one's *reason* to choose what one ought to do in given circumstances. Reason is combined with prudential judgment to determine whether and how one's ethical obligations apply in particular circumstances.

At base, then, *ethics always involves choice and judgment.* As regards judgment, humans make two kinds of ethically related judgments: those about ethical obligations, that is about what one ought to do or ought not to do; and those about the ethical values, that is, about what things are to be seen as good or evil in themselves. Furthermore, ethical judgments apply not only to the person who makes them, but to others as well. *Our personal ethical judgments imply that the same judgments ought to be made by others confronted with the same circumstances. We do not only make judgments about how we should act, but also about how others should act.* What we reserve to ourselves ethically we may not deny to others; what we ethically permit for ourselves, we must permit for others as well. Thus, if we affirm that torturing prisoners is wrong, the fact that the enemy tortures prisoners does not permit us to escape ethical responsibility from doing so ourselves.

To be ethical, the soldier must realize that he or she is not only an actor in the ethical drama, but also a spectator, advisor, critic, and, ultimately, a judge. The professional ethics of any profession, certainly the profession of arms, must allow its members to perform all these roles. Although an ethical judgment is intensely personal in terms of the consequences for the individual making it, once it is made there is the clear implication that what a person may have done in particular circumstances is justified as appropriate for other persons to do in the same circumstances. In this way, all members of the profession become responsible for the actions of all other members. The actions of one affect all, and the actions of all affect one. Otherwise, professional ethics becomes little more than individual preferences, i.e., not ethics at all.

A Definition of Ethics

When talking about the meaning of ethics, at least two types of activity come to mind. First, ethics has to do with the way one thinks about ethical questions. Here ethics involves ethical reasoning and is a branch of philosophy that requires the mental application of knowledge about questions that arise in the mind of the actor concerning ethical dilemmas. More to the point of military ethics, however, is a view of ethics which sees at its core the observance and undertaking of ethical *actions*. By this, one means living up to the obligations and precepts expressed in a professional code of ethics and observing the obligation to make difficult choices when ethical obligations conflict. From this perspective, then, ethics has to do with the translation into human affairs of ethical precepts requiring or prohibiting certain actions.

In this view, ethics has to do with observing obligations and knowing why it is one observes them. It is worth pointing out again that mere compliance with specified precepts or obligations is not an ethical act unless one is aware that one is carrying out an obligation and knows why. At the very heart of the study of ethics are the concepts of obligation, responsibility, knowledge, ethical reasoning, judgment and, of course, the necessity to choose which obligations take precedence over others in circumstances where ethical precepts conflict.

A rough definition of ethics is the art of observing those obligations that are appropriate to a person's roles in the social order. *Military ethics can be defined as the art of observing those ethical obligations and precepts that are appropriate to the soldier's role within the profession of arms.* Membership in a profession is likely to present the individual, and certainly the soldier, with specific kinds of circumstantial difficulties in the application of ethical principles that inevitably must be taken into account in the ethical equation. Thus, it is unlikely that the lawyer or clergyman will ever face the question of having to destroy a building which the enemy has turned into a combat position and which also contains innocent civilians. Nor is it likely that the soldier will ever have to decide what information given him by a client may not be revealed even to a judge. In short, the circumstances in which ethical principles have to be applied are important elements in ethical action within a profession.

To be more precise, *ethics is defined as making choices between competing obligations when the circumstances in which the obligation must be carried out will not permit one to observe both.* Viewed in this way, ethics is a form of *promise keeping* rather than simply following rules. Making deliberate choices is at the centre of ethics, as is knowing *why* one has chosen one obligation over another. It is lack of understanding of this point that sometimes leads to a confusion of ethics with law, character, and religion. One of the oldest distinctions made by ethical thinkers is the difference between law and ethics. Law is the formal dictate of the state, which may or may not have an ethical content in any given case. Moreover, all laws bind the citizen equally, so that the individual is forbidden to choose what laws to obey and which ones not to obey. The freedom to choose that is central to ethics is absent in considerations of law. Accordingly, one cannot escape responsibility for an unethical act simply because the law has made the act legal. Saddam Hussein's genocidal attacks against the Kurds with chemical weapons that killed thousands were accompanied by all the procedures required to make the attacks legal under Iraqi law. The killing was legal, but it was not ethical.

Among the more frequent errors in thinking about ethics is to confuse ethics with the character of a person. Character addresses what the individual is or is not, that is, possessing or lacking certain virtues. Character says nothing, however, about what the person does, and ethics is always about what a person does or fails to do to another person. It is tempting, perhaps, to believe that a person of generally good character will automatically act in an ethical manner. But this is obviously not always the case. Thus, a soldier who is honest, courageous, and prompt may just as easily make the decision to torture a prisoner to obtain information as a soldier who is not. *People of good character are just as capable of making bad ethical choices as people of bad character are capable of making good ethical choices.* The old adage that, "the more he spoke of his honour, the faster we counted the spoons", carries sound advice.

The confusion of ethics with religion is, perhaps, more easy to understand since it often seems that some of our most basic ethical principles are drawn from religious sources. And that is true. But the difficulty arises when one attempts to explain *why* a principle like "thou shalt not kill" applies or does not in a given circumstance. The difficulty is rooted in the fact that religion can only offer *statements* of principles, not *reasons* why they ought to be followed. This is because religion is based upon faith in a set of propositions, which, by definition, are not susceptible to proof or disproof in the empirical world, whereas ethics relies on the unique human capability to reason to demonstrate why something is or is not right. As such, neither debate nor explanation about the existence or applicability of religious precepts can be conducted with someone outside the faith itself. How, for example, does the ethicist answer the claim by radical Muslims that God has willed that all apostates from the Islamic faith may be killed? It is certainly true that some basic ethical principles are identical to principles drawn from religious faith. But the *reasons* why these similar principles may or may not apply in given circumstances are surely not the same.

To say that law, character, and faith are not the same thing as ethics is not, of course, to say that these things are unimportant to our ethical lives. It is, however, to caution that law, character, and faith are often not very good guides to making ethical decisions. One is on much safer ground relying upon the application of human reason, although this, too, is hardly foolproof. As a simple rule, humans may never escape their responsibility for making ethical decisions by claiming that law, character, or faith takes priority over reason. History is full of racial and religious slaughters, often done in full compliance with the laws of the state by persons of strong faith and character that are terrible testaments to the need for this simple rule.

Obligations and Responsibility

C entral to any notion of professional ethics are the concepts of obligation and responsibility. There are all kinds of obligations, but the ones of particular concern to the soldier are ethical obligations. Ethical obligations acquire a special character insofar as they are recognized as involving grave questions of right and wrong. An obligation to be prompt, for example, is not regarded as possessing the same ethical gravity as insuring that one's troops are not squandered in combat. Ethics involves keeping promises, especially those promises perceived to be of some grave consequence when they are not kept. Not every obligation is an ethical one, and not every ethical obligation is of equal importance. Moreover, the weight of obligations change relative to the circumstances in which they must be observed. Thus, the obligation to come to the aid of another acquires greater ethical weight on the battlefield than it does in the schoolyard.

Obligations

Much of the confusion about military ethics stems from the failure to understand the nature of obligations and what they require. Obligations have to do with *voluntary actions*, not mere behaviour. If one focuses only upon behaviour, one falls into the behaviourist trap which considers the totality of human ethical action as evident only in behaviour. From this point of view, one is only what one does, and no distinctions are made among humans who act out of good intentions, bad intentions, tradition, habit, coercion, or blind fear. Observing obligations obviously involves something that goes beyond mere behaviour. Obligations involve voluntary human actions.

Voluntary actions imply the freedom to do otherwise, that is, they imply a certain freedom from overt coercion as well as from the more subtle coercion that may lurk in habit or tradition. Observance of an ethical precept out of habit or coercion is not really acting out of ethical obligation. *An act of ethical obligation implies the ability not to do what one ought to do.*

Obligations also imply the *ability to act*. A fundamental proposition of any ethical theory and the moral judgments that it makes about human action is summarized in the axiom "ought implies can." There can be no basis for judging actions as ethical or unethical when the ability to perform the action is absent. *Obligations are ethically binding only when it is reasonably possible to execute them.* If one is going to impose ethical obligations upon members of the military profession, the soldier must have the ability to carry them out.

Obligations are also concerned with the activities of reason. For fulfillment of an obligation to involve voluntary action, it must be based in that intellectual activity that we call reason. Accordingly, one must *consciously know* when one is obliged and when one is fulfilling an obligation. If an individual is not rationally aware that he or she has an obligation, then no obligation can be said to exist in any true ethical sense. This does not mean that the community or profession cannot impose sanctions on that person on the grounds that he or she *should* have reasonably known that an obligation existed. From the perspective of ethical judgment, however, it is difficult to argue that a soldier should be held responsible for not doing what he or she ought to have done when the person is reasonably unaware of what they should have done. This is one of the stronger arguments for the formulation of an ethical code for the military profession and for institutionalizing ethical training within it. Soldiers cannot reasonably be held responsible for obligations specific to the profession unless they are first made aware of them. A formalized code of military ethics is one of the surer ways of educating members of a profession of their ethical obligations, although it is not the only way.

The argument that obligation involves reason implies that a soldier must not only be aware that he or she is fulfilling an ethical obligation but also why they are fulfilling it. A soldier who complies with an ethical precept without knowing why it must be complied with is not truly carrying out an ethical obligation, but only exhibiting obedience. This raises an interesting point about ethical codes. If it is true that people have to know why they observe obligations, it is also true that they are not likely to develop reasons as to why they ought to comply until they develop and are aware of a code specifying a set of ethical precepts. Merely complying with an ethical code does not constitute ethical action. The soldier must understand that an obligation is present and that he or she must observe it because there are sound reasons for doing so.

An important element of obligation is choice among the available alternative actions. For an ethical obligation to truly be such requires that alternative claims upon the soldier be recognized and rejected in favour of observing the ethical precept. This necessity for choice not only implies the recognition of alternative claims expressed in terms of other obligations, but also recognizes that the presence of coercive forces may present the soldier with a serious dilemma. Thus, soldiers cannot ethically do some things even if they are threatened with punishment, coercion, and even loss of life. If, for example, one recognizes that intentionally killing children is evil in itself, then the soldier who is ordered to kill children under the penalty of punishment or even his/her own execution and does so is not acting ethically. If the soldier recognizes that the initial obligation not to kill children is what is binding in these circumstances, the fact that there is a coercive element operating in the ethical equation merely constitutes an alternative claim. If the soldier is to act ethically, he or she must reject the alternative claim and refuse to carry out the order to kill the children. If the soldier carries out that order, however, then the fact that there was an alternative claim in the form of a threat of punishment or even a threat to his/her own life does not remove the soldier's ethical responsibility.

The essence of ethical judgment and of observing ethical obligations also involves the recognition that the soldier may have to choose among competing obligations some or all of which, in the abstract, bind equally, that is, they are not mutually contradictory. There is, for example, no inherent contradiction between being a citizen and a soldier, but one cannot have an obligation to be both a pacifist and a soldier. When one obligation is clearly superior to another, the necessity for choice does not present much of a problem. For example, a soldier rushing to be on time for morning formation may ignore that obligation in order to aid a person injured in an auto accident that the soldier witnessed. A true ethical dilemma exists when a soldier is confronted with two equally compelling ethical obligations under circumstances that will not permit him or her to carry out both. In these circumstances the soldier must make an ethical judgment as to which obligation is more compelling using reason and the understanding in his or her own mind as to why one has chosen once course of action over another. To remove the element of choice from ethical decision making and to substitute obedience to orders or even to law is to detach ethics from voluntary human action, to transform all ethical issues into mere questions of who obeys whom, that is to say, into questions of power.

Grave ethical dilemmas do not usually constitute a source of constant concern for most individuals in most professions on a day-to-day basis, although they are likely to arise more frequently in the military. Ethical decisions are not concerned with trivialities, and rarely concern the routine operations of our lives where grave ethical issues are not raised very often. Moreover, the tendency for humans to construct highly complex, socially differentiated structures also removes the loci of decision-making for many of the serious issues of life, greatly reducing the ethical burden. *Not every disagreement involves an ethical issue and not every unclear course of action involves an ethical choice, nor is every refusal to comply with instructions necessarily based in ethical considerations.* In normal day-to-day activities, most people comply with existing standards and rules because they do not appear to them to raise ethical questions and, most often, do not. There is, of course, the danger that existing norms can institutionalize unethical practices or, at the extreme, degenerate into a "banality of evil." But for most people most of the time in relatively free societies, this is only a marginal risk.

On the other hand, observing obligations does not always mean taking action in compliance with the norms of a profession. If one imparts an ethical quality to the notion of obligation, the course of action chosen must be undertaken because it is believed to be ethically right. If so, an ethical course of action can be either to obey or disobey. One of the elements of ethical judgment is the willingness to make decisions among competing ethical claims when to observe one is to obviate the other. To raise the question of ethical obligation and choice is to be aware that the sword cuts in both directions. The soldier must be aware that while he or she has an obligation to observe the obligations of the profession, at some point they may well have an obligation to violate some professional precept because of other obligations by which they are bound. Thus, a solider may refuse to deploy with his/her unit to war because as a citizen he or she has come to the conclusion that the war itself is not just. The necessity for ethical choice is simply inescapable, even in military affairs.

How, then, do people acquire obligations, and how do they come to feel obligated? Obligations are acquired within a social environment and are closely bound up with the social process and conscious human action and behaviour are largely, though not completely, a product of social environments. Accordingly, the process of acquiring obligations and the way in which they become recognized as such may also be said to be a social process. Indeed, humans have some obligations to other humans simply as a result of being human and thus part of the human community, so in that sense are born with certain obligations. But a sense of *professional* ethics and its obligations can in no meaningful sense be said to be innate and is acquired voluntarily. The reason is that professional ethics seeks to identify specific obligations as they apply to the circumstances that are most likely to confront an ethical agent as he or she acts as a member of that profession. Since human beings as human beings are not members of any profession at birth but only become members later on, it is clear that the acquisition of obligations related to a profession requires membership in the profession. Hence, the inculcation of professional ethics to which the soldier is obligated is closely tied to the social process of group membership.

Since ethical judgments imply that one's own actions would be right for others in similar circumstances, it is also clear that the multiplicity of individuals involved in a group provides an important dimension to professional ethics, namely judging the actions of other members as ethically acceptable or unacceptable. Membership in a profession, therefore, implies that one will act in a certain way and confers expectations on the rest of the group. Specifically, membership in the military profession requires the soldier to act in ways relevant to the profession that are judged to be ethical by the other members of the profession. Membership in any profession implies and requires certain ways of acting, as well as a willingness to accept the standards of the group as a yardstick for judging those actions. Thus, people in the military are expected to act in different ways than lawyers, physicians or clergy. Furthermore, all are expected to have different priorities and values relevant to their ethical behaviour within their professions for the precise reason that the circumstances under which the soldier is expected to act and the kinds of ethical questions that are likely to arise will be different than for members of other professions. When one voluntarily joins a group, therefore, one is prepared to accept the obligations of membership in that group.

It is important to note that *the professional obligations which bind members of the profession to act ethically are acquired freely and by deliberate choice.* No one, after all, is required to become a member of any profession. Thus it is that over time, people assume a number of social roles and group memberships, many of their own free will. With each role or membership come expectations as to what constitutes right behaviour relative to that role. Figure 3.1 portrays in graphic form the multiplicity and complexity of social roles and group memberships that might be acquired by a soldier.

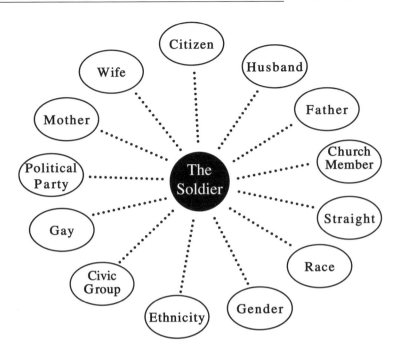

Figure 3.1 – Sources of Competing Ethical Obligations

While the soldier might place his/her professional affiliations at the centre of his or her ethical universe, it is readily apparent that the acquisition of other social relationships generates other ethical claims that must be considered. Thus, a soldier may also be at one and the same time a husband or wife, a father or mother, a sister or brother, a son or daughter, a parent, a grandparent, a member of a church, a citizen, a taxpayer, a home owner or renter, a voter, member of a political party, race or ethnicity, an officer or enlisted, etc.. Each of these social roles carries with it expectations of proper behaviour. In principle, none of these expectations conflict so that, for instance, there is nothing inherently contradictory between being a good soldier and being married or a member of a church. What is clear, however, is that the circumstances in which a soldier may be forced to act can easily raise conflicting ethical claims arising from the ethical expectations of the different roles he or she occupies. It is not difficult to imagine a soldier who refuses to fight on the grounds that his/her church has declared a war to be unjust, or that a soldier may resign from the profession of arms itself in order to care for an aging and helpless parent. In cases like these, the soldier is making an ethical judgment that one moral obligation is more important and more binding than another.

The assumption at the root of all ethics is that people ought to carry out their obligations when the circumstances permit them to do so. *Membership in any group implies expectations of behaviour because without such expectations any form of social organization would be immediately destroyed, and social life itself would be impossible.* No one, for example, would long remain in the banking business without the expectation that borrowers would repay their loans even though it may be to their financial interest not to. Nor would medical care amount to much if the patient could not trust the physician to be diligent in his/her practice. If the principle of ethical egoism, that people should do whatever they wish to further their own interests, were to be universally applied, then lying, cheating, betrayal, and treachery would become the norm of human activity. *There would then be no basis for social life at all; what would exist would be a war of all against all.*

The argument of the ethical egoist that individuals may do what they wish to further their own interests as they perceive them, that is, not to observe their obligations whenever it is inconvenient to do so, cannot be sound since the egoist cannot realistically countenance the same behaviour on the part of others with whom the egoist has to deal. To do so would be to negate any kind of social intercourse except conflict. The assumption of certain obligations by individuals and the relative assurance that they will be reciprocated at least to some degree rests at the foundation of any type of social organization. It most certainly rests at the very roots of the profession of arms. It is these expectations that come to constitute obligations. When these expectations are joined with the other characteristics of ethical behaviour, namely, reason, choice in the face of alternative claims, judgments of others' behaviour, and voluntary action, the observance of obligations in an ethical sense begins.

Since ethical obligations are strongly rooted in the social process, a soldier may therefore acquire several distinct sets of obligations derived from the various social roles that the soldier simultaneously occupies along with his or her membership in the profession of arms. In some situations, the soldier's obligations to one social group or role might conflict with his or her obligations derived from membership in another group. When this happens, the ethical dilemma surfaces and the soldier must choose which obligation will take precedence and know why it does so. This is the crux of ethical choice and making ethical judgments, and there is no certain way in which one moral obligation can be assessed *a priori* to be greater than another apart from the circumstances in which they must be observed.

Responsibility

Another important aspect of ethics is the fact that individuals can never escape responsibility for their ethical choices. One of the characteristics that distinguish humans from all other species is their ability to make conscious reasoned decisions about why they think things are right or wrong. In this sense, all human beings are ethical agents who are responsible for their actions and for their consequences. To abandon one's ethical judgment to another or even to subordinate that judgment to another is almost to cease to be human, that is, to become a tool of another's will. In defence of unethical action, the claim of absolute obedience to one's superiors can therefore never properly express the relationship of one human being to another.

Human beings always remain ethical agents responsible for their actions. This idea is firmly rooted in Western law and ethical tradition. Whether one looks to the Fifteenth century doctrine of *respondeat superior* ("let the superior be responsible"), or the notion of just war, or the more recent cases of the execution of General Yamashita for war crimes or the Nuremberg trials, it its clear that Western society has long held that soldiers cannot escape ethical responsibility for their actions by transferring that responsibility to others. As General Order # 100 of the United States Field Manual of 1863 put it, "Men who take up arms against another in public war do not cease on this account to be moral beings responsible to one another." Soldiers always remain ethically responsible for their actions, and are held to be ethically responsible for what they do precisely in terms of what they promise to do and not to do. Soldiers are responsible for observing the stated ethics of the military profession that they agreed to abide by when they entered upon special membership in the profession of arms. For the military, then, the soldier's ethical responsibility requires the specification by the profession itself of those ethical precepts that are most likely to apply within the military environment. *The caretakers of the profession must set the ethical standards of proper military behaviour being consciously aware of why the obligations bind as they do.* Soldiers who execute the precepts of the code without knowing why are engaged only in acts of obedience. Ethical actions involving judgment, choice, and responsibility are the antithesis of blind obedience. Members of the profession must understand that a sterile loyalty to a stated code is ethically meaningless unless the precepts are understood and its obligations undertaken willingly. One cannot avoid ethical responsibility by blindly observing a code.

All ethics, then, is prescriptive or proscriptive. As simple as this idea is, however, it is not without its opponents. In democratic societies where individualism is strong, it is often argued that teaching and inculcating ethical values does not involve the specification of precepts taken as obligations. Instead, it is assumed that the way to teach ethics is to offer a range of ethical perspectives to the individual and have him or her choose whatever perspective seems congenial. This is a view of ethics as descriptive rather than prescriptive. Perhaps in teaching general ethics, one can present a range of ethical perspectives as long as the purpose is only intellectual exercise and not the inculcation of ethical values. But if the goal is to establish a professional ethical perspective with a view toward having the individual soldier exemplify it, then one must specify what set of ethical precepts the profession prefers and provide the reasons why. This misunderstanding of ethics was acutely evident in the statement of one of the U.S. Naval Academy's commandants who described ethical instruction at the academy in the following terms. "They [the cadets] were exposed to several sets of ethics and morals. They could take their own and keep them or accept others. I didn't care what kind as long as they had a system of their own." The idea that teaching and inculcating ethics involves only the presentation of a number of ethical perspectives from which the individual may extract those precepts with which he or she feels comfortable is called *descriptive ethics* and is a contradiction in terms.

All ethics must either proscribe, i.e., dictate, that the individual not do certain things or prescribe, i.e., dictate, that he or she do certain things. It is precisely this binding quality, this sense of ethical imperative, which separates ethical obligations from descriptions of preferences. To think that an individual may pick and choose among a series of ethical perspectives simply because he or she is comfortable with them is to misunderstand the normative nature of ethics. This is especially so in the military profession which, with its stated obligations and responsibilities, is set apart from the larger society it serves. In general, if all perspectives of right and wrong are equally acceptable, then there is no basis at all for making ethical judgments. Specifically, what distinguishes professional ethics from general dissertations on ethics is precisely this prescriptive or proscriptive quality that imposes serious ethical obligations upon the individual.

The claim that one can inculcate ethics in the soldier by exposing him/her to a range of ethical perspectives and having him or her choose those precepts which are found acceptable to the individual implies, at the very least, that ethical obligations need not be specified by the profession itself, that is, that a code of ethical behaviour is not required to ensure that the soldier acts ethically. This is a curious application of the notion of free enterprise to the discipline of ethics. To suggest that the profession has no responsibility in this regard is to negate the very nature of the profession which, by definition, must posit as its reason for being a set of precepts, values, obligations, and responsibilities which apply directly to its membership and separate it from the larger society.

To deny the need for an ethical code for a profession is to assume that a collectivity of its members, officers and soldiers, whose ethical precepts are fundamentally personal ones, will somehow spontaneously generate a sense of ethics that is applicable and acceptable to the professional community as a whole. But precisely the opposite is true. It is possible to have a community ethic which can be used to integrate and socialize individual members to that ethic as the price of membership in the ethical community that is the profession. It is unrealistic, however, to attempt to produce an ethical community from a collection of individual ethical perspectives. *In this sense it is important that a profession not only have a shared purpose, but also possess a sense of shared values which are central to any definition of the shared purpose.* It is the values of a profession that define membership and govern the actions of its members.

Those who suggest that ethics cannot be taught or enforced in an organizational setting like the profession of arms because ethics in a highly personal concern are simply wrong. In point of fact, the ethics of a profession is not a highly personal concern. The ethics of a profession is a *community* concern. It is membership in the profession that lends a particular set of obligations their binding quality. Individuals who cannot accept the ethics of the profession must, therefore, remove themselves or be removed from it. It is a contradiction to suggest that the military profession will have no code of ethics and still remain a profession in any meaningful sense of the word, or, equally so, that the profession has a code of ethics from which members may freely select those precepts with which they agree while rejecting others. Both of these conditions negate the very essence of a profession.

Without a professional ethic, the soldier risks becoming an armed bureaucrat. One of the burdens of the military profession is a tendency of many outside the profession to confuse the profession of arms with a bureaucracy, and then complain that the military seems to have lost its ethical compass. Being a member of a profession is categorically different from being part of a bureaucratic apparatus. The rules are different, the ethical requirements are different, but most of all the degree to which judgment is required and the extent to which responsibility must be assumed are categorically different. The idea of the soldier as an "armed bureaucrat" is entirely contrary to the ethical concept of the profession of arms.

In the first place, the purpose of a bureaucracy is to routinize decision-making and to eliminate judgment, that is to administer rules as Max Weber noted "without respect to persons." The bureaucrat carries out rules formulated by others which the bureaucrat has little or no part in formulating. The bureaucrat is not asked to agree or disagree with the rules, only to execute them. The bureaucrat is not really engaged in ethical action, the voluntary carrying out of obligations, as much as he or she is engaged in behaviour, merely carrying out rules regardless of whether he or she understands why they are there. The fundamental task of the bureaucrat in practice is not to observe obligations, but to obey existing rules. In doing so, the scope of accountability is narrowed and the bureaucrat may escape legal responsibility, and hope to escape ethical responsibility, should anything go wrong. The defence in such circumstances is that the bureaucrat executed the rules required by existing regulations. Because the bureaucrat followed orders laid down by his superior, he or she would argue that they, not the bureaucrat, must bear responsibility. This was exactly the defence offered by Hitler's *Waffen SS* to escape responsibility for their crimes. It was also the defence offered by the American soldiers involved in the killing of civilians at My Lai in Vietnam and Haditha in Iraq. But again, the ethical soldier is not an armed bureaucrat.

It ought to be clear that the actions taken by bureaucrats are not at all what we generally mean by ethical action. Ethics involves judgment and promise-keeping instead of rule-following. Instead of the bureaucrat's rulebook, the soldier must have a code of ethics. The code itself is relatively general and the way its precepts will apply in any set of circumstances is often unclear and depends heavily upon the soldier's ethical judgment. However, while the bureaucrat is engaged in merely carrying out rules, the soldier cannot be permitted to engage in merely carrying out the code. *The generality of the profession's ethical code requires that the soldier understand the basis of the code's precepts so that the soldier must not only carry out the obligations of the profession, but must also know why he or she must do so.* The soldier, in short, must always exercise ethical judgment. The soldier is engaged in the rational action of discerning why one obligation binds more than another in a given set of circumstances, and why he or she must chose one obligation over another. Accordingly, the last refuge of the armed bureaucrat is to execute rules as a means of escaping both legal and ethical responsibility. *The soldier must always exercise ethical judgment and can never escape the legal and ethical responsibility for these judgments.*

If soldiers are to be held responsible for the ethics of the profession, then the profession's ethical code must provide three things. First, it must make soldiers capable of recognizing ethical dilemmas that may be involved in their actions and decisions. One cannot expect the soldier to make sound ethical decisions if he or she does not recognize the existence of an ethical problem in the first place. Second, soldiers must be taught how to reason through ethical questions by becoming adept at ethical reasoning. If a soldier does not understand why professional precepts are binding, it is unlikely that he or she will ever know how to apply them in changing circumstances. Third, the ability to recognize ethical dilemmas and reason one's way through them should force the soldier to clarify his or her own ethical values and obligations. All human beings must be responsible to their own consciences for what they believe to be right or wrong. For soldiers, there will often be instances in which their other obligations as human beings will conflict with the obligations acquired as members of the profession of arms. When these conflicts arise, grave ethical choices must sometimes be made. Choices between one's role in the military and other roles can be resolved only when the soldier understands his or her own values. Once again it must be stressed that membership in the profession of arms and observing its code do not constitute the sum of one's ethical being. Establishing standards of ethical action within the profession thus serves as a stimulus to identifying and understanding the soldier's other ethical obligations. In this sense, an ethical soldier is also an ethical human being.

Misconceptions About Ethics

D ifficulties in properly understanding ethics usually arise as a consequence of misunderstandings concerning some of the basic concepts, definitions, and distinctions upon which the discipline of ethics rests. One purpose of the foregoing chapters is to clarify some of these basic concepts and definitions. This said, there are those who believe that the establishment of a professional ethical code for the soldier is unworkable or even undesirable, and that any ethical values within the profession of arms that are not also widely evident in the civilian society at large either cannot be made to work or raise the spectre of praetorianism. This chapter identifies the major objections to the use of professional ethical codes and tries to answer them. For the most part, these objections seem to be based upon misconceptions about the nature of ethical obligations.

The first objection concerns the claim that ethics involves universal precepts. Such precepts are said to be fundamentally unworkable as guides to human action because no ethical code can specify *in advance* all the circumstances in which an ethical precept might apply. No ethical code can specify every situation to be covered by general precepts and so it is impossible to devise a code in which the precepts of the code never conflict. It is the very nature of life to be uncertain and there is no point to trying to reduce this uncertainty by prescribing behaviour in advance. This objection is not, however, sufficient to support the proposition that one cannot develop a working code of ethics, nor does it negate the value of an ethical code for a profession.

To argue that an ethical code is useless because it cannot specify in advance what ethical action ought to be taken in every possible circumstance is to confuse an ethical code with a body of law. It is the nature of laws to address *specific instances of behaviour* and to detail how one must behave in these circumstances in order not to be guilty of illegal behaviour. Ethical codes, on the other hand, set forth *general principles* as to what one ought to do. The important distinction between laws and ethical codes is that laws require obedience without any understanding as to why the law necessarily binds one to obey it. Ethics, by contrast, sets forth general principles about what one ought to do and requires that the individual know why the precepts constitute obligations. In addition, codes of ethics require the application of ethical judgment in order to decide *how* a precept might apply in given circumstances. Laws not only require no such judgment, they often prohibit it. No one may legally choose which laws to obey and which to ignore. Unlike ethical precepts, all laws bind equally regardless of circumstances. Laws are dictates of the state that may or may not have ethical content. Ethics by its very nature always addresses the ethical content of human action. It is in the very nature of ethics to set forth principles of action rather than to specify in advance how a precept will apply in different circumstances. Only ethical judgment with its attendant choice among alternatives and ultimately voluntary action can determine the application of ethical precepts.

The view that ethical precepts should spell out the specifics of ethical conduct in all circumstances is called *apodictic ethics*. An example of apodictic ethics is expressed in the Ten Commandments, the precepts of which are presumed to bind absolutely in all cases regardless of circumstances. But it is not difficult to imagine circumstances when they would not. Thus, the command "to honour thy father and mother" cannot possibly bind other children of a family if they are aware of circumstances of child abuse. The abused as well surely has no obligation to obey or honour parents in this situation. Another obligation, namely to promote one's own physical survival or to prevent another human being from being hurt, clearly takes precedence. The other children are obligated to report the abuse to the police. The crux of ethical deliberation is to choose one obligation over another when one cannot observe both. If it were possible to specify in advance all applications of an ethical precept, the need for ethical judgment would be eliminated altogether, as would any uncertainty in human affairs. Ethical judgment would be replaced by a handbook of rules or laws, once more confusing obligation with obedience and action with behaviour. As long as there is uncertainty in human affairs, ethics will be required to help guide moral action in difficult circumstances. Uncertainty in human actions is exactly what gives ethical precepts their meaning.

A second objection is that ethical codes are useless because some precepts may conflict in some circumstances and that codes do not provide guidelines as to which precept should be observed. To suggest that ethical codes are useless because some of their precepts may conflict in some circumstances is to misunderstand the nature of both obligation and ethical choice. With regard to conflicting precepts, there is a distinction between *prima facie* duties and actual duties. An actual duty is what an individual ought to do in a particular situation. A *prima facie* duty is what the individual ought to do if no other considerations interfere. A *prima facie* duty is what normally would be an actual duty if no other ethical considerations intervened. As to the precepts of an ethical code, they are properly seen as statements of *prima facie* duties, that is, those things that ought to be done if no other circumstances or ethical considerations were involved.

Of course a code should not contain within it a contradiction of its *prima facie* duties, for such duties supposedly constitute ethical precepts that one ought always to try to observe. But given the conditions under which human beings must act, an ethical precept may be outweighed by other obligations or indeed by other *prima facie* duties. It must be remembered that the ethical code for a profession is never the sum total of the individual's ethical obligations, any more than his or her life within the profession is the totality of the soldier's ethical life. Accordingly, an ethical code for a profession pertains only to the activities usually encountered in circumstances relevant to that profession. Individuals may perceive contradictions between the requirements of their profession and the obligations they have acquired through membership in other social groups such as their church or family. In these instances, one is left with the very human problem of ethical choice.

The argument that the precepts of a code will sometimes conflict and, therefore, are useless in deciding which ethical action ought to be done is not sound, for ethical precepts within a legitimate ethical code do not conflict. A valid ethical code cannot require two obligations which are mutually contradictory. Thus, no code can oblige one to be both a soldier and a pacifist at the same time. What confuses the individual as to which obligation is more compelling are the *circumstances* in which the precepts have to be applied. The tension in the mind of the individual rather than among the precepts of the code creates contradictions. In any case, it is the essence of ethical action to make choices. One can only ethically fail to observe an obligation when it is in conflict with another obligation judged to be more compelling, and when both obligations cannot be observed at the same time.

While circumstances may require individuals to choose among precepts of the code, this does not mean that the precepts themselves are not legitimate obligations. Just because circumstances present the agent with a conflict does not mean that the original precepts have no ethical worth or that they are not instructive as to how one ought to act. A conflict between ethical precepts of the same code arises out of circumstances and only reinforces what we have said from the beginning: that ethical agents must make choices and that choice and judgment are at the centre of ethical acts.

Conflict is a frequent condition of ethical action, and it is conflict that makes the necessity of ethical judgment obvious. To argue that conflicting precepts negate the value of an ethical code is to misunderstand the nature of ethical judgment. Ethical judgment often involves uncertainty, and deliberation arises from the attempt to apply an ethical precept in circumstances that complicate choices. It is nonsense to try to establish a code of ethics that eliminates the need for ethical deliberation and judgment. If such a code could be developed, it would not be an ethical code at all as much as it would be a handbook of rules. However, such a handbook would not be for human beings as we know them, people with free will capable of choice, but for unthinking automatons. Under these circumstances ethics would no longer require personal promise-keeping but only impersonal rule following.

As long as human beings remain what they are, conflicts between obligations will arise. This does not mean that one ought not to clearly delineate what one's obligations are in a profession or in one's life. Nor does it mean that all obligations can be observed equally well under all circumstances. It most certainly does not imply that obligations are meaningless because they are difficult to observe, or that ethical precepts are not worth stating because they create difficulties of choice in given circumstances. Simply put, it is difficult to see how anyone can act ethically without first being aware of the set of ethical precepts one is ideally expected to observe or that generate *prima facie* obligations. The fact that the precepts of a code of professional ethics may be made to conflict by circumstances says less about the value of ethical precepts than it does about the nature of ethical choice and the conditions under which it must occur.

A third objection that critics of military ethics raise involves the question whether the ethical precepts of the military profession constitute absolute or relative values. If they are absolute, so the argument runs, then they are precepts which the soldier must apply the same way in all circumstances. Since few, if any, such precepts can be readily identified, the critics insist that if military ethics involves absolutes they become impossible to serve as guides for human action in an empirical world. If, on the other hand, military ethics consists essentially of precepts that are only relative obligations, then the precepts of military ethics are not absolute statements of right and wrong, and are changed and focused essentially by circumstances. Thus, ethical precepts become meaningless as guides to ethical judgment since one can never know which precept will apply or how it will apply. From the perspective of absolute ethics, therefore, the ethical precepts of the profession of arms are useless because they are impossible to observe empirically, while from the view of relative ethics they are equally meaningless because they do not provide adequate guides to their application in different circumstances.

The argument reveals a basic misconception about the nature of ethics. In the first instance, whether or not the ethical precepts of the military profession are to be regarded as absolute or relative, one point should be clear: *ethical precepts have application only within the circumstances in which they must be observed.* The claim that ethics is based on relative precepts is really not a tenable position to begin with. To suggest that universal ethical precepts are somehow of less worth to human beings because they apply only in variable empirical circumstances is to miss the point of what ethics is all about. It has value in that it serves to actualize the values codified in the precepts themselves precisely in terms of the circumstances under which a human being will realistically have to attempt to implement them. This is also why the ethics of the military profession is different from the ethics of the legal profession. Thus, if one is going to talk about the tension between absolutes and relatives as they apply to the precepts of military ethics, it should be understood from the beginning that the fact that ethical precepts must be applied in empirical circumstances and that these circumstances have a bearing upon how these precepts will apply does not change the obligatory character of the ethical precepts themselves.

The debate between absolute and relative ethics is often joined by pointing to the tension between what has been called an *ethics of absolute ends* and an *ethics of responsibility.* The central proposition of an ethics of absolute ends affirms that nothing is ethically sound except adherence to a set of absolute values. Obligations to absolute values logically permit no modification by empirical circumstances. One is required to observe ethical precepts regardless of the circumstances in which they arise. What is most important is the ethical attitude of the agent; indeed, this is the only concern. If the individual's *intentions* are good, then the consequences of his or her actions are not strictly relevant to the ethical quality of the act. This perspective is not acceptable as the basis for an ethic of the military profession because while it is necessary to consider the intentions of an individual in assessing the ethical soundness of any act, motives cannot be the sole factor in judging whether or not an act is ethical. In some circumstances even those pursuing the noblest of goals can precipitate disastrous consequences.

Actions can never be ethical if they do not take account of consequences. If one accepts the doctrine of *homo mensura* in the ethical sense that human dignity is the value that determines all other values, then what we do to our fellow human beings is of utmost importance. It is clear in a very common sense way that not only intentions but also consequences are important. It is true that human beings make judgments about the ethical quality of an act by taking into account the intentions of the agent, that is, the value of what the individual tried to do. But we reserve a more important place for assessing the *consequences* of the act. The idea that absolute values can and ought to be pursued in an empirical vacuum makes no sense, for human beings can only act in empirical circumstances. The constraining effects of these circumstances cannot simply be wished away. The implication of an exclusive concern for intentions, that in the pursuit of ethical ends one can freely generate unethical consequences, is tantamount to the abandonment of ethical responsibility. It was this kind of thinking that gave rise to the religious wars in the West following the Middle Ages. The doctrine was expressed in the motto, "let the principle be served though the world perish," and justified the wholesale slaughter of thousands on the grounds of the absolute value of "God's will." Similar thinking lies behind the *jihadist* doctrine of radical Islam and the more recent refrain of "Bomb them all. Let God sort it out." One cannot affirm that a code of military ethics resides totally in an ethics of intentions directed toward absolute ends without risking an ethical and empirical catastrophe.

In contrast to the ethics of absolute ends is an ethics rooted in the responsibility of the agent. The ethics of responsibility presumes that the individual does not adhere to an absolute set of values or, indeed, even pursue good intentions. Rather, the individual tries to act in such a way as to effect the most humane consequences of his or her actions. The standard of ethical judgment is the consequence resulting from one's actions. While bad consequences can make a well-intentioned act unethical, good intentions do not in themselves constitute an ethical act. However, for an act to be ethical, the individual must realize that he or she is observing an obligation and must have knowledge as to why the obligation is worth observing. Thus, from our perspective of the ethics of responsibility, the exclusive focus on the consequences of the act is insufficient as a standard of ethical action. *Assessments of ethical action must include an examination not only of the consequences but also of the actor's intentions.* Neither by itself is sufficient.

Neither the ethics of absolute ends nor the ethics of responsibility is sufficient to support a code of military ethics. The pursuit of absolute ends as a kind of self-centred ethical task is rejected as potentially ethically catastrophic for a profession that deals directly with the lives and deaths of large numbers of human beings. At the same time, concern for the consequences of the soldier's actions cannot be seen as the sole determinant of ethical action. Rather, the soldier must have an awareness of his or her obligations and their value as such. The issue of absolute versus relative ethics leads us to the following proposition: for a code of professional ethics to be valid, it must stipulate precepts which members of a profession hold to be good in themselves as *prima facie* duties; that is, the precepts possess some intrinsic merit that transcends bad application. Thus, for example, one ought never to harm innocent civilians is a *prima facie* duty, but one which the circumstances may prohibit with the result that "collateral damage" may readily accompany the attempt by the soldier to carry out a legitimate mission. At the same time, these precepts cannot be isolated from the empirical world in which the soldier must act. The precepts of an ethical code taken together must, therefore, also "work" in those circumstances that the soldier is most likely to encounter.

Ethics "works" if, when an individual acts in terms of the precepts relative to given circumstances, the values and goals expressed in the code will tend to be achieved or at least approximated in the empirical world. For example, if a code requires that an individual do something, like minimizing civilian casualties, then to do that must be regarded as good and also possible to do, given the circumstances under which the individual is expected to act. If the soldier attempts to minimize civilian casualties in those circumstances, the consequences of the soldier's action will also be judged as good, all other things equal. Thus, one cannot separate the intentions of the individual and the values he or she seeks to obtain from the consequences that result from the attempt to obtain them.

If the precepts of a code of military ethics are neither absolutes nor relatives, what, then, are they? The answer is that *they are ethical imperatives*. If one applies the principle of universality, then the reason to see ethical precepts as imperatives of action becomes clearer. The *principle of universality* states that when one renders a moral judgment in a particular situation in pursuit of particular ethical goals one implicitly agrees to render the same judgment in any similar situation. More importantly, it also means that if one judges one's own action to be ethical in certain circumstances, one is committed to render the same judgment upon the acts of others who act the same way in similar circumstances. *In this way humans tend to universalize lessons and judgments into rules of action and codes of ethical precepts as guides for others to follow.*

The idea of an ethical imperative may also be pressed further, as Immanuel Kant did when he introduced the concept of the *categorical imperative.* Kant held that an individual "ought to act only on that maxim which one can at the same time will to be a universal law." The idea is that while certain codes of ethics and ethical judgments are fashioned relative to anticipated circumstances, they can nevertheless be universalized into propositions and precepts that serve as standards of judgment for the actions of others in similar circumstances. Thus, an ethical imperative dictates what human beings would choose if they saw clearly, thought rationally, and acted disinterestedly and benevolently.

There are, then, few truly absolute obligations, those that apply in the same way to all human beings at all times regardless of circumstances. When we speak about ethical imperatives, we usually mean those ethical precepts that hold for all human beings who must act in the same circumstances. Absolute precepts are seen to bind regardless of circumstances, while ethical imperatives depend to a greater or lesser extent upon the circumstances in which they must apply.

Ethical precepts are instructions as to how one ought to act under certain circumstances. We universalize them to check their ethical validity. If one judges an act to be good, one is implying that one can universalize that precept so that other soldiers who act the same way in the same circumstances would be entitled to the same positive judgment. One could validly raise a precept to the level of a maxim or law in the Kantian sense and develop a number of "universal" imperatives. All the concept requires is that one be prepared to explain and justify one's actions relative to extant circumstances, not only for oneself but also for other individuals confronted with the same choices under the same circumstances. The universalization of an ethical precept is not just a lexical activity. One does not codify simply to codify. Rather, one "elevates" a precept or a code of precepts requiring certain actions in order to test one's sense of ethics by theoretically applying it to all. In terms of a profession, the ethics of the profession is extended to its membership through its ethical code.

While the application of ethical precepts depends upon circumstances, the precepts themselves are imperatives in their own right. They receive additional worth in human affairs by their applications and the judgments that result from them. Yet, the precepts of professional ethics should have sufficient value in themselves so that the consequences of their application can be judged in terms of how their application approximates their realization. One of the criteria for judging ethical actions is whether or not the consequences of one's actions tend in fact to achieve the values specified in the precepts. If they do, one might then surmise that the act was an ethical one, all other things equal. The point is that the assessment of consequences is tied to the intrinsic value of the principle as specified in the code. Thus, if the precept affirms that soldiers ought to minimize civilian casualties in carrying out military operations, then one can assess the consequences of the actions taken by the soldier in carrying out his combat mission in terms of the degree to which the precept was achieved.

From the perspective offered here, it can be said that military ethics consists of a set of precepts that have been raised to the level of ethical imperatives in that they affirm that all human beings who find themselves in the same circumstances as soldiers within the profession of arms are justified in acting the same way. The tension between absolute ethics and relative ethics is, in the proper context, not so much a tension as a confusion in conceptualization. Absolute ethics can never be pursued without regard for consequences, nor can human actions be judged in terms of consequences without proper regard for the intentions of the agent or the values expressed within the ethical precepts which guide the soldier's actions. Values, intentions, and consequences must all be considered in judging the ethics of an act.

Situational Ethics

The confusion surrounding the issue of absolute and relative ethics often manifests itself in the problem of situational ethics, a term that is often misused and much misunderstood. Situational ethics is usually thought to be the simplistic notion that any decision that takes into account the circumstances or situation in which the soldier must act negates the value of the ethical precepts he or she should observe. This notion is false. As noted earlier, all ethics must take into account the circumstances in which the soldier is required to act, just as it must consider the conflict of obligations and the consequences that follow from the choice of one obligation over another. To claim that the circumstances of one's actions will to some degree condition the manner in which an ethical precept applies does not constitute a case for situational ethics, any more than it constitutes a case for the dilution of the value of the original ethical precept.

It has been observed in this discussion that the pursuit of absolute ends without regard for their empirical consequences is also not a legitimate ethical position. The command, *fiat justicia pereat mundus* ("let justice be done though the world perish") is not only a very difficult precept to observe, but it is likely to lead to great ethical problems in most applications. More than that, the notion that the pursuit of absolute ends can validly ignore empirical circumstances and consequences misses the point of the debate between ethics of responsibility and absolute ethics. The whole point of ethics involves discovering what one ought to do under particular circumstances. It involves deciding what precepts apply in those circumstances and using judgment in their application. For an individual to consider the circumstances in which an ethical precept applies neither makes the case for situational ethics nor diminishes the value of the precepts that the individual must observe. Ethics and the circumstances of their application are inevitably bound up in ethical action.

What exactly is situational ethics and why isn't it possible for a code of military ethics to be situational in character? Situational ethics is a philosophical perspective that affirms that basic judgments about what obligations ought to be observed are always purely particular ones. Ethical obligations are held to be always relative to a particular set of empirical circumstances in which one finds oneself at the moment. No attempt is made to make the circumstances relevant to any general ethical precept or, more importantly, no general ethical precept is made relevant to any given set of circumstances. *Situational ethics claims that the individual determines what is ethical exclusively in terms of the information and knowledge available to him or her in the circumstances in which he or she finds himself at a particular moment.* It is, therefore, impossible to universalize any principles of ethical action as imperative precepts simply because each situation is affirmed to be unique. Thus it is that the individual approaches each situation in which he or she must act as ethical *tabula rasa* ("a blank slate"), lacking any governing ethical precepts.

The reasons why situational ethics cannot form the basis of a code of military ethics are obvious. *Situational ethics offers no standards to determine what is ethically acceptable or unacceptable.* Apart from a set of particular circumstances, no experience can be generalized into precepts of ethical action since circumstances are always affirmed to be unique. In this situation, one can only act "rightfully" on the basis of information gathered through intuition while *simultaneously* experiencing the circumstances themselves, that is, one simply "knows" what is right and wrong on this basis without any ethical instruction or, as in the case of the existentialist, one "decides" what to do and in so doing the individual "becomes what he/she has done." The difficulty is that situational ethics is unable to develop any precepts of ethical action that would have any meaning at all outside the completely unique circumstances in which they occur. Since each set of circumstances is unique, the fact that one acted one way in some circumstances does not imply that one ought to act the same way in similar circumstances. Strictly speaking, situational ethics is not a code of ethics at all.

Situational ethics actually offers no way of deciding what one ought to do or not to do, because on its own terms it offers no basis for affirming larger ethical precepts that could serve to influence future ethical acts. Moreover, it offers no basis for deciding what is right or wrong since what is judged to be such is completely and exclusively tied to the circumstances of the moment in which the ethical agent finds him or herself. One cannot, therefore, use one's past experiences or the experiences of other members of a profession to help decide what one ought to do in the future. Finally, situational ethics offers no basis for ethical education since all ethical decisions are completely tied to unique circumstances. There is, then, nothing to teach. *Ethical education that deals only with ethical singularities is not ethical education at all.* If the essence of ethical education involves specifying what ethical precepts one ought to observe while inculcating a mode of ethical reasoning that helps one apply these precepts in varying situations in which they might arise, then situational ethics cannot offer any basis for the soldier's ethical education.

Ethics Don't Work

A final objection regarding military ethics is the argument that one cannot specify the central values of the military profession because to do so is a wasted exercise. This position claims that all ethical codes are naive because they can be misapplied by evil individuals, and the existence of a code of ethics does not guarantee that it will be followed. Of course, the mere promulgation of an ethical code for a profession will not guarantee compliance in all cases, although some studies do suggest that the promulgation of a code does indeed increase the degree to which ethical behaviour is observed within a population.[1] Yet, the fact that some individuals fail to observe the code does not negate the value of the code or its precepts. Codes of professional ethics state what its members ought to do.

One cannot realistically expect soldiers to observe ethical obligations unless they first know what those obligations are. Accordingly, the first step in trying to inculcate ethical values in the military professional is to promulgate a clear set of ethical precepts.

In order to hold the soldier responsible for unethical acts, it is first necessary to formulate a standard that tells us what precept has been violated. Unethical behaviour cannot be corrected without some standard against which to measure the soldier's behaviour as ethical or unethical. The inculcation of ethics as a way of both preventing and correcting unethical practices requires a set of precepts which establish the standard of ethical action. The existence of a good code of ethics says nothing about bad practice except that it is bad, and clearly the fact that a code may be violated does not diminish the value of the code as such.

Regarding violations of a military code of ethics, soldiers must understand that carrying out ethical obligations often involves having to reconcile conflicting obligations and to judge which ones are to be observed and which ones overridden in given circumstances. The fact that a soldier chooses to override one obligation in favour of another does not make the overridden obligation any less of an obligation in the *prima facie* sense. To conclude that obligations are valueless when they cannot be observed because of the circumstances and to abandon them because they are less than clear in all circumstances is to abandon *any* sense of ethical commitment whatsoever.

In the absence of a code of ethical precepts for the profession of arms, what would guide the ethical choices and actions of the profession's members? The answer is that there would be no guides beyond those of the ethical preferences of the individual soldier. There would be no precepts that bound the actions of all members of the profession. *Ethical precepts of some sort are required to set standards of professional ethical behaviour.* That these standards may be violated from time to time says nothing about the value of the code itself. The fact that individuals violate a code of military ethics is irrelevant to the need and value of the code for the profession as a whole.

Endnote

1.   See Donna B. Ayers and Stephen D. Clement, *A Leadership Model for Organizational Ethics* (Indianapolis, IN: U.S. Army Administration Centre, 1978), 89 for more on this point.

A Special Need

T he need for ethics in any area of human endeavour ought to be self-evident. Without some standards of behaviour and the ability to judge that behaviour, peaceful social intercourse becomes impossible. In a general sense, the one element that makes human society possible is the expectation on the part of one's fellow human beings that individuals will observe their obligations. In the most basic sense, observing obligations in a willing manner is what we call ethics.

All social actions require some regulation or the potential for social violence increases. The propensity for civic violence is magnified in any society in which people form organized groups and have at their disposal sufficient resources that can be put to destructive purposes. While social action requires some regulation, the question remains as to where this regulation originates. Some believe that man is inherently self-regulating and can be relied upon by his nature to pursue that which is good. Historically, there is very little evidence to support the truth of this proposition. As Admiral James Stockdale has observed, "Humans seem to have an inborn need to believe that in this universe a natural moral economy prevails by which evil is punished and virtue is rewarded. When it dawns on these trusting souls that no such moral economy is operative in this life, some of them come unglued."[1] Or, as Woody Allen put it, "it may be true that the lamb will lie down with the lion...but the lamb isn't going to get a lot of sleep!"

While ethics is required in order to make human society possible, and while regulation of human action is needed to achieve the "good" society, ethics does not function apart from society. It is human beings who create notions of right or wrong, and it is human beings who observe ethical obligations. It is humans who engage in ethical action, and it is humans who render judgments about the ethical quality of the actions of others. Whatever transcendent value it may also have, ethics is, for purposes of this discussion, a human discovery, and the need for ethics seems an absolute requirement for human society to exist in relatively peaceful circumstances. To claim that society requires ethical standards for reasonable social intercourse to survive does not imply that a separate set of ethics should be applicable to the military profession. It is clear, however, that the military does indeed have a special need for a set of ethical precepts to govern its actions. The fact is that the military is a profession, it proclaims itself to be a profession, its members feel it is a profession, and non-members recognize it as a profession. At the very least a profession requires a defining set of obligations that mark it as different from other professions. It is inconceivable that a profession should not make some statement of how it differs from what other people do or are expected to do. *It is important to understand that it is the values and obligations of the profession, the moral burden levied upon its members, and not the required technical skills and abilities that makes a profession altogether different from other forms of social organization.*

Not only must a profession clearly state those values and obligations which make it different, but a profession must also encompass an *ethic of service* rather than an *ethic of self-interest* to distinguish it from other kinds of organizations. What distinguishes a profession from a mere occupation is the stated sense of special ethical requirements that binds its membership. *This "special ethic" must include the requirement that members observe their obligations not only in addition to their self-interests but also, in some instances, instead of their self-interests.*[2] Given the risks that soldiers face, the requirement that one may be obliged to observe obligations "even unto death", to quote Saint Paul, by itself truly constitutes a special and unique sense of ethics, obligation, and responsibility.

All true professions, then, must possess ethical codes that distinguish them from other forms of social organizations and from other professions. There can be no military profession without a code of ethics that states the obligation of service to a larger group, society, the nation or people that is to a higher cause than the profession itself. The pursuit of "enlightened self-interest" within a profession can never be truly legitimized by its code of ethics. Thus, the mafia has an "ethical" code that binds its members under penalty of death. But this alone does not make the mafia a profession. The code of the mafia is designed to further the interests of the individual *mafiosi*, and there is, of course, no pretense that the mafia is serving any higher social value. What makes the ethics of the profession of arms different from the ethics of other forms of social organization—all social groups have rules—is precisely the requirement of service to others which resides at its centre.

The military may well have a greater need for ethics than any other profession because its task involves the systematic application of social violence against other human beings. The consequences of unethical behaviour within the military environment are potentially far more devastating than in civilian life. A society may well be able to tolerate a wider scope of unethical behaviour, among its other groups and even professions, largely because the consequences of that behaviour are likely to be restricted to a relatively small number of people. The consequences of unethical action by soldiers, however, especially on the field of battle can be catastrophic for they can immediately affect hundreds or even thousands of people. This is, no doubt, what Major R.I. Aitken of the Canadian Staff School had in mind when he said,

> The consequences of a degenerating ethical climate are bad enough in time of peace; they would be disastrous in war. War places men under unparalleled pressure, no matter where in the forces they serve. At all levels tough decisions must be made—decisions that cost lives. There is no room for anything but an eye toward the common good here. Mutual trust is indispensable if the forces are to operate the way they must. The whole structure of discipline and esprit de corps will disintegrate if officers cannot see past their own wants and aspirations.[3]

The tension between individual self-interest and service to the community within the profession of arms must always be resolved by the soldier in favour of the community. To possess a corps of leaders guided mostly by self-interest is to risk enormous ethical and human desolation on the battlefield, to say nothing of the threat such a profession might pose to the democratic civil order.

The special nature of the military task, the systematic application of violence against other human beings, makes the development of ethical standards for soldiers even more necessary. In time of war the soldier finds himself/herself surrounded by death. Being both witness to and cause of so much human suffering can have profound psychological effects if the soldier cannot comfort him or herself with the fact that he or she acted as humanely and ethically as possible in the circumstances. The horror of war drives human beings mad. In every war in this century the number of psychiatric casualties has been twice as large as the number of soldiers killed.[4] And the rate of stress casualties is growing as the conventional battlefield is replaced by the unconventional battlefield. Psychiatric casualty rates in Iraq are twice what they were in Vietnam and three to four times the rate they occur in the civilian population, a function of fighting an unconventional war in an urban environment. It is not only the fear of being killed that drives the soldier to psychiatric collapse. As Lieutenant-Colonel Dave Grossman notes in his book, *On Killing: The Psychological Cost of Learning To Kill in War*, it is the realization that one has killed another human being that consumes the soldier with guilt and drives him/her over the edge of sanity.[5] The stress resulting from killing increases with the proximity of the act, that is, how close to the victim one was when the killing occurred. The environment of urban combat increases the probability that the soldier will know with greater certainty that he or she has in fact killed another person, increasing the probability that the soldier will suffer psychological effects. To some degree, the soldier's conviction that he or she has acted rightly in such circumstances goes a long way in mitigating some of these effects.

Combat confronts the soldier with terrible ethical choices. There is the fear of threat to his or her own life that must be overridden if the soldier is to function at all. No other profession confronts its members with such arduous conditions of mere existence. There are also the deaths of innocents—civilians, children, the aged, the young—that sometimes occur as a result of the soldier's actions. Thus, a soldier might order an air strike against an enemy gun position located on the second floor of an apartment building knowing full well that there is a good chance that innocents are also in the building and may be killed. Worse, after the strike the soldier is likely to see the results of his decision when the enemy position is cleared. It is in the nature of urban combat that the soldier is most often likely to see results of his or her actions. Somehow, the soldier must learn to cope with the guilt.

But the most difficult burden that must be born by the soldier is the realization that he or she has caused fellow members of the profession to die, be wounded, or even driven mad. It would be of some comfort if, as the movies often portray, that death and wounding on the battlefield was largely accidental, the consequence of simply being in the wrong place at the wrong time. This is, however, mostly not the case. Every soldier in a position of leadership, from squad to regiment, knows only too well that whenever he or she gives an order to subordinates to do something, the odds are that someone is going to be hurt or killed as a result. A platoon commander who orders a squad to clear a house becomes responsible for what happens to the soldiers in the squad. *No other profession requires its members to spend the lives of its fellow professionals in the legitimate conduct of its responsibilities. Combat leaders at every level of command, therefore, must live with the ghosts of the men and women whom they have caused to be slain, wounded, or driven mad. Without a strong ethical foundation, few soldiers could long carry this awesome psychological burden.*

Without a clear sense of professional ethics to sustain and guide the soldier, there would be no basis for giving meaning to the special ethical responsibilities that the soldier is forced to bear as a condition of membership in the profession of arms. There would be no means by which all the killing, dying, and suffering could be made meaningful in human terms. Without ethical values, death in war would have no more meaning than death in a slaughterhouse. Perhaps this is what the Germans were getting at when they determined that the word *Schlacht* would mean both "battle" and "slaughter." Without some reassurance from the ethical code that what the soldier has done may be made right, we would be forced to confront the terrible conclusion that the men and women who were sent to their graves or the insane asylum as a result of what we ordered them to do had no human value beyond their value as mere tools to accomplish the task set before them by their superiors. *Without ethics, sacrifice is demeaned to mere utility.*

Military ethics is also what makes it possible for the soldier to keep his commitment to the common good by subordinating his or her legitimate career interests to those of the profession and the civilian community it serves. Without an ethical code of service to sustain them, soldiers, especially those at the higher ranks who must advise their civilian overseers, would find it very difficult to provide their superiors with the often harsh truth. If the soldier cannot find the courage to sacrifice career and advancement possibilities to the larger communal good by telling the truth to superiors even if it requires admitting our own failures, then civilian authorities will be unable to trust the military professional's judgments and recommendations. The result, if history is any guide, is likely to be disaster for the country. As with Vietnam, there has not been a single officer of higher grade who has resigned in protest over the failed policies pursued by the United States in Iraq. Without a clear ethical code to sustain the soldier, dissent from accepted policy, even when the soldier considers that policy to be harmful to the nation, is difficult to accomplish. If one is to be expected to meet the grave challenges of one's life in an ethical manner, one likely will do so only if one has lived an ethical life in meeting the lesser challenges.

Without a clear ethic for the military, there is no way to socialize new members to the profession. The young soldier must be taught from the beginning that the moral burdens he or she is expected to bear are different from the moral burdens of all other professions. It is the ethical code that specifies these burdens and attempts to guide the soldier so that his or her actions are consistent with the profession's values. Without a clear code of ethics, there would be no way to teach the novice how and why the profession of arms is different and why these differences are crucial to what is expected of the soldier. In these circumstances, the profession risks taking to itself individuals who see the profession as just another occupation where advancement depends upon pursuing self-interest after the fashion of the business corporation. The soldier risks becoming an entrepreneur instead of a public servant.

An ethical military is also necessary for a representative form of government to survive and prosper. This is a point most often overlooked in the United States, Canada, and Britain where democratic institutions and practices have been secure for more than a century. But in Europe these institutions have been established only since the end of World War II. Prior to that, there were glaring examples of military establishments threatening the democratic states. The German army betrayed the Weimar Republic, the Spanish army the Spanish Republic, precipitating a civil war, and the French army undercut the Third Republic. As late as 1958, French officers attempted to assassinate President DeGaulle while others went over to open rebellion in Algeria. In the United States, a substantial number of the officers of the Confederate armies in the Civil War had been serving Federal officers when the war broke out, including Robert E. Lee who had been commandant of West Point and refused command of the Union armies in order to support the rebellion. Since the end of the Cold War, the world has witnessed the replacement of many autocratic regimes with representative ones. Many of these new democracies inherited military establishments that were themselves undemocratic and under the control of conservative aristocratic elites (especially the officer corps) who did not share the democratic values of the newly elected political regimes. The result has often been *coup d'états* or other unlawful interference in the democratic processes by these military establishments and even open civil war as in Serbia. There is great need for these undemocratic military establishments to be educated in the new values and ways of behaviour required by a military within a democratic state. Central to this effort is education in military ethics.

An ethical military is absolutely necessary if these and other democratic regimes are to survive over the long run. Military establishments by definition are the only organizations within the polity that possess a monopoly on the instruments of deadly force. *The only barrier between the military's control of deadly force and its subordination to civilian authority is the ethical barrier imposed by the military's commitment to its ethical role as subordinate and responsible to the democratic process itself.* Without these ethical restraints, no civilian authority can count itself safe. Moreover, if the military were to be ruled by the ethics of self-interest so evident and celebrated in Western democratic societies, there would be no ethical barrier to prevent the military's forceful intervention in the political process whenever it deemed it to its interests to do so. In which case, of course, the military establishment would be indistinguishable from a mafia and become a threat to the democratic order itself, as sometimes happens in new democracies. Weary may be the head that wears the crown. But the fact that civilian authorities can get any sleep at all with an armed military in their midst is due to the ethical restraints imposed by the military upon itself. *Without a military ethic establishing the ethical commitments of the profession to the democratic state, representative government would not be possible.*

The need for military ethics is also evident in that most crucial of professional obligations, the need to engage in mortal combat. The military's loss of some of its traditional values and their replacement with the values of the marketplace has sometimes led to the abandonment or distortion of important ethical precepts to the point where combat effectiveness itself is affected. In all the familiar arguments for efficiency, cost-effectiveness, and administrative streamlining that have been marshalled to justify the adoption of business values and practices within the military, one fundamental truth as often been overlooked: from the point of view of combat effectiveness, the adoption of some business practices and values can work against the social cohesion of combat units that is so vital to their effectiveness under fire. Thus, many of the same practices developed by business enterprises that work so well in the civilian sector can actually undermine the combat capability of the military.

The key to any successful military profession is its ability to develop combat units that will remain intact and perform their mission under the terrifying stress of battle. Unit cohesion is not the result of weaponry or the quality of troop training, although these certainly do contribute. Unit cohesion is the result of strong social bonds of shared attachment among members of the battle group which, in turn, is a function of sharing the same hardships, the same risks of death or injury, a common fate, and having one's leaders in clear evidence during combat. In this basic socio-psychological sense, the motivation of military units has not changed throughout history.

Modern management practices and values adopted from the business corporation on the grounds of cost-savings and efficiency can erode the social attachments basic to unit cohesion by destabilizing leadership elements, disrupting unit stability through frequent rotation of small unit leaders, and demonstrating that the risks of combat do not fall upon leader and led alike. As a result, military units become incapable of sustaining the pressure of combat and can crack apart, as they often did in the American Army during the Vietnam War.[6] If the bonds of social cohesion are weakened, no amount of ideology, patriotism, home front support, or even the imperatives of the military system itself will prevent disintegration. At the extreme, the adopted practices and values become ends in themselves and persist even when they work counter to military success. The battle of the Somme provides a classic example.

The overall commander of the battle, British general Sir Douglas Haig, wished above all to maintain control of events. Planned by staff officers, priority was placed upon obtaining this objective. Regimental commanders were forbidden to advance with their troops, being ordered instead to remain behind in their command posts in order to man the new communications technology of the day, the telephone, so that they could file regular reports to the staff as to the progress of the advance of their regiments. In order to afford the artillery control over its firing schedules, the infantry was ordered to advance at a walk. They were forbidden to run or even to hit the ground to avoid enemy fire lest an impromptu advance of a regiment or two disrupt the rolling barrage. Finally, whenever a regiment reached its objective, it was required to stop in place and wait for other units to reach their objectives. Regiments were forbidden to advance further because this would remove the ability of the higher-level commanders to control the advance. The result was a disaster. Only at the battle of Cannae when Hannibal destroyed the Roman army in 216 B.C. did more soldiers die in a single day than at the battle of the Somme in 1916.

The gradual encroachment of business techniques upon traditional social organizations and institutions like the military began with the Industrial

Revolution in the Nineteenth century. Its progress was greatly accelerated by the events of the Second World War. Faced with the necessity of organizing and coordinating the multiple centres of economic and social power to mobilize manpower and resources on such a grand scale, Allied war planners turned to the only model available that had some experience in the field of resource organization on this scale that was at the same time consistent with the values of democracy and free enterprise: the business corporation. The United States, the birthplace of the Industrial Revolution and the inventor of schools of "scientific" management, led the way under the command of General George C. Marshall. Close coordination between the United States and its allies ensured the spread of the business model as the main mechanism of military coordination to other countries, although at greater or lesser rates of adoption once the war ended.

The symbiotic relationship between the military and the business corporation has continued to the present. The rise of huge defence budgets supporting large standing military establishments as a response to the Cold War had much to do with both how and why this relationship developed and sustained itself. Throughout the 1950s, Western military establishments exhibited more of the planning, internal control, auditing, and evaluation techniques of business corporations. Paradoxically, these practices were adopted eagerly by some of America's allies, most notably Great Britain and Canada, whose own military budgets were shrinking and who, therefore, hoped to obtain more economic efficiency by adopting the new business techniques. By 1960, the American military had so thoroughly integrated civilian business practices that the appointment of Robert S. McNamara as Secretary of Defense, a man whose only previous experience had been to produce automobiles, seemed unusual to no one. Himself the very model of the successful executive, McNamara signalled the rise of a new breed of military managers that would now staff the military establishment.

The symbolism of McNamara's influence ran even deeper. He was the ideal corporate man, and during his tenure the American military moved closer to the modern business corporation in concept, tone, language, and style. The military officer became thoroughly identified with the corporate executive to the point where the functions and responsibilities of command were perceived to be identical to the functions and responsibilities of management. Now higher-ranking officers competed with one another to obtain "command assignments" where control over ever larger budgets increased one's professional standing and chances for promotion. More and more of the military's officers were sent to graduate schools to obtain advanced degrees, the overwhelming majority of whom received degrees in business management and administration. The traditional values, habits, and practices of the military way began to erode under the impact of new administrative skills, staff reorganizations, computer models of decision-making, and the redefinition of the criteria needed to succeed within the profession itself. Military leadership in the traditional sense became obsolete. Indeed, it became unnecessary to a successful career. The machines, new administrative doctrines, and a corps of military managers would show the way. The era of the automated battlefield had arrived, soon to be replaced by the electronic battlefield and its computer-based techniques.

Had military establishments been more selective in their adoption of business practices and values, it is questionable whether the damage would have been so serious. But the military establishments of the West to varying degrees adopted not only the technologies of business, but also much of its language, style, and ethics. However gradually and subtly, the military ceased to be perceived as a unique element set apart from society or, at least, did not have to be so to function properly. The extent of the metamorphosis could be seen in the practice of referring to lower-ranking officers, those expected to carry the burden of leadership with combat units, as middle-tier managers. In Canada, the regimental system, one of the primary mechanisms of soldier socialization, officer education and development, and unit cohesion was abandoned along with the decentralization of promotions. In many cases, the officer corps itself has come to believe that leadership and management are one and the same thing, and that mastery of the techniques of the latter will suffice to meet the challenges of the former.

Military social systems, especially the small unit social subsystems that are expected to bear the burden of killing, are categorically unlike anything in the business world and to confuse them is a mistake. No one truly expects a soldier to die for the business corporation or for the careers of its executives. But the expectation that the soldier will carry out his or her duty even unto death, that soldiers will live up to the "clause of unlimited liability," remains a very real expectation and possibility in the military. Consequently, the forces that compel an officer or platoon sergeant to fulfill his or her obligations to him or herself, their commands, their superiors, and their profession are categorically different from those that press the corporate executive or foreman to fulfill their obligations. The circumstances under which the obligations of the soldier must be observed are extremely different from those of the corporate officer. *The truth is that combat leaders are not managers of any sort if only because one cannot manage soldiers to their death. They must be led by those who share the risks and hardships that all must face equally if leadership is to be effective.*

Military organizations that are successful in withstanding combat stress require high levels of individual identification with community goals to compel individual action. This sense of belonging is what defines a truly cohesive military unit and motivates the soldier to stand and fight and to risk death in the service and protection of his comrades. The adoption of business values within the military environment threatens to erode this sense of belonging. In a free enterprise, post-industrial, democratic economic system, business "ethics" is dictated largely by calculations of cost-effectiveness and efficiency which, in turn, are directed solely to the maximization of profit. One often hears from business executives that "my first obligation is to my stockholders," thus denying any serious obligation to the community or common good. The assumption is that one's private interests are identical with the common good. Indeed, business practices that even harm the common good may be "ethically" acceptable to the business executive if they are legal and profitable! The values of the modern business corporation thus constitute the negation of professional ethics in the sense that they assume the pursuit of individual self-interest to be the highest "ethical" value. In a colossal leap of faith for which there is scant empirical evidence, such pursuit is affirmed to result in the emergence of a community of interests and values by "an invisible guiding hand," without any responsibility to attain it being borne by the individual and his or her actions. Accordingly, on this model, the individual has no direct responsibility for developing and following ethical norms that address community needs. The "ethics" of business is not really ethics at all as much as a doctrine justifying the rapacious pursuit of self-interest and enshrining the individual as predator. To the degree that such "business ethics" is permitted to penetrate and become lodged in the profession of arms, central ethical precepts of the profession required to sustain its effectiveness in battle can be dangerously eroded.

The adoption of business values undermines the traditional values of community service, dedication to one's comrades, and necessary sacrifice. As a consequence, career management becomes the ultimate means to the ultimate value—one's own promotion. The cumulative impact of this change has been the rise of "the officer as entrepreneur," the person adept at managing his or her career by manipulating the system, mastering its technology usually defined in terms of administrative and managerial techniques, having his or her "ticket" punched by rotating through a number of assignments in a short time, and obtaining the "right" assignments in order to qualify for the next promotion. The entrepreneurial officer and the ethics that motivate him or her constitute one of the problems afflicting modern military establishments.

The adoption of the ethics and practices of the entrepreneur constitutes a severe and corrosive force within the military profession because it eats at the very moral foundations of the profession itself, a sense of selfless service to the community and to one's fellow soldiers. It is encouraged and sustained by a hundred different policies and bureaucratic practices, ranging from an officer evaluation system that almost all agree is inflated and measures nothing but trivialities, to the practice of rotating officers through a series of assignments and schools in keeping with the preposterous doctrine that every subaltern is a potential Chief-of-Staff. Many of these practices are imposed upon the military from without by public law by public officials who seek to impose well-meaning measures of efficiency and cost-effectiveness but who sometimes do not comprehend the moral basis of military service. In so doing, they unwittingly weaken the ethical precepts that bind soldiers together in the cause of serving the common good.

If the ethics of the business enterprise is not effective in producing cohesive military units, what is the military profession to do? What guidelines if not cost-effectiveness, efficiency, and good management—all values highly regarded by the larger civilian society as well as by its elected representatives—should an effective military establishment adopt? Some business techniques, of course, are useful. In the management of *things—* spare parts, munitions, food supplies, etc.—modern computerized management techniques work well enough and ought to be employed by the military. *But in the area of developing fighting units, good leadership is required, and good leadership is not the same thing as good management.* By and large, any managerial technique that erodes the personal ties between soldiers and their leaders—rapid turnover in leadership assignments, individual instead of unit replacement and rotation, proliferation of staff assignments, use of administrative control devices at the small unit level, centralized promotions for the lower ranks, to mention but a few—ought not to be employed.

The military profession requires models of organizational control and development that stress personal ties, social interaction, ethics, stability of leadership, and community identification with the profession itself. The point is that such "pre-modern" organizational forms rely heavily upon the interpersonal interaction and identification of its members with one another rather than upon an amorphous, faceless bureaucratic structure to compel suitable behaviour. Institutions like the British or Canadian regimental system or the German system of *Lehrbatallionen* used to sustain the cohesion of German combat units during World War II or even the legion structure of the Roman army come to mind as exemplary. One cannot, of course, dismantle the military bureaucracy, nor would that be advisable. What must be attempted, however, is to prevent the penetration of those practices and values derived from the business model beyond non-combat elements of the profession so that they do not corrode the social attachments that are the basis of the fighting units.

Not all of the ills of the military profession can be attributed to a lack of ethics. This said, many of these ills emerged because the members of the profession have acquiesced in policies they felt to be wrong. Perhaps, over time, they have done so in defence of their careers or, more likely, because there was little support for resistance within the military bureaucracy or in the larger society and political establishment. Ethics in the profession of arms operates within a far more complex organizational setting than in other professions, and within that setting rewards and punishments should be meted out in support of ethical precepts. Without institutional support within the profession for its own ethical precepts, soldiers and officers will find it difficult to resist the power of the organization. Without a clear code, written or unwritten, the soldier confronted with an ethical dilemma can find him or herself pitted against the organization and its formal values of success, personal advancement, and loyalty to superiors. In these circumstances, the organization is likely to prevail.

Endnotes

1.   James Bond Stockdale, "Taking Stock," *Naval War College Review* (February, 1979), 2.

2.   Lewis Sorley, "Competence as an Ethical Imperative: Issues of Professionalism," Paper presented at the Southeast Regional Conference of IUS, Maxwell Air Force Base, Montgomery, AL. (June, 1979), 6.

3.   R.I. Aiken, "The Canadian Officer Corps: The Ethical Aspects of Professionalism," *Canadian Forces Staff School* (unpublished paper) April, 1979, 16.

4.   Richard A. Gabriel, *No More Heroes: Madness and Psychiatry In War* (New York: Hill and Wang, 1987), 86.

5.   David Grossman, *On Killing: The Psychological Cost of Learning to Kill in War* (Boston: Little Brown, 1995), Chapter 7.

6.   Richard A. Gabriel and Paul L. Savage, *Crisis In Command* (New York: Hill and Wang, 1978), 42.

Making Ethical Choices

T he complexity and uncertainty that attend making ethical choices is reason enough for individuals to want to simplify the task and to make it less uncertain. *There is, alas, no simple formula for making many ethical choices.* One is often forced back upon the process of ethical reasoning that leads to a *prudential judgment* that is almost always likely to be uncertain to some extent. A prudential judgment is defined as one in which reasonable people could disagree if they were equally well-informed and well-intentioned. Thus, it is the nature of prudential judgments to be uncertain especially when they are made with unavoidably incomplete information under the pressure of time in difficult circumstances which compel the individual to usually choose between less than ideal alternative courses of action. Prudential judgment is making the best choice one can under the circumstances. Prudential judgments lie at the centre of the soldier's ability to make difficult ethical choices.

Prudential judgments must always be preceded by a general sense of *ethical awareness* that conditions the soldier to be sensitive to ethical issues. It is here that the dangers of excessive legalism and apodictic codes present a danger to the soldier's ability to act properly. If the soldier is incorrectly trained only to follow a body of laws or to execute an apodictic, often religiously based, code, then the soldier becomes predisposed to limit his or her ethical awareness only to the terms addressed in the code or set of laws. Under these circumstances the soldier is likely to overlook those ethical issues that are not already addressed by the codes and to regard those that are addressed as easily solvable by following the codes. Thus, the soldier risks becoming like the general who told his soldiers that the struggle in Iraq was between good and evil because "Islam is a work of the devil!" The false promise to simplify one's ethical decisions is purchased at the risk of ethical catastrophe by placing a large range of ethical problems beyond the dictates of the codes and at the same time diminishing the soldier's ethical autonomy and responsibility by encouraging the soldier to follow the code or body of law regardless of the consequences.

The first requirement of the ethical soldier in making moral choices, then, is that he or she be aware of the potential ethical difficulties attendant to their actions and that their ethical autonomy and consequent responsibility not be diminished by the need to confront difficult choices in difficult circumstances. This means that the soldier has an obligation to try and think through difficult situations in order to do what is right and not do what is wrong. There is a great danger, especially in combat situations, that one will immediately react to the circumstances as they present themselves at first glance with little in the way of systematic thought regarding the ethical difficulties that might accompany the circumstances. While this is surely understandable, it can result in grave ethical difficulties. The soldier will be held responsible for his or her actions in any case, and rightly so, thus every effort must be made to deal with the ethical complexities that accompany the soldier's actions.

Two additional points are worth making with regard to the soldier's responsibility to make prudential judgments in dealing with ethical dilemmas. First, the soldier's burden does not end when he or she renders their best judgment. As noted earlier, ethics has to do with *public* acts so that there is every reason to assume that what the soldier did or failed to do will become known to others, certainly to military superiors. This means that the soldier's decision is likely to be subject to further review in calmer times by military or civilian authorities, and that the soldier will be held responsible for the consequences of his or her decision by this review. The review process, formalized in the military by the court martial or judicial investigation, is one of the primary means which the military profession possesses to ensure that its basic ethical precepts are being observed by its members. *In circumstances of grave ethical difficulty, the soldier is wise to assume that the profession itself is watching, that his or her actions will become known, and that the profession will judge whether or not the soldier's actions support or violate the ethical precepts upon which the profession itself rests.*

Second, making ethical decisions is not the end of the soldier's responsibility. Having made a decision that selects one course of action over another, *the soldier must then find the courage to act upon this prudential judgment and attempt to carry out the decision.* Otherwise, an ethical decision becomes an attribute of personal virtue rather than ethics. It is insufficient to know what is the right thing to do; the soldier must also attempt to do it. Unfortunately, having made the decision to do the right thing does not guarantee that the individual has the courage to attempt it. In a scene from the movie, *Scent of a Woman*, U.S. Army Colonel Slade tells an assembly of young men that in every ethical crisis of his life he always knew what the right thing to do was. "I always knew what the right path was," he says. "Without exception I knew.

But I never took it. Know why? Because it was too damned hard!" Courage is a product of *character*, not ethical reasoning.

There is no formula for reaching prudential judgments. All that can be done is to specify the factors that are important in the decision-making process. The difficulty is, of course, that one cannot specify in advance which of these factors should be regarded as more important than the others, nor can the order in which they are considered be determined ahead of time. The intellectual process by which ethical decisions are reached may to vary from individual to individual as will the ethical weight that the individual assigns to each factor. That is why prudential judgments are always somewhat uncertain. All that can be done here is to identify and explain the primary elements that ought to be considered by the soldier when attempting to reach a prudential judgment. These are: (1) the facts and circumstances of the situation, (2) intentions, (3) means, (4) consequences, and (5) what ethical precept governs the action.

Facts and Circumstances: Ethical problems arise from the confluence of circumstances that confront the soldier and strongly shape the environment in which the soldier must make ethical choices. The first step in any ethical decision is to comprehend as completely as possible the facts of the matter, that is, the circumstances that he or she faces. This is often not an easy task, especially in combat, where stress and rapid change may make it almost impossible to know what is happening. *If the soldier concludes too quickly what the situation is, there is the risk that he or she will overlook important factual information that can change the nature of the ethical problem with which he or she has to deal. And that is the point: the definition of what the ethical dilemma is flows directly from the circumstances that define the ethical dilemma.* Failure to ascertain the circumstances as much as conditions permit risks failing to identify the ethical problem the soldier faces or even to recognize that there is an ethical problem at all. Lieutenant-Colonel Hal Moore, commander of the American battalion at the battle of the Ia Drang Valley in Vietnam summed up the difficulty nicely when he said that in battle a soldier must ask himself, "What is happening? What is not happening? and, What can I do about what is happening?"

By way of example, let us assume that a rifle squad operating in an urban area in Iraq comes upon an insurgent position located on the second floor of a five-story apartment building. The insurgents take the squad under fire and the squad leader must decide what to do. He/she decides to engage the position and destroy it. What is the ethical problem the squad leader faces? At first glance, there appears to be no ethical problem at all in deciding to destroy the enemy position. On further reflection, however, the squad leader realizes that the enemy position is embedded in an apartment complex where innocent civilians may be located in nearby apartment units. There may even be people held against their will in the apartment from where the insurgents are firing. Note that the definition of the ethical dilemma faced by the squad leader is different in all three cases precisely because the circumstances in which the squad leader must make an ethical choice are different. Thus, the ability to comprehend the facts or circumstances in which the soldier finds him or herself is crucial to making sound ethical choices.

Intentions and Ends: It is immediately clear that the soldier's understanding of the circumstances and the ethical difficulties that arise from them influences the soldier's intentions and ends he or she will attempt to achieve. In the case of the rifle squad, the decision to engage and destroy the gun position presents, in itself, no ethical difficulties. In other circumstances, however, the ends for which one acts may not be ethically neutral. What does a commander do if he or she has to deal with an insurgent position that is using civilians as human shields? Or how does one obtain information from a prisoner that might be vital to saving lives? Thus, the intentions or ends one seeks to achieve by one's actions can have important ethical consequences.

One of the most common ethical mistakes made by soldiers is to regard the *ends* for which they act and their *intentions* as the most important factors in their ethical decisions. This is not surprising in a profession that emphasizes mission accomplishment and obtaining results in situations of great stress and danger. Nonetheless, *it must be clearly understood that the rightness of one's goals and intentions are only one factor in the ethical equation, and most often not the most important factor.* Thus, the goal of weakening the will of the German military to resist and bringing World War II to a close was a good end. However, bombing the civilian population of Germany's urban centres when most German military units were already deployed on the eastern or western fronts far from the cities raises grave ethical issues of criminal behaviour. The same seems true of the air strike on an Iraqi air raid shelter full of civilians in the closing days of Operation Desert Storm in 1991. The shelter was known to house the families of Iraq's highest-ranking military leaders. A radio link connected the shelter to the headquarters of the general staff. On the basis of this radio link, the shelter was defined as a legitimate military target and struck by two bunker-busting bombs killing more than 600 women, children, and old people. The rationale behind the decision was that the destruction of the families of high-ranking military officers might provoke Iraqi officers to turn against the civilian leadership, remove it, and bring the war to a close. However, good intentions or noble ends are not sufficient by themselves to render an act ethical. The soldier must learn to look beyond his or her good intentions in making ethical decisions.

Another common error in ethical judgment is a willingness to accept the evil of the moment on the grounds that it will prevent a greater evil or produce a greater good later on. As a general principle, this is never acceptable and one must observe the axiom of Saint Paul never to "do evil that good may come." Note that there is often no claim that the means employed to achieve the good end are not evil in the first place, only that their employment is justified on the grounds that some higher good will eventually follow. Thus the problem of using evil means remains and evil means are always ethically unacceptable. There is, too, the problem of the proximity of the good end that will supposedly be achieved by evil means. How certain can one really be that the good will eventually result from committing the present evil? How long will it take for the good to be realized? The claim that a greater good will follow from evil means is but another way of saying that the actor's good intentions or noble goals are the sole important factor in ethical judgment. This is not true.

An example of the reasoning that often attends this ethical error was evident during the Vietnam War as part of the Rolling Thunder air campaign against North Vietnam. A B-52 strike was planned against the assembled crowd gathered to celebrate the graduation of the class of new physicians from North Vietnam's only medical school. Almost the entire graduating class was killed, along with many of their families and physicians on the teaching faculty. The justification for this horrible act was that to the degree the North Vietnamese army and its insurgent allies, the Viet Cong, could be deprived of medical support in the field, the "kill-rate" of wounded enemy combatants would rise, and enemy morale would fall, thus reducing their combat effectiveness. Thus, the employment of inherently evil means, the killing of civilian doctors, was justified on the grounds that a greater good, a reduction in the combat effectiveness of the enemy, would eventually follow. It did not. But even if it had, the bombing of the medical school would have been wrong.

Note that the above example is not the same thing as the soldier having to choose between two evils, since it is clear that one could have chosen to do nothing, that is, either not bomb the medical school or find another means to reduce enemy combat effectiveness. *At times the soldier may find himself in circumstances that present no ethically acceptable choices.* When this is the case, the soldier must try and choose the lesser of two evils if the soldier cannot avoid the circumstances altogether. One must, however, be very careful in deciding which evil is indeed the lesser, and the choice must not be in favour of something that is truly evil and something that is only a lesser good. In war, ethical judgments can be very complicated indeed.

Means: The choice of means to implement a decision involving an ethical problem sharply reflects the soundness of the soldier's ethical judgment and is an important consideration in any later attempt to assess the ethics of the soldier's actions. *The means chosen to obtain an end or fulfill an intention must be proportionate to the end or intention itself.* In fact, good ends can be made bad by the employment of unethical means and ethical means can equally be made unethical if put to the service of evil ends. Thus, one can expect no ethical credit for being kind to prisoners who are on their way to being executed, or for using quick and painless methods to execute them since killing prisoners in any case is unethical.

The squad leader trying to neutralize the gun position in the apartment complex (a good end) has an ethical responsibility to choose appropriate means to achieve this end. The circumstances are complicated by the likelihood that there are civilians in the other apartments and although the squad leader cannot know for certain, perhaps civilians being held by the insurgents in the same apartment where the gun position is located. What is the squad leader's course of action? The answer is to neutralize the insurgent position while minimizing the danger that innocent civilians will be killed in the process. The means at the squad leader's disposal range from calling in an air strike, a helicopter missile attack, using a shoulder-fired missile, or employing an infantry small-arms assault. Which of these means is most likely to achieve the objective of neutralizing the insurgent position *and* minimizing the potential harm to innocent civilians? Note that the squad leader must balance *both* considerations in making his or her prudential judgment, although he or she does not necessarily have to give *equal* weight to each consideration, only *appropriate* ethical weight to each. Thus, the gun position must be neutralized even at the risk of civilian deaths, but due consideration must be given to minimizing these deaths. Suppose, however, that the squad leader did not have any less violent (kinetic?) means at his disposal and that there was no way to destroy the insurgent position without demolishing the entire apartment complex with an air strike placing two Mark IV 500 pound bombs on the complex. Under these circumstances, it would be unethical to bomb the apartment complex because the choice of such means to a good end is both unethical and disproportionate. The air strike requires the squad leader to accept the obvious evil of killing civilians *as a prior condition* to attaining the good of destroying the insurgent position and violates Saint Paul's axiom not to do evil in order to achieve good. The act cannot be carried out without destroying the innocent first. The squad leader must find another way.

Consequences: The soldier is responsible for the consequences that result from his/her actions. The degree of ethical responsibility for consequences is dependent upon an assessment of three factors: the soldier's intentions, the degree to which the consequences could have been reasonably foreseen, and the proximity of the consequences to the soldier's actions. As a general rule, evil intentions always render the act evil even when the consequences of the intended act do not materialize. Thus, a person who attempts to shoot another but who misses his/her victim can still be held responsible even though no evil consequences resulted. A soldier who shoots and kills a non-combatant while checking his/her weapon to ensure that it is empty has wrought terrible consequences but without any evil intent. Although the soldier may be guilty of carelessness, the soldier has not acted unethically even though he or she has killed another human being. Intentions, therefore, are central to assessing ethical responsibility.

But intentions alone are not sufficient for judging the consequences of an act. What did the soldier intend when he/she threw a hand grenade into the insurgent bunker? No doubt to neutralize the actions of the enemy combatants. But what if there were civilians held hostage in the bunker and they, too, were killed? Clearly the soldier cannot be held responsible for their deaths on two grounds: the soldier did not intend them to be killed and the soldier could not have *reasonably foreseen* that they were present. The squad leader who called down an air strike on the insurgent position in the apartment building, on the other hand, can be held responsible for the deaths of the civilians precisely because he could have reasonably foreseen that civilians were in the other apartments.

For a soldier to be held ethically responsible for the consequences of his or her actions, the consequences must be reasonably proximate to the act, that is, the consequences must be directly tied to the action and not separated by an inordinate amount of time. Thus, a squad leader might order his/her squad to clear an area around a school that has been used as a sniper's roost. In doing so, one of the soldiers glimpses movement in a nearby culvert and fires at the motion he/she senses in the bushes. A civilian hiding from the patrol is hit and killed. The squad leader cannot be held ethically responsible for the death even though it was his/her original action that set events in motion that ultimately resulted in the death of an innocent person. It is an old military adage that "a commander is responsible for everything his troops do or fail to do." This may be true in the sense of command responsibility, but it is not true of individual ethical responsibility. Human actions often set into motion chains of events that no one intended or could foresee. The further away in time and space a consequence gets from its originating action, generally the less is the agent's ethical responsibility.

Governing Ethical Precepts: The soldier's awareness of each of the factors mentioned above is not by itself sufficient to make him or her able to render an ethical judgment. The soldier must now determine which ethical precept or general principle will guide his or her assessment of the factors involved, that is, how to assign them relative ethical weight in reaching a decision. *Because the soldier has many sources of ethical obligations, he or she may legitimately draw upon the basic ethical precepts of any one of these sources to guide his or her actions.* Thus, it is possible that the soldier may draw upon his or her religious obligations, conclude the war is unjust, and refuse to fight. More likely, however, the soldier will draw upon the ethical precepts of the military profession itself which are likely to be the most relevant to making ethical judgments within the circumstances the soldier is most likely to confront. Thus, one of the important functions of a profession's ethical precepts is to aid the soldier in making ethical choices by providing a larger frame of ethical reference within which other relevant factors may be assessed.

With regard to the actions of the soldier in combat, the soldier might begin his or her process of ethical reasoning by first determining the general ethical precept that will apply to the circumstances confronting the soldier. That principle may be "all humans have a right to live and ought not to be killed." If left at this, however, the precept is of only little help for it is often the soldier's task to kill the enemy. The soldier must continue to think through the problem. A corollary principle of the first is that "one has a right to one's own life." If so, then the soldier has a right to his or her life and may exercise the appropriate means to remain alive. This proposition permits the soldier to kill anyone who is trying to kill the soldier. Thus, soldiers have at least some ethical claim to justification in killing those on the other side who are trying to kill them. *Killing in war, then, if not always ethical is at least not always unethical if restricted to combatants.*

But this proposition is less than ideal since it is possible to kill large numbers of enemy soldiers through long-range artillery and air strikes even when they present no proximate threat to one's life. To deal with this difficulty, the profession can affirm as an ethical precept that "soldiers may only kill enemy combatants." But since "every human being has a right to live," every effort ought to be made to limit the violence against *all* human beings, whether soldiers or not. A precept which seeks to apply only minimal violence in war, therefore, would meet acceptable ethical standards. If violence is only a means to achieve ethical ends, then the soldier ought to use only that violence necessary to achieve those ends at the same time reducing the chances for unforeseen consequences. Thus, the squad leader in our previous example ought to choose those means that achieve the end of neutralizing the insurgent position with minimal violence. The profession's general ethical precept also implies clearly that enemy wounded or prisoners ought not to be killed since they no longer constitute any reasonable threat to the soldier's life. Non-combatants, of course, may not be killed for the same reason.

Following this line of reasoning further, the soldier might deduce the following corollaries to guide his or her actions in combat that can be reasonably derived from the first precept that "all humans have a right to live and ought not to be killed." The soldier may conclude that: (1) Soldiers have a right to their lives and may defend themselves against anyone who tries to take that life. (2) Human beings ought not be killed except under pressing circumstances of personal danger so that violence must be limited and proportionate to the ends intended to be achieved. (3) Human beings who do not present a threat to life, civilians and other non-combatants, may not be harmed. (4) Those who no longer present a threat to one's life, wounded enemy and prisoners, may not be killed. As this example illustrates, armed with a knowledge and understanding of the basic ethical precepts of his profession, the soldier has at least a reasonable chance of being able to reason his or her way through to prudential judgments and increase the chances that he or she will at least attempt to do the right thing on the battlefield. As in other areas of human endeavour, there are no absolute guarantees of ethical action in warfare.

But what of the peacetime soldier? Most soldiers are likely to experience combat for only a small part of their military careers. It is important, then, for the profession's precepts to provide ethical guidance for dealing with those ethical dilemmas that arise during times of peace. Modern military establishments provide many critical functions to the elected leaders of a democratic state that go beyond defending it with their lives. These peacetime functions include offering advice on budgets, weapons systems, research, and even overseeing novel social programs such as affirmative action, bilingualism, and racial integration that sometimes lead the way for their adoption by the civil society. In some military establishments, such as Turkey and Israel, military service is the primary mechanism for achieving literacy and the social integration of disparate ethnic, racial, and linguistic groups. The point is that the military profession performs other vital functions besides combat, and it is equally important that these peacetime roles be performed in an ethical manner.

The ethical precept that governs the soldier's actions in peacetime is "the soldier serves the common good of the nation above all other interests." Thus, the self-interested free-market ideology commonly evident in the larger society and which is presumed legitimately to motivate civilian employees is rejected as the guiding ethical precept for the peacetime soldier. Instead, the soldier's obligation is always to pursue the common good even at the expense of his or her own interests. The ethical corollaries that follow from this precept are: (1) The soldier must always tell the truth in dealing with civic and military authorities. (2) The soldier must speak truth to power, that is, provide competent and honest advice to elected and appointed leaders. (3) The soldier who witnesses corruption must expose it. (4) A soldier may ethically protest a policy that he or she believes is detrimental to the nation. This protest may include resignation from the profession itself or even the refusal to follow orders. These corollaries follow from the profession's own precept that the soldier's primary obligation is to serve the common good.

The ethical burdens of the soldier in war and peace are heavy burdens indeed and starkly different from those borne by members of other professions in the usual conduct of their professional activities. Moreover, the horrors of war do not provide an excuse for the soldier to escape these burdens. Quite to the contrary. The unique characteristic of the ethical soldier is that he or she must carry out their ethical obligations under conditions that make ethical choice more difficult, not easier. *The inhumanity that is attendant to war is never an excuse for the soldier to become inhumane.* The soldier must strive instead to retain his or her ethical moorings while awash in a sea of blood, fear, and death, to lessen the violence and reduce the killing, to cherish human life when it can be saved, and to stay the hand of death and destruction whenever possible. In order not to make the horror of war worse, the soldier must seek the ethical solution to the terrible dilemmas that soldiers face. The soldier must seek the way of the ethical warrior.

Professionalism

T he proper role of the soldier in Western society has not changed much over the past two thousand years. Society has always had need for the soldier, and the values and functions required for a military establishment to be effective in its role of protecting its host society have remained relatively constant over time. There is not much in the *Iliad* that the modern warrior would not find familiar, and military professionals still study the accounts of ancient battles for insights into how to fight modern ones. Beyond the technologies and lessons of war learned from the past, the virtues and values of commanders and troops long dead are with us still if only because the reasons why men and women seek the profession of arms have not changed much over the centuries. Major Aitken of the Canadian Army expressed this well when he said,

> "The tasks and obligations of the soldier have not changed appreciably over the years; indeed in light of the weapons of mass destruction now at our disposal, the military has more of a social responsibility than ever before. Therefore, regardless of the erosion of moral and ethical standards in the society at large, the soldier must, as a condition of his survival, demonstrate an ethical stance which is above reproach."[1]

Whereas the tools and technologies of the profession of arms have changed, the modern soldier must still possess the same personal leadership and character, take essentially the same actions on the battlefield, and establish the same close bonds with his or her troops and peers to be an effective commander as did the commanders of antiquity.

The literature on military effectiveness confirms the truth of this observation. In his *Face of Battle*, a study of the battles of Agincourt, Waterloo, and the Somme, John Keegan found that despite changes in military technology and even the cultural values of the larger societies, the requirements of military effectiveness, defined in terms of those things a leader had to do to establish unit cohesion, remained unchanged over time.[2] Alan Lloyd, in his study of British soldiers in World War I, demonstrated that leadership effectiveness depended upon the ability of the leader to establish strong personal bonds with his men and that this in turn had very much to do with the leader's example of personal bravery and a willingness to share the risks and hardships with his soldiers.[3] The consistency of a leader's behaviour as a force for military effectiveness was documented in Shills and Janowitz's study of the German Army in World War II. They discovered that the battlefield cohesion of German units was largely a consequence of the strong interpersonal relations among soldiers and leaders.[4] Samuel Stouffer, in his study of the American Army in World War II, came to the same conclusion, as did Paul Savage and I in our study of that army during the Vietnam War.[5]

The role of the leader and of what might be called military virtue as they contribute to the effectiveness of military units does not seem to have changed over the centuries perhaps because human nature itself has not changed. The profession of arms, even in our modern post-industrial societies, represents one of the few social roles that have survived intact over time. It is not too much to claim that unit cohesion is crucial to the ability of military establishments to perform effectively, and to the extent that good leadership contributes to cohesion, then since the battlefields of the future, conventional and unconventional, will present an even greater intensity of combat stress, therefore in the future even greater degrees of unit cohesion will be required for the soldier to function well or at all. The future will probably require military professionals who are more than ever certain of their own values and actions. To ensure success in the future, military professionals will have to relearn the lessons of the past.

Professionalism

Many of the difficulties evident with the leadership corps of modern democratic armies can be traced to a failure of their members to realize that what they are asked to do as military professionals is anthropologically quite different from the tasks required of other professions and occupations in the larger society. This confusion of roles and objectives has led some members of the profession to attempt to pattern their values and actions after those of the larger society, and even after specific successful businesses and other occupations within it. If the soldier is to understand why the profession of arms is different from other professions, he or she must understand why members of all professions incur different kinds of obligations from those of other types of social organizations that do not enjoy professional status. How, then, is a profession different from other social groups in a society?

The very word "profession" is an honorific term denoting that there is something special about a profession that is not shared by associations like other social organizations and businesses. *The term itself implies that membership is akin to a vocation or special calling by people who "profess" to live by certain values rather than an association based upon mutually shared material interests.* It is precisely because of the honorific aura of professions that almost every occupation or business wants to be known as professional. Thus, sports figures, cosmetologists, realtors, morticians etc., all like to refer to themselves as professionals to share in the honorific aura even while there is nothing special in any sense about what they do. A true profession has certain distinguishing characteristics which set it apart. One difference between a profession and an occupation is that the profession is recognized as performing a service that is more important to the common good than other tasks generally are. Thus, the medical profession which deals in the treatment of illness and saving of human lives or the clergy that attends to spiritual needs or lawyers who serve justice as well as the law are all considered to be more valuable to the society than, say, the selling of vacuum cleaners.

It is the "service" that the professional renders in an altruistic manner to his "clients" as part of serving the common good that is the "first ethical imperative" of a profession. The profession of arms certainly meets this imperative by its responsibility to protect the very existence of the society itself by its willingness to risk the lives of its members in doing so while engaging in the nasty, but often necessary, business of killing other human beings. Moreover, unlike other professions whose "clientele" is relatively small, often a few hundred people at best, the military's "client" is the nation itself. Quantity confers a quality all its own, as Napoleon observed, so that in terms of sheer numbers, the responsibilities of the military profession exceed that of any other profession. Indeed, it can be argued that unless the military profession does its job well, no other profession, vocation, organization, or business can hope to function at all.

Modern democratic post-industrial societies are premised largely on the pursuit of self-interest with most social relations based on mutual utility. But the soldier is obligated to carry out his or her task even to the detriment of his or her self-interest. As Lewis Sorely has cogently observed, "in military service involving combat the obligation to serve the general interest is typically to do so *instead* of rather than *in addition to* one's own self-interest, even to the extent of sacrificing one's life."[6] In a true profession, members must at times carry out their obligations not only in addition to their own interests but instead of them. This places the obligation of sacrifice at the centre of the profession of arms.

Another element that sets a profession apart from other forms of social organization is a code of ethics that governs the actions of the membership in rendering their obligations to their clients. Without a code of ethics, there is no standard against which the actions of the profession can be measured, and there is no clear statement of what the profession does that separates it from other occupations. Without a clear sense of what the profession is all about, it becomes extremely difficult to socialize new members to it in terms of the special obligations required of them. *Thus, a code of ethics for the profession of arms is a necessity.* A profession that has no code of professional ethics is not a profession at all, for there is nothing for its members to "profess," namely the values that govern their actions beyond their own self-interest. Without a code of ethics, the critical means for linking the individual actions of its membership to the expected actions of the profession in carrying out its obligations to the common good are absent.

All professions, of course, require the possession of special knowledge or expertise by which the profession lays claim to a special competence. But the possession of expertise in itself does not constitute a profession. A computer technician, for example, possesses a special competence, and in a general sense "serves" his or her clients. But no one would seriously claim that a computer technician is a member of a proper profession. To note that a profession requires some special competence is only to point out that its membership must be competent in carrying out its special obligations. Expertise *per se* does not constitute a truly special quality since in complex post-industrial societies occupational specialization of one kind or another sets one group apart from another as a matter of course.

Of course the military profession has requirements for special knowledge and expertise that rest in the clear task of the military to carry out the systematic application of violence in the service of the state. This is what military establishments do, and the possession of special expertise and competence is linked directly to those skills required in combat. Moreover, the skills of the soldier are not otherwise available in a society and can only be legitimately acquired and practiced within the confines of the profession itself. Thus, the profession of arms certainly meets the requirement that a profession possess special competence and that this competence be exercised only in the service of the common good.

Professions also require that their performance be subject to rational analysis and standards of competence enforced by peers.[7] The military, therefore, is not a priesthood in that its claim to special competence is overtly measurable. Simply put, bad armies are defeated on the battlefield or threaten the state. The military must be competent in the application of its special knowledge and that competence must be subject to analysis and measurement. Standards of competence and performance must be subjected to review by superiors and peers. *The profession has a responsibility to police itself, ensuring that its standards of competence are met and that it is carrying out its obligations in a manner that serves the common good.* Those who do not meet the standards of professional competence and ethics must be driven from the profession by the superiors and peers of the membership itself. Thus, the profession must have a certain degree of autonomy so that it becomes self-governing and responsible for regulating its membership.

The military can never be self-governing to the same degree as other professions for obvious reasons. The military is an instrument of the state and its political masters necessarily and rightly have an obligation to oversee and control it. Nonetheless, except in the areas of grand strategy or social policy which are as a matter of course dictated by political superiors, the profession retains an autonomy in which appropriate authorities within the profession have a direct responsibility for insuring that it is meeting its standards of competence and ethics. It is in this sense that the profession is self-governing. At the same time the military has autonomy of action in enforcing its standards insofar as it has its own law, courts, jails, as mechanisms of enforcement. It does not rely upon the larger society's means of enforcement to ensure the proper behaviour of its members.

A profession must also possess a sense of corporateness.[8] Members of the profession of arms must believe that what they do is more important than what other professions do, that they are crucial to the survival of the nation. This sense of special corporateness or belonging should, however, not be permitted to degenerate into a narrow specificity of outlook on the part of the soldier. In order to prevent this "isolation of the intellect," the profession must provide broad training and education to help its members fit their role in their profession into the larger concerns of all human beings. While the soldier must be a proficient technician, he or she cannot be allowed to become a mere technocrat whose possession and application of the skills attendant to his or her special competence are applied in an ethical vacuum. *It is the profession's responsibility to develop a proper concern for the ethical dimensions that accompany the actions of the soldier.*

In this regard, it is vitally important for the soldier to understand that to be a good soldier is not the equivalent of being a good human being, and that there may come a time when the requirements of the profession will conflict with other obligations to people to whom the soldier has strong ethical commitments. The recognition of these conflicting obligations and their solution constitute the nub of ethical choices that cannot be avoided. The profession of arms must never become a refuge for those who abandon their other ethical obligations, ignoring them in deference to their purely professional obligations. To carry out the obligations to the profession without regard for the soldier's other obligations is to court ethical disaster. The soldier must realize that his or her professional life is not the sum total of their obligations or their ethical existence.

The Military is Different

The profession of arms is different from other professions in democratic civil societies in four aspects: *scope of service, degree of responsibility, extent of personal responsibility, and monopoly of service.* With regard to its scope of service, the responsibility of the military profession is simply greater than that of any other profession. The military is responsible for the very survival of the civic society and the sheer number of people that the profession must address in its service is larger than that of any other profession and encompasses the entire society. No other profession, not even the medical profession in times of epidemic, can be construed as being responsible for the very survival of the society.

The degree of ethical responsibility of the military profession is also greater. No other profession has responsibility for the lives and deaths of such large groups of people. The argument does not speak only to causing the deaths of one's adversaries, but also to causing the deaths of one's fellow citizens, those placed in the care of the profession. No other profession has the awesome responsibility to spend the lives of others, one's fellow citizens and soldiers, in order to fulfill its obligations to the common good. Sometimes it is easier to meet one's own death than to be responsible for sending other soldiers to their deaths in the legitimate conduct of one's professional responsibilities. To those who do not know, there is a tendency to regard death and injury in battle as largely accidental. The truth is that the responsibility of military leadership includes the need to sacrifice the lives of one's own soldiers in pursuit of battlefield objectives. This "trading" of human lives and wounds for a piece of terrain, a crossroad, or any other military objective imposes upon those who must make such decisions—and they are made by all members of the profession at all levels of leadership—an awesome ethical responsibility from which there is no escape. No other profession requires sacrificing the lives or breaking the bodies of one's fellow professionals in order to carry out one's responsibilities to the common good. *The level of ethical responsibility that the members of the profession of arms take on is both greater and more frequently confronted than that shouldered by other professions.*

Unlike other professions, the requirement of service for members of the military is total and encompasses what General Sir John Hackett has called "the clause of unlimited liability" that obliges members of the profession to give their lives in the performance of their professional duties. In a paraphrase of Saint Paul, the soldier must be willing to "fight the good fight, tell the truth, and finish the race" even at the cost of his or her own life. General Hackett summed up the extreme degree of personal liability expected of members of the profession of arms thus:

> "The essential basis of military life is the ordered application of force under an unlimited liability. It is the unlimited liability which sets the man who embraces this life somewhat apart. He will be (or should be) always a citizen. So long as he serves he will never be a civilian."[9]

No civilian profession requires the sacrifice of one's life in its service, whereas the military may lawfully and regularly require it. The clause of unlimited liability separates members of the profession of arms from *all* professions in civilian life.

Another characteristic of the military profession that separates it from others is the military's monopoly on the skills it practices. In other professions, one may leave one's place of practice and still practice elsewhere. A doctor may leave one hospital for another, a lawyer for another firm, or both may even offer their skills in private practice. But once a soldier leaves the military, he or she is outside the profession forever. One could, of course, become a soldier of fortune, but one would still no longer be a member of a profession *per se*. No other professions maintains a monopoly of practice in the sense that one must either belong to it totally or not practice one's skill at all. While other professions sometimes exclude members from practicing, that is clearly not the same thing as having a member in good standing prohibited from practicing because of the monopoly of the service offered.

When the military is examined in terms of its scope of service, degree of moral responsibility, extent of personal liability, and monopoly of service, *it is clear that the military is not just a profession but a profession unique among all others*. It is a profession that requires a high degree of competence, expertise, and service to others, perhaps more than any other profession. It is a profession that will require that one be prepared to die in its service. If only for this reason, the profession of arms is a unique social institution. It is unique because it imposes special obligations and requires special people to fulfill them. It is hardly surprising, then, that this special institution must to some degree be separate from the society it serves in order to carry out its commitments to it.

The military profession in a democratic society has three clients: the legal-civic order it has sworn to preserve and protect, the larger societal order, and the members of the profession itself who have assumed the obligation of unlimited liability. There can, therefore, be no question of a military profession that becomes so self-serving that it does not serve its clients. A profession that serves only itself, as is the case with some military establishments in non-democratic societies, is no longer a profession but a private enterprise whose concern is the interests of its memberships instead of its clients. *But to say that the military must serve the larger society is not the same thing as saying that the profession be completely like that society.* Given the special nature of the military profession and of its obligations and responsibilities, it seems obvious that a wide range of societal practices and values cannot be permitted in the military either because they do not work or because they erode the values and obligations of the profession itself. And since the society cannot (and ought not) to become like the profession in terms of the obligations it must observe, some degree of separation of the profession from the larger society is required for it to be able to carry out its obligations.

There is a range of individual behaviour that is accepted or at least tolerated by the larger society that is corrosive of the ties that bind the profession. Recreational drug use, for example, seems readily tolerated without any serious effects on the larger social order. But within military units it can alter the ability of the unit to perform under fire, to forge interpersonal ties that bind members of the unit together, and affect the operation of equipment adversely. Another example might be the habit of being late for appointments. Being late for deadlines in the military can be deadly. Other examples easily come to mind. Unless one is prepared to argue that it does not matter whether the military is effective or not, it seems obvious that some forms of tolerable social behaviour in the larger society must be restricted or prohibited altogether within the profession.

Another reason why the military has to be to some degree separate from the larger social order is that some of society's *values* are simply unworkable in the military environment. These values erode the values of service and special obligation, which rest at the core of the military profession and cannot be tolerated. Lieutenant-General Robert Gard has described this problem.

> "Vital to combat operations and therefore a necessary part of traditional military professionalism is a set of values which are to some extent contrary to those held by civilian society. Military organization is hierarchical, not egalitarian, and is oriented to the group rather than to the individual; it stresses discipline and obedience, not freedom of expression; it depends on confidence and trust, not *caveat emptor*. It requires immediate decision and prompt action, not thorough analysis and extensive debate; it relies on training, simplification, and predictable behaviour, not education, sophistication, and empiricism. It offers austerity, not material comforts."[10]

General Gard is emphasizing a singular fact of the military mission: because it aims at special service to the larger community as opposed to self-interest, inevitably certain values in the larger society run contrary to this idea of selfless service and, therefore, tend to dilute the professional values of the military way. This lack of value congruence is particularly acute in Western democracies where the highest values are placed upon the individual and his or her wants and needs. The emphasis on the individual can become so strong that individual desires completely eclipse communal needs, a circumstance that appears more evident when volunteer military establishments find themselves fighting wars for which whatever political support once was present has now been lost. In the profession of arms, the individual has value as part of a group, not as an individual *per se*. The strong emphasis on individualism evident in modern societies cannot be permitted free rein in a military context.

If some behaviour is not conducive to military effectiveness and some values unacceptable because they erode the moral foundations of the profession, then the profession is responsible for protecting itself and its members from such behaviour and values. The profession must establish and enforce its own values and standards of behaviour that can serve as ethical reference points for its members. Thus, *responsibility for maintaining the military's professionalism rests with the profession itself and its members. The profession must be the keeper of its own flame or be prepared to watch that flame extinguished in the winds of hostile values that blow through the larger society.*

Some fear, however, that a military profession whose values are not identical to those of the larger society runs the risk of creating a "state within a state" that could present a danger to the civil society. This fear appears to be based more upon ideology that solid reasoning. To suggest that the profession of arms need not be separate from the society that it serves is to misunderstand the dynamic of group formation in a democracy. In fact, no societal group ever demonstrates a perfect congruence to the values and behaviour of the larger society. This is true of sports teams, business corporations, fraternal organizations and other professions, and it is true of the military profession. Moreover, there is no necessity for such complete congruence to protect democracy. It might even be argued that it is impossible to establish a direct congruence of values between the society and any societal sub-group since a wide range of the subgroup's activities are not at all relevant to the values of the larger society. For example, the decision of a football team to execute a certain play has no bearing at all on societal values. Thus, the value connections between social groups and the larger society are not all equally important nor, indeed, are they equally relevant to the subgroup's behaviour in any given instance.

Membership in any societal subgroup, therefore, includes a wide range of values and behaviour that is irrelevant to larger social values. Much of what people do in groups on a day-to-day basis has absolutely no relationship to larger social values, and the question of such a relationship rarely, if ever, arises, at least in democracies. The day-to-day training and responsibilities of the soldier are likely to have little to do with larger social values, and questions of conflicting values within the military does not seem to arise more frequently than in other groups. To expect a high degree of value congruence between different subgroups and the larger society is to misunderstand both the nature and dynamic of people in groups and the nature of democracy itself.

A fundamental distinction between democratic and totalitarian governmental forms is that in a democracy there are wide areas of social intercourse in which the writ of the state does not run. Only totalitarian societies require the ideological values of the larger social order to penetrate and apply to *all* aspects of group activity. The major premise of totalitarian societies is precisely the claim that certain values explain the total behaviour of both individuals and groups within the state. Democracies, on the other hand, affirm that there are large areas of human endeavour even among groups created by the state itself in which the writ of the state runs in only the most general sense or even not at all. The fear that sub societal groups such as the military may develop values that threaten the democratic state is rooted in an ignorance of the nature of group dynamics and of what motivates people to join groups.

General Walter "Dutch" Kerwin, USA, has summed up the dilemma of those who fear that the military will come to present a threat to democracies if it is permitted to hold its own values and a degree of social distance from the larger society. General Kerwin notes that the military is of necessity different from a civil society. Those who do not understand this fundamental fact miss the point of military professionalism.

> "We face a dilemma that armies have always faced within a democratic society. The values necessary to defend that society are often at odds with the values of the society itself. To be an effective servant of the people the army must concentrate not on the values of our liberal society, but on the hard values of the battlefield...We must recognize that this military community differs from the civilian community from which it springs. The civilian community exists to promote the quality of life; the military community exists to fight and, if need be, to die in defense of that quality of life. We must not apologize for these differences. The people...are served by soldiers disciplined to obey the orders of their leaders, and hardened and conditioned to survive the rigors of the battlefield. We do neither our soldiers nor our people any favors if we ignore these realities."[11]

General Kerwin's point is an extension of the definition of professionalism. Professions require different obligations and responsibilities from their members than one finds in the civilian society. These require that some values, rights, and privileges of the civil society not be permitted free rein within the profession for very good reasons. The choice is either to separate the profession from its civil order on the grounds that it must do so to remain what it is, a profession with special obligations, or else to dilute that very professionalism by turning the military establishment into one more civilian occupation congruent with the larger social values some of which are antithetical to basic values of service and sacrifice. We can, of course, choose the second course, but we cannot do so without losing our profession in the process.

The crux of the argument for not separating the military from the civil society rests on the proposition that every person in uniform is a citizen first and a serviceman second, and that any attempt to separate the defended from the defenders presents a potential threat to the democratic state. But the fact is that most Western democracies and a number of those emerging in the states of the former Soviet Union now have all-volunteer militaries, in fact already separating the defenders from the defended. None of these post-Cold War militaries has yet to present a danger to their civilian leadership. Where we most often find military establishments that threaten their civilian overseers is in those states of Latin American and Asia that still have conscript armies but whose officer corps are comprised of either traditional or revolutionary elites openly hostile to democratic values. In Turkey, we witness the strange paradox of a conservative military occasionally intervening in the political process to *preserve* democratic institutions! Thus, there does not appear to be any relationship between all-professional military establishments, at least in the West, and a tendency for these establishments to threaten their respective democratic institutions.

Those who fear the prospect of the military profession becoming a threat to the civic order appear to overlook the fact that such a state of affairs would be equally unacceptable to the military itself! The nature of military professionalism is to render selfless service to the democratic society it serves. Any military establishment that violated this basic value would be quickly recognized for what it was, a mafia-like gang of armed thugs. *There is no inherent connection between the adoption by the military profession of values that are based on a degree of necessary separation from the values of the larger society and any tendency of that profession to become an overt threat to the state.* The profession of arms can never be legitimately separated from its basic loyalty to the democracy it serves or the processes that sustain that democracy and the legitimacy of its elected leaders. The degree of necessary separation concerns only sets of sub societal values and norms of behaviour that are openly dysfunctional and corrosive of the values necessary to the military profession and its conduct of effective military operations.

The issue of the military becoming a threat to the civil order has been grossly exaggerated on ideological grounds. The question is not one of praetorianism as much as harsh pragmatism, of the necessity to make choices enforced by the nature of the military task. Even the most liberal democracies could not long survive without an effective military institution or, at very least, could hardly afford to take the risk of trying to do so in an uncertain and dangerous world. The need to separate the military from the civil society has been recognized by the society's political leaders in their willingness to create within the military a set of institutions that renders it virtually autonomous and self-governing on a day-to-day basis. Thus, military establishments have their own court, codes of law and regulations, police, trial procedures, judges, court of appeals, and even their own prisons. All these institutions exist and function quite apart from the larger society and with society's approval. To a large extent, then, the social distance between the society and the profession already exists. To insist on a congruence of all but the most basic values of society and profession runs the risk of either militarizing the state, as in totalitarian societies, or civilianizing the profession to mirror the larger society as much as possible. Neither path serves the profession or a democratic civil order well.

Endnotes

1. R.A. Aitken, "The Canadian Officer Corps: The Ethical Aspects of Professionalism," *Canadian Forces Staff School*, unpublished thesis, (April, 1979), 20.

2. John Keegan, *The Face of Battle* (New York: Vintage Press, 1976).

3. Alan Lloyd, *War in the Trenches* (New York: David McKay, 1977).

4. Edward A. Shills and Morris Janowitz, "Cohesion and Disintegration in the German *Wehrmacht* in World War II," *Public Opinion Quarterly* 12 (1948).

5. Samuel Stouffer, *The American Soldier* (Princeton, NJ: Princeton University Press, 1976). See also Richard A. Gabriel and Paul L. Savage, *Crisis in Command: Mismanagement in the Army* (New York: Hill and Wang, 1978).

6. Lewis Sorely, "Competence as an Ethical Imperative: Issues of Professionalism," Paper presented at the IUS Regional Conference, Maxwell Air Force Base, Alabama, (June 4, 1973), 3.

7. Arthur J. Dyck, "Ethical Bases of the Military Profession," *Parameters* (March, 1980), 40.

8. Samuel P. Huntington, *The Soldier and the State* (Cambridge, MA: Harvard University Press, 1967), 67.

9.   Sir John Hackett, *The Profession of Arms* (London: Times Publishing Company, 1962), 63.

10.   Robert G. Gard, "The Military and American Society," *Foreign Affairs* (July, 1971), 699.

11.   Walter Kerwin, "The Values of Today's Army," *Soldier* (September, 1978), 4.

Challenges to Professionalism

M odern democratic societies are organizationally and sociologically complex. That complexity gives rise to a number of challenges to the professionalism that rests at the core of the military and its special ethics. The problem is that democratic organizational and social structures are "modern" in the sense of being organized and operated on "rational" lines while institutions like the military must be organized and operate along "pre-modern" or interpersonal lines. Rational organizations cannot take cognizance of the differences and worth of individuals while premodern institutions must do precisely that in order to create and sustain the social forces that produce cohesion and attachment among their members. No soldier is willing to die for an organization's efficiency, but he or she might risk his or her life for the close friendships he or she has made within an institution and for the values the institution represents. This contrast between modern and pre-modern organizational forms and the different ways that they create meaning for individuals challenges the professionalism of military establishments.

Democratic military establishments are subject to five challenges which arise from within the modern societies they serve: psychological egoism, occupationalism, managerialism, confusion with bureaucracy, and specialization. All of these have one thing in common, the underlying assumption that the individual's pursuit of self-interest somehow leads to the highest form of human fulfillment. With regard to group life, the corollary assumption is that the pursuit of self-interest will necessarily result in a sense of community interest recognized and shared by all members of the group. A further corollary is that the pursuit of self-interest can never truly be contrary to the good of the community which, in any case, has no real existence apart from the collective of individuals which comprise it. The whole can never be greater than the sum of its parts. This same set of assumptions forms the value foundation of most Western capitalist democracies and is characteristic of most modern forms of social organization.

The difficulty is, however, that these assumptions are open to serious question from a variety of perspectives. With regard to the military profession, it seems clear that one cannot have a sense of professional community obligation that will not at some point require the individual soldier to forego his or her self-interest in order to secure the interests of the community. At the same time, one cannot form a community of military professionals in which communal obligations bind the soldier apart from his or her self-interest if one assumes that the individual's self-interest is the highest operant value. These contradictions not withstanding, the challenges to military professionalism can converge with great force and threaten to erode the ethical centre of the profession itself.

Psychological Egoism

The threat from psychological egoism arises from its claim to be a valid ethical perspective that can supplant the ethic of community service as the foundation of the military profession. Proponents of egoism argue that a community ethic transcending the interests of the individual is simply not workable. All that is possible, they claim, is the ethics of real individuals fashioned from the specific circumstances in which they find themselves at the moment. This view is clearly expressed by a young officer in an article entitled, "The Career Officer as Existential Hero," and makes a case for the role of psychological egoism in a military career as an alternative ethic within the military profession.[1] It is worth exploring because it offers a good example of the view that psychological egoism can provide the basis for community ethics within the armed forces.

The author argues that such "old ideals" as duty, loyalty, honour, sacrifice, and service to others no longer have meaning for the modern generation of soldiers and officers. These values are "external commitments" that are forged in the profession and superimposed upon the individual soldier. Since they are rarely if ever internalized by the soldier, they quickly collapse under the stress of war and are never really honoured. The author argues that allowing the soldier to develop his or her own set of "internal commitments" will serve as a better motivator for the soldier.

> "I only ask that they not try to influence me into accepting their motivations. Truth, after all, is a relative quantity; the environmental factors influencing the graduates of the service academies of thirty years ago have changed; thus the motivational factors must also change."[2]

The logical consequence of this position is that since one cannot create a set of community ethics within the military profession (or any other profession for that matter) that are different from those of the larger society, individuals within the profession need to adopt those ethical values that are congruent with the larger society. Thus, "what is required today is the projection of an image of the career officer consistent with the aspirations spawned by the contemporary society. Senior officers...must respect the claim to a different motivation by not trying to force their motivations upon us."[3] It is, therefore, only the individual who develops whatever motivations lead him or her to enter military service, and the larger professional community in which the soldier claims membership may or may not share these motivations. In either case, the individual soldier reserves to him or herself the right to develop whatever values or goals they see fit. Because people are social beings, whatever values motivate them in any group are essentially those that will motivate them in the larger society. Thus these motivations must be the same.

The psychological egoist also suggests what the role of the military ought to be vis-a-vis the individual soldiers who comprise it.

> "A true profession must provide the opportunity to work with and for people, the opportunity to influence others, the opportunity to master a discipline, and those aspects which make the military and the naval profession particularly appropriate for the fulfillment of an "existential commitment—the opportunity to develop a level of personal and professional excellence and have it meaningfully challenged in positions, the opportunity to do battle with potentially overwhelming adversaries, and the opportunity to aid in the conquest of man's last two frontiers, space and the seas. Dedicated service to our country will follow."[4]

The duty of the military profession, then, is to provide *opportunities* for individual fulfillment and in taking advantage of such opportunities the soldier will confront circumstances in which he or she must make choices. It is in making these choices that the psychological egoist finds meaning in the world and personal life. The egoist is what he or she decides. Humans are to be judged by the consequences of their acts and man is only what he decides to do. The role of professional standards is only to provide opportunities within which the soldier may make choices and in doing so come to define him or herself. The idea that the individual may have obligations to the profession that transcend the circumstances in which decisions are made is rejected. It is simply assumed that once the individual decides what he or she wishes to do, dedicated service to the profession and country will follow. *It is presumed that there is no fundamental tension between what the individual soldier wishes to do in any given circumstances and what the military profession and professional ethics require him or her to do.* It is in "doing one's thing," so to speak, that the individual defines him or herself and thus renders service to the profession and the nation.

Several criticisms may be directed at this theory of professionalism. First, egoism undercuts any notion of service to the community as a basis for military professionalism. While one may witness such service, it results only tangentially from the fact that the individual is "defining himself" in the larger professional or social context and could have just as legitimately made the opposite decision. There can be no question of the soldier having to sacrifice individual interests for the community good. Egoism posits a distinct difference between *external* commitments and *internal* commitments. Values imposed from without are not really values at all. Only those values that evolve from within are likely to be meaningful to the individual and compel observance. While no one would dispute that internalized norms are excellent motivators, two points are worth considering. First, in some instances external communal values may be the only ones available or the only way to compel observance to a necessary, but difficult, course of ethical action. Second, there ought to be an intimate connection between external and internal values. Humans are social animals and live in organized groups. Much of what is meaningful to humans is obtained through group membership. This is especially true with regard to the norms of the military profession which are not found outside the profession itself. Thus, in a society based largely on self-interest and egoism, where but in the profession of arms would an individual find values of service and sacrifice? If values are only internally derived, then we must resign ourselves to a profession based on self-interest and self-actualization.

Most individuals find great meaning in their personal lives largely as members of some group. Frequently, the external values of the group become internalized and become effective stimuli for ethical actions within the group. Without a clear statement of these external standards, especially those ethical standards and precepts most relevant to the profession's responsibilities, it is difficult to see how an individual within the profession could arrive at these standards at all. Even if it were possible for an individual to arrive at these standards by intuition or, perhaps, through experience, it is by no means certain that a community of individuals would end up discovering the same values. It seems obvious that internal values will only develop within group settings, and that they evolve more quickly and more clearly insofar as the group itself sets certain standards that must be observed as the price of belonging to the group. To suggest otherwise is to claim that somehow individuals within a community can spontaneously arrive at identical values without the group first setting forth what those values are.

Yet another criticism of psychological egoism can be directed at its claim that "truth, after all, is a relative quantity." The fact is, however, that a profession must offer a statement of values and ethics that transcends its membership and defines what the profession is all about. In this pragmatic sense, truth is not a relative quantity at all. *If the profession does not profess an ethical centre or set of obligations that constitute the true values of the profession, then, quite simply, it is not a profession.* To suggest that professional values and norms are merely relative ethical qualities is to suggest that professionals may hold grossly different values about what constitutes their obligations to the profession and what the obligations of the profession to the community are. It is absurd, for example, to suggest that a physician who feels comfortable with values condoning the extermination of the mentally ill or physically handicapped should be allowed to put those values into practice as a physician simply because he or she "feels they are meaningful." No one could in good conscience consent to this physician being allowed to remain a professional in good standing.

The question of whether or not truth is relative, however, is not as important as the egoist's claim that values and standards have no meaning apart from the individual who holds them. If this is so, then ethics of any sort is impossible since ethical judgments on the meaningful actions of others would have no basis upon which they might be made. *The very foundation of military professionalism, as well as all ethics, requires that the values and ethics of the profession have existence and meaning apart from the willingness of the individual to observe them.* Only when the individual willingly commits in advance to observe such values even before he or she can know the circumstances in which the values might have to be applied can he or she truly be granted membership in the profession. It is not possible for the profession to tailor its values to a multiplicity of individuals who manifest a range of conduct, even contradictory conduct, and still claim it is a profession.

With regard to the egoist argument that the values of individuals are "spawned" by those of the larger society, it can be pointed out that people live in social groups and different social groups tend to develop different values appropriate to the activities of their members. Thus, academic groups have different values from, say, bowling leagues because their activities are different, although both are "spawned" by the larger society. *There is no demonstrable requirement that the values of military professionalism be inextricably tied to the values of the larger society or that the motivational forces that work in the larger society necessarily work as well or at all in any of society's subgroups.* Quite to the contrary. A large number of societal subgroups require motivational forces that do not work in the larger society but are still requirements for membership. One would be hard pressed, for example, to explain recruitment to the clergy on grounds of economic self-interest. The claim that there is a fixed set of motivational factors that serve the individual regardless of the social setting or circumstances in which he finds himself is false. Some motivational factors are appropriate to some social groupings and completely inappropriate to others.

Nowhere is the egoist more disturbing to the military professional than in the claim that social groups exist only to provide individuals with *opportunities* to which they may react and in doing so define themselves. In reacting to these opportunities, individuals make decisions that define "who the individual is." The egoist's stress on opportunities obscures the fact that the military profession has far more to do with *obligations* than with opportunities. To suggest that the reason for being of the military profession is to create opportunities for individuals is to do nothing less than to negate any ethical standard as to *how* soldiers *ought* to act since the egoist claims that the challenge comes from responding to circumstances in which soldiers find themselves *at the moment*. It is critically important that the military profession set standards of how soldiers ought to act in order to guide them when they have to act. The egoist claims that this is unnecessary in that soldiers will "know" how to act either through intuition or the relevant information that presents itself by the circumstances in which the soldier finds it necessary to act. But the contradiction is obvious. If the only basis for ethical action is intuition or information provided by the circumstances themselves and, as the egoist claims, every set of circumstances in unique, then one can learn nothing from one's own experiences. Thus, for the "existential hero" there is no basis at all for obligations to bind since obligations must bind soldiers *before* they find themselves in the circumstances in which they must act.

The fundamental thrust of psychological egoism as a threat to the professionalism of the military is its denial of the ability of human beings to create ethical rules to govern human conduct in anticipation of that conduct. As a corollary, it becomes impossible to devise ethics within the confines of the profession itself. Egoism is corrosive of the ethics of military professionalism, as it is of any sense of obligation apart from that which the individual discerns to be imposed by the circumstances of the moment. The military profession has an obligation to deal with this challenge forcefully by emphasizing and enforcing its own ethical standards.

Occupationalism

Occupationalism claims that the profession of arms and the soldier's service in it is no different than being employed by and working in any other occupation in the civilian sector. As Western societies moved toward the post-industrial democratic age, they began to develop bureaucratic forms of socio-economic organization, at the same time developing highly econometric methods for analyzing the performance of these organizations. One consequence was the idea that the military establishment could be treated exactly as any other occupation in terms of analyzing and evaluating its performance. It was assumed that people entered and remained in the armed forces for the same reason they entered and remained in any other civilian occupation. The focus of analysis in employing econometric models was upon "hard" data such as wages, amount of free time, paid vacations, working conditions, status, etc., all factors easily measurable by statistical techniques. The result of this approach, in fact a necessary precondition of being able to utilize its methodology at all, was the conclusion that the military did not represent any special form of human organization and, therefore, did not require any different motivation for its members. In short, the profession was thought to be not meaningfully different, if at all, from any other civilian occupation or business. If so, then what motivates individuals in the larger social context—the pursuit of power, prestige, income, status, etc. defined in terms of self-interest—also motivates the soldier. This assumed similarity of motives permitted the application to the military of a wide range of techniques that had proven useful in the organization and management of civilian business.

It may well be that certain concerns of business executives and employees are of equal moment to officers and soldiers. But even if the same motivational forces *initially* attracted individuals to military service, it is unlikely that these same forces could *sustain* soldiers in the profession for very long. Econometric formulas cannot explain why soldiers are prepared to risk their lives and, in some instances, sacrifice their existence in service to their comrades. In simple terms, *econometric models do not work on the battlefield because death and injury in combat is always an irrational economic choice for the one injured or doing the dying. Whatever it is that motivates soldiers to do these things, it surely is not an economic calculus.*

Occupationalism presents a threat to military professionalism because it may transfer the inequalities of the larger society into the profession. Once military service is defined in essentially economic terms and motivation of the soldier is rooted in economic egoism, any notion of selfless service and sacrifice that transcends individual self-interest is weakened. It is nonsense to claim that the military can recruit and hold soldiers in service largely on the grounds of economic self-interest and at the same time maintain that the military is a profession based on selfless service to its clients. The use of economic formulas for recruitment and retention fundamentally diminishes the ethical and professional supports of the military establishment.

Occupationalism was initially forced upon the profession by its civilian overseers in an effort to save money and analyze performance in terms of cost-effectiveness. After a while, the military establishment itself developed a corps of officer-managers who willingly embraced the new measurements. In the end, the movement away from vocationalism represents a movement away from professionalism and toward occupationalism, a corrosive force eating at the ethical foundations of the profession itself.

These developments can have potentially devastating effects on the ethics of the profession. As the military moves away from being perceived as a special calling or vocation toward being perceived as just another occupation, the military's self-image and the popular image of the profession change markedly. As long as the military views itself as a vocation, the populace can rightly expect it to adhere to high ethical standards. At the same time the officer and soldier believe that their adherence to these ethical standards is what sets them apart from civilian occupations. There exists, then, a wide recognition that military service requires a sense of special obligation and responsibility that permits the members of the profession to have their role legitimized precisely in terms of their service to the community and to the profession.

With occupationalism, however, the military has become more job-oriented, and the perception of its role has changed. The public, paradoxically, still expects adherence to ethical standards while simultaneously perceiving and treating military professionals no differently than other employees. The military is assumed to be motivated by forces of self-interest while at the same time the populace continues to require the military to perform selfless service. The difficulty arises once the military becomes widely perceived as just another occupation (as it already has in most countries with volunteer military establishments), when success within the profession is measured by terms synonymous with the values of the business executive (promotion, good assignments, status, etc.), and when military professionals in dealing with their civilian overseers are required to function in a marketplace environment that is often more conducive to ethical precepts (ethical egoism, for example) that run contrary to those of the military profession. Under these circumstances, one fears that the profession will suffer an ethical breakdown[5] as it attempts to adjust to this powerful hostile environment and in doing so risks becoming indistinguishable from other self-interested business enterprises. If the motivational, organizational, and leadership practices of the military professional become more and more like those of the professional manager and business executive, there is a great risk that an erosion of professional ethics and the special identity that supports them will occur. One cannot destroy professionalism in the name of economics and at the same time expect that the military's sense of special obligation, selfless service and sacrifice to the common good will long remain intact.

Managerialism

Managerialism is defined as the penetration of the profession by values closely associated with those of the civilian business enterprise. If military service can be equated with civilian business, then there is no reason why many of the business organization's managerial techniques cannot also be applied to the military. Modern managers believe that the application of business management techniques, such as cost-effectiveness, personnel management, centralized promotions, human relations specialists, computer purchasing, and financial control can just as easily be applied to the military establishment. No doubt this is true. But the key question is how much of this can be accomplished without disturbing the basic nature of the military profession.

Over the last two decades many of the military's traditional and successful mechanisms of control, organization, and accountability have been replaced in Western armies with mechanisms adopted from the business corporation. Some of the traditional powers of commanders over promotion in the ranks have been taken away and centralized in remote personnel centres. Often leave and pass policies are no longer subject to disciplinary requirements by local commanders but are guaranteed by central managerial authorities as conditions of the soldier's "employment." Soldiers no longer live in barracks once they leave basic training, but in two or three-person rooms, despite the fact that the traditional housing arrangements have been shown to be among the strongest institutional supports for building unit cohesion.[6] Cost-effectiveness and budget monitoring are often the most important requirements to which commanders have to attend so that many spend more time satisfying bureaucratic requirements than with their troops. The establishment of a readiness system in which paper reports and surveys are substituted for actual field readiness inspections and performance tests routinely produces false assessments of actual combat fighting ability. All are examples of managerial techniques within the military that have proved less than useful to strengthening the fighting ability of the profession.

Among the most damaging aspects of managerialism has been the adoption of managerial values. The importance of self-interest to career advancement has made itself felt mostly in the officer corps of volunteer armies. In *Crisis in Command*, my colleague and I described a number of managerial values afflicting the American officer corps after Vietnam that were traceable to the transformation of the military from a vocation to a business. Some or all of these practices can be found to a greater or lesser extent in every volunteer army in the West. These practices include careerism, ethical relativism, the need to be "a team player," lack of dissent, lack of resignations in protest of policy, an officer corps in peripatetic motion continually punching its "tickets" in order to position itself for the next "deep zone" promotion, and sending too many officers to staff and professional schools despite the inability to employ most of them in positions for which they are extensively trained. Often advanced degrees are pursued only with a view toward post-service employment, thus the proliferation of Masters of Business Administration degrees among staff officers.[7] One can discern the tendency among managerial officers to refer to captains and platoon lieutenants, the key commanders in the military's killing units, as equivalent to "middle-tier managers."

Central to the threat posed to the profession by managerialism is the proposition that military leadership can be equated to or even replaced by modern managerial practices, that literally, "men can be managed to their deaths." Resource management, the management of things, has become dangerously equated with leadership. *This change in values threatens to erode the warrior ethos of leadership and to replace it with managerial technique on the ground that ability in one is equivalent to ability in another.* This substitution of managerialism for professional military leadership can have disastrous consequences in war where it works against unit cohesion and the confidence between leaders and led that is vital for an army to fight well. The American army during the Vietnam war is an example of what can happen when managerialism is substituted for professional leadership, values, and competence. That army suffered a battlefield catastrophe in which units would not fight, officers were assassinated, and troop rotation made it a deadly practice to have the least experienced soldiers walk point. To meet the challenge of managerialism will require a leadership corps that recognizes the difference between good leadership and good management and does not confuse one with the other.

Confusion with Bureaucracy

If there is anything more disheartening than trying to make the soldier into a businessman, it is trying to make the soldier into a bureaucrat. This confusion is inevitable given the tendency to view the military as no different from any other organizational form. There is, however, a fundamental difference between the soldier and the bureaucratic manager, and that is the values that motivate each. The bureaucrat is charged with executing rules that are designed to limit initiative and discretion. *The purpose of a bureaucracy is precisely to limit innovation by routinizing responses to the environment to only those circumstances that the bureaucracy can foresee.* By executing rules "without respect to persons," the bureaucrat avoids responsibility for consequences and minimizes the need for judgment. The ultimate goal of the bureaucrat is to follow orders, minimize risks, and move upward in the organization by following the rules of promotion to his or her own advancement.

The role of the soldier is radically different. *The crux of military leadership is the ability and willingness to exercise judgment in unforeseen circumstances. This is the core of command in battle.* But if judgment is central to good leadership, then the soldier's code of ethics meant to guide him or her in making command decisions is not equivalent to a set of bureaucratic rules. For the soldier, a code of ethics represents a set of governing norms encouraging judgment and initiative. While the bureaucrat must always follow orders, the military commander must make judgments;

where the bureaucrat shuns initiative, the commander must seize it; where the bureaucrat avoids responsibility, the commander must willingly accept it. While it may be possible to make a good leader a good bureaucrat, one is unlikely to succeed in making a bureaucrat a good leader. The continued confusion of leadership with managerial bureaucracy remains a self-inflicted wound from which many military establishments suffer.

Unless due care is taken, bureaucratic organization and values will tend to transform the profession's leadership corps into managerial functionaries. Central to the task of resistance is a clear ethical code that supports the precepts of military professionalism. The code must necessarily extol courage, both ethical and physical, flexibility of action, and a willingness to make decisions, take risks, accept responsibility, and exercise judgment. It is precisely these qualities that have historically marked effective leadership and professional officership, and they are in as much demand today as they have been throughout history.

Specialization

As the military's organizational structure became more complex, specialization of function became a necessity. Colonel Richard Rosser notes that specialization within the military has tended to reduce professionalism,[8] and that specialization tends to become overspecialization and works against commitment to the profession and substitutes for it a narrow commitment to one's own area of special skill:

> "Perhaps the biggest challenge to the concept of military professionalism is the need for specialization in all ranks. Young men in the service increasingly think of themselves as meteorologists, economists, electrical engineers, political scientists, and nuclear physicists. If they have a commitment, it is primarily to their particular profession or discipline and secondarily to the military profession."[9]

The short career lengths of many volunteer armies exacerbate the effects of specialization by forcing people early on to look beyond their period of military service to second careers in order to sustain their families and provide education and medical insurance for growing children. As a consequence, they often seek to acquire skills within the military that they can use in the civilian economy after they leave service at a relatively young age. It does not help, of course, if military retirement benefits are inadequate, as they usually are. Specialization, both as a force within the military and as an anticipated reaction to leaving it, lessens the member's sense of commitment to the profession as a way of life. *Here it must be recalled that what marks a person as a member of a profession is his or her willingness to bear the special ethical burdens and responsibilities that are imposed on it by the profession's code of ethics. It is not the soldier's possession of special skills nor even his or her proficiency in practicing them that makes a soldier a professional.*

Specialization has not, in itself, necessarily undercut military professionalism. Given the amount of time the soldier spends in the profession, his or her career can be structured to offset the pull of whatever specialty he or she possesses. Although the soldier possesses skills, the key point is that he or she still practices these skills within a military environment, and the challenge is to ensure that the pull of the environment is sufficiently strong to sustain the soldier's primary interest in remaining a member of it. In other professions, specialization does not seem to reduce commitment. There is far greater specialization within the professions of law and medicine, for example, than there is in the military. And yet members of these professions seem to have little problem identifying with their professions. Perhaps this is a function of lifetime membership and practice which affords personal identity and financial rewards over a longer time than is typically permitted for the soldier.

Paradoxically, a soldier does not usually spend a significant number of his or her career assignments in a specialized skill field. An examination of a typical career officer who attains general officer rank would show that in a period less than twenty-five years that officer would have "punched through" approximately eighteen different assignments, spending only a few months in each of them. Most military promotion systems encourage the creation of generalists by rotating officers through a number of assignments. This, of course, works against creating a corps of specialists who are likely to be found in the more technical services like the air or naval forces. Thus the system itself is likely to mitigate the negative effects of excessive specialization, at least among the officer corps.

The fact is that specialization by itself is not an overwhelming force. It presents a major challenge when it is found in combination with other more virulent challenges that weaken the profession in other ways. Barring that, the application of technology and specialization has seldom caused a weakening of the military profession by itself. The Roman army, for example, was the most technologically sophisticated armed force for its time, and yet was able to maintain a stunningly high degree of professionalism. The same was true of Napoleon's army. Technology and specialization are most likely to have negative effects when the profession is unsure of itself, already weakened by other corrosive forces. Without some degree of specialization, it is unlikely that a modern military force could sustain itself. The true challenge of specialization is not to rid the profession of it, but to control it and have it serve the goal of enhancing professionalism.

A profession under siege by occupationalism, managerialism and the values of business, that confuses itself with bureaucracy, that allows psychological egoism to erode its philosophical base, and permits specialization to cut across communal ties is at great risk of ceasing to be a profession at all. Under these conditions, the military establishments of Western democracies are in danger of becoming entrepreneurial enterprises, vehicles for fulfilling career aspirations. The basic tension is between an *institution* with a developed sense of corporate ethics and an *organization* governed largely by mechanistic values of utilitarian efficiency.[10] The two are opposites and ultimately irreconcilable, especially in the profession of arms where the responsibilities of the soldier are so serious and the requirements for ethical behaviour so obvious.

Endnotes

1.   David G. Deininger, "The Career Officer as Existential Hero," *U.S. Naval Institute Proceedings* (November, 1970), 18-22.

2.   Ibid., 22.

3.   Ibid.

4.   Ibid.

5.   Alan J. Futernick, "Avoiding an Ethical Armageddon," *Military Review* (October, 1979), 17-23.

6.   Larry H. Ingraham, "Drugs, Morale, and the Facts of Barracks Living in the American Army," paper delivered at the 13th Annual Anglo-American Psychiatry Association, Plymouth, England (October, 1978). For more on this subject see by the larger official study by the same author, *The Boys in the Barracks* (Washington, DC: Walter Reed Army Institute of Research, 1978).

7.   Richard A. Gabriel and Paul L. Savage, *Crisis In Command* (New York: Hill and Wang, 1978).

8.   Richard R. Rosser, "Civil-Military Relations in the 1980's," *Seaford House Papers* (1970), 68.

9.   Ibid.

10.   Richard A. Gabriel, "Acquiring New Values in a Military Bureaucracy: A Preliminary Model," *Journal of Political and Military Sociology* (Spring, 1979), 89-101.

Some Responses

Responses to the challenges facing the military profession generally fall into two categories. First, there is the convergence response which claims that the military will remain an effective combat force only if it succeeds in bringing its archaic values into line with those of the larger society. Second, there are those who think it possible to return to a "golden age" during which they believe the military to have been almost completely isolated from society or, in a curious corollary, one in which society was strongly supportive of the military because of a value congruence between the values of the profession and those of the society. Neither of these alternatives seems appropriate or workable considering how the challenges to professionalism operate today.

Those who would return to a so-called "golden age" when societal values strongly supported military values might have considerable difficulty describing just when this period in Western history existed apart from times of war when patriotism and support for the military always tends to rise. There does not appear to ever have been a time in Western societies when these conditions of support obtained. In the United States, for example the military has always had to confront the antagonism of the larger society. Russell Weigley notes in this regard that:

> "Historically...the army and its values have tended consistently to seem so alien to the rest of society that for the army the times have almost always been troubled....The tensions between army and society have been great enough that, for American soldiers attempting faithful service to the values of both, dilemmas of moral integrity are not altogether new."[1]

In 1912, Colonel Emery Upton was so upset at relations between the army and its civilian overseers that he charged openly that the military profession was being "perverted" by civilian policies.[2] In Britain, too, the army has been historically regarded with distrust since it was often an instrument of domestic suppression by the king. The solution to this distrust was to deprive the military of a source of manpower by refusing to institute a draft, thus keeping the army small and making every effort to station it abroad. When military men lament the fact that they are not loved by the very society which they serve, they can take some consolation from the fact that it has almost always been so. For most of the last two centuries, military professionals have had to establish and enforce their own standards and values in the face of societies whose values were patently contradictory to military values and sometimes openly hostile to the very existence of a standing military force. To hope for a return to an age when the military enjoyed the respect and support of the civilian populace is to seek a time that never was.

The lack of an historical tradition of popular support for the military profession is not surprising considering that Western democracies and even the autocracies of Latin America and some former Western colonial societies have been predicated upon the pursuit of economic self-interest. These societies are unable to generate values congruent with the military profession's ideals of sacrifice and service. To attempt to make them do so would likely have required the militarization of the state more than the liberalization of the military. But in earlier eras, military professionalism was not the result of a congruence of values at all. Indeed, the opposite seems to have been true. Military establishments sustained and developed habits of good officership, cohesion, and discipline within the profession despite the fact that the larger society did not support these values. This was helped to some degree by the physical isolation of military posts and garrisons from the populace at large.

The reverse of the congruence strategy suggests that one can fashion a response to the challenges to professionalism by ensuring that the profession's values converge with those of the larger society. Thus,

> "Military professionalism must ultimately be grounded on the premise that military ethics converge with the ethical values of the larger society. A military system in a democratic society cannot long maintain its credibility and legitimacy if its ethical standards significantly differ from the civilian values of the larger society."[3]

When the values of the military are brought into line with those of the civil society, therefore, the result will be a profession secure in its own sense of service and obligations and more effective in carrying out its responsibilities. What is the evidence to support this claim?

If one is going to talk about the convergence of military and civilian values, one must first be clear as to the terms of discourse. If one is addressing the values of the society as they are meant in the general sense and their relation to the military profession, it is obvious that some degree of congruence already exists. *To the extent that the military's existence only makes sense in terms of its service to the state and society, there already is a convergence of fundamental values. No democratic society could tolerate a military establishment that did not see its primary role as service to the civic order.* In this sense, then, to suggest that convergence is required to sustain a sense of military professionalism may be stating the obvious, that is, to require that the profession be a profession. One the other hand, if by sustaining military professionalism through convergence one means that the values operant on a day-to-day basis of the larger civil society should be transposed into the military, then one makes a serious error. Over the last three centuries, most civil societies of the West have been fundamentally antithetical to the values of military professionalism. This is true not only as regards the highest social values of self-interest and individualism, but also insofar as the societies demonstrated values and practices that worked against military effectiveness. *If the strategy of convergence is taken to imply that the military must bring its own values and practices into line with those of the civil society, the price of convergence, assuming it is possible at all, is likely to be a military profession without a true sense of professionalism.*

Convergence as a strategy for responding to the challenges of military professionalism is a two-edged sword. If one democratizes, liberalizes, and civilianizes the military, the fear arises that the military will be unable to carry out its responsibilities in an effective way. From what we know of the causes of unit cohesion and military effectiveness, it seems clear that many of the practices, values, and norms of civil society simply will not work in the military environment. Thus, convergence in one sense runs the risk of producing a military establishment whose values are in fact congruent with those of the civil society but which is unable to effectively carry out is mission. Convergence could easily erode military professionalism by eroding the military capability of the profession itself.

An even greater difficulty is implicit in convergence. If the profession were to conclude that it was being weakened by the importation of civilian values and practices that were reducing its ability to fight, the profession might face a truly grave dilemma: the choice of silently watching the profession being destroyed in a sea of hostile values, or deciding that the civic order has become a threat to the existence of the profession itself. The danger of the strategy of convergence is that it lays out the logical rationale for a strike at the state by the military in order to survive as a profession. If the only nexus of military professionalism rests in society's larger values, that is, if no military establishment is permitted to exist unless it adopts civilian values, then when the military finds itself failing in its capacity to fight, the temptation to "reform" the society as a way of "reforming" the profession may be irresistible. Of course, this is precisely what happens when a traditional military establishment, often elite, class-bound, and autocratic, decides to intervene in the political process and "reform" newly established democratic societies like those of Chile or Guatemala.

The assumption that military professionalism and effectiveness will somehow follow from a convergence of military and civilian values is a proposition for which there is little if any evidence. What evidence there is suggests the opposite. Western military establishments have proved themselves capable of remaining professional institutions and of conducting effective combat operations in the face of a lack of popular support, and sometimes outright hostility, from their societies. The Roman legions, for example, remained a disciplined and cohesive fighting force long after Roman society had become manifestly corrupt. The German armies of World Wars I an II continued to fight long after their civic societies had been pounded into dust and could no longer function. The example of the French army at Dien Bien Phu suggests that the overt support of the larger society is not necessary to sustaining an effective military establishment.

None of this is to say that this support is not desirable, but only that the military profession is so different from civil society and requires such different obligations and responsibilities that it is unrealistic to expect civil orders rooted in self-interest to meet the requirements of professionalism by forcing the profession to make its values congruent with those of the society. The reality is that the military must be the guardian of is own values, codes, practices, and discipline that contribute to its professionalism and, ultimately, combat effectiveness. To be sure, the military ought never to forget that its own honour and professionalism are rooted in service to the state and its civilian masters. There is no evidence, at least in most Western societies, that a necessary contradiction exists between a sense of military professionalism and the larger democratic values of the civil polity.

What, then, is the profession to do? At least three directions of professional development seem possible. The first posits that the military has historically been isolated from the values of its host society. This is not to suggest that the profession does not share the fundamental values of the society. Indeed, the profession's reason for being is its service to the society. But the values associated with an effective military cannot be the same values of a civil democratic society rooted in self-interest. *Some degree of separation of the military from the larger society's values is a basic condition for sustaining military professionalism.*

A number of studies reveal that soldiers, especially officers, tend to reflect the socioeconomic characteristics of the larger societies from which they came.[4] At the same time, however, they have a distinct perspective of their profession that differs from that found in the society at large. Soldiers tend to see themselves as having to make greater sacrifices than the average citizen, as well as being a repository for the best traditional values of the civil order. The point is that membership in the profession seems in itself to result in a degree of social distance from the society, and this social distance or value isolation allows professional values to take hold in the soldier. Some soldiers may well feel that the civilian populace has low regard for what they do. In fact, a series of opinion polls taken in democratic societies over the years tend to show that the military remains one of the most prestigious institutions in the eyes of the general populace.[5] Most often the civilian population tends to view the military with high regard. In the United States, for example, the military remains among the most respected public institutions even though the war in Iraq has little public support. If the military is to successfully deal with the challenges it faces, its most basic requirement is that it remain a profession, and to accomplish this it must remain apart and distinct from the values of the civil society.

Clotfelter and Peters, in a study of the effects of civilian-military social interactions on the attitudes of military professionals, found that increased interaction by soldiers with civilians tended to have no effect on reducing the soldiers' sense of separateness and professionalism. When that interaction was negative in tone, the effect was to reinforce the soldiers' feeling of being a member of something special.[6] They also found that officers saw themselves as a distinct social group, as upholding the best traditional values, as requiring and giving greater dedication to the society than civilians, and they see their profession as involving greater sacrifice and responsibilities than even other professions.[7] What Clotfelter and Peters' data suggest is that the military profession is already separated from the larger society to some extent and that separation reinforces professional values by inculcating in the soldier a sense of belonging to a social institution that is different and special.

A second way that the military can reinforce its professionalism is by understanding the source and condition of the profession's core values. Historically, the source of the profession's values has been the profession itself. One of the reasons why the challenges to professionalism are so dangerous is precisely because they tend to erode these core values. It is important for the profession to realize that it has the primary responsibility for preserving its own uniqueness, just as the medical profession must preserve its own unique status by setting values and enforcing them. *The military cannot expect the larger society to provide or support the values most appropriate to the profession.*

Most of all, the profession must be prepared to defend its core values from assault from without and erosion from within. A major criticism of the modern military is its spotty record in successfully controlling the impact of hostile external social forces on its members.[8] Successful professions are those that succeed in forming barriers around themselves that mitigate and control these negative influences. The American military, for instance, is often criticized for failing to protect itself and acclimatizing too readily to civilianization, occupationalism, and managerialism as a way of sustaining support among other powerful government and private pressure groups for its budgets. The task of dealing with these difficulties is not easy, but neither is it impossible.

For those who are concerned that the military may become too isolated, it is worth emphasizing that a thoroughly professional military is far more easily controlled than one that closely reflects the momentary values of the larger society.[9] Military establishments become dangerous to the civic order precisely when they become too closely identified with the values and aspirations of the populace they protect. The risk is that the development of revolutionary conditions within the population may provoke strong sympathy within the "people's army," leading to dangerous consequences. Reginald Brown has noted that a strong sense of military professionalism eliminates a range of action that the military can legitimately take during times of social unrest.[10] Professional military establishments are more likely to defend the existing socio-legal order than attack it even in times of great social disturbances. Brown concludes that military professionalism is less of a threat to civilian authority than it is a force for confining the overt *political* response of the profession to very narrow channels. In the West, then, a number of professional and authoritarian military establishments have successfully coexisted within their host societies without difficulty. In practice, there appears to be no contradiction between a liberal democratic civil order and the presence within it of an authoritarian military profession. Both attempt to do different things and require different values.

The third direction that military professionalism might take is to develop and enforce a clear code of ethics. The codification of the profession's responsibilities as precepts to govern the actions of its members clearly implies that those who cannot or will not observe these responsibilities must leave the profession. Military service is not for everyone. Professionalism means living up to the requirements and expectations and carrying out the obligations that define membership in a group bearing special responsibilities. *Often military professionalism is confused with following orders and "doing one's duty." However, duty is the servant of ethics, not a substitute for it.* An example of the confusion is evident in the following statement:

> "The military professional is susceptible to influences external to the profession, albeit in a less pervasive way. Buffeted by these various forces, the individual professional is nevertheless expected to follow the lifestyle and accept the morality and ethics of the profession that primarily evolves from a monastic focus and horizontal network. Although the profession operates within the context of the morality and values of the political-social system, these dilemmas are relieved by adjusting individual lifestyles to the expectations of the profession. Thus the perspectives of the profession become the dominating morality and ethics of the individual officer. Institutional articulation of integrity, duty, honour, country and officership are substituted for the individual's own sense of morality and ethics."[11]

The above is an adequate description of the process of value socialization that attends the person who enters a profession. But it wrongly interprets the role of ethics in the professional environment. One's professional ethics, to reiterate, does not constitute the ethical obligations of the whole person, and to maintain that it does is to risk turning the soldier into an armed bureaucrat who follows rules rather than making ethical choices. To be sure, professional values can never promote evil as such; but the soldier draws his or her ethical obligations from a number of sources besides the profession. At best, the ethical values of the military profession are adequate guides in those situations most relevant to the activities of the military profession.

Even then the soldier cannot abandon his or her other ethical self without becoming deformed and deforming the profession as well. The observance of obligations without understanding, choice, and knowledge of consequences is not ethics or duty. It is a perversion of both.

A clearly stated code of ethics would go a long way to helping the military profession retain its moorings in a sea of hostile values but will not, by itself, eradicate the challenges facing the profession. At least two additional elements are required. First, the soldier must be provided with adequate training to develop an ability to recognize ethical dilemmas that are likely to arise in the conduct of his or her profession. Second, the soldier must be trained in ethical reasoning and the knowledge of how ethical choices are properly arrived at, and to find the courage to resolve those dilemmas in an ethically acceptable way. If this means, as it may well, choosing between the obligations of his or her profession and those acquired elsewhere, then that is the very nature of ethical choice. *One cannot escape ethical responsibility by substituting obedience for difficult choices.*

All professions, including the military, must understand that tensions sometimes arise between the individual's personal sense of ethics and the ethics of his or her profession, or among any number of other sources of ethical obligation that bind the soldier. The problem is not to try and bring the values of the individual soldier into perfect symmetry with those of his profession, for such tensions will always remain and arise since the soldier's professional ethics are not the totality of the soldier's ethical self. The soldier cannot escape the difficulty of choice and remain an ethical agent. The profession must recognize this central fact as it attempts to establish, promulgate, and enforce a code of ethics for its members, and then train them in the ways of ethical thinking.

Life, its challenges, and ethics are quite different in the profession of arms than in other occupations and professions in the civil society. As a profession, it might even be said that the military is categorically different. If the military gains its legitimacy from the recognition that its reason for being is to serve and protect the civil order, there can never be a question of a military professionalism that transcends the society as long as the civic order itself does not by its own actions become evil in itself, as it did in Germany in the 1930's or in Iraq under Saddam Hussein. The challenges confronting the profession require that the military devise strategies to meet them. At least three directions of future professional development are suggested. First, in order for the profession to prevent an erosion of its professional values and ethics the military must keep a certain social distance from the society. Second, with regard to generating, protecting and inculcating values appropriate to the behaviour of the profession's members, the military is itself responsible for accomplishing these tasks. It can expect little help from outside. Third, the very centre of the profession requires the establishment of an ethical code that clearly defines the responsibilities and ethical obligations of its members. The more the profession is permitted to become like the civilian society in values, habits, and practices, the less like itself it will remain.

Endnotes

1.   Russell F. Weigley, "A Historian Looks at the Army," *Military Review* (February, 1972), 26.

2.   Ibid., 33.

3.   Sam Sarkesian and Thomas M. Gannon, "Professionalism," *American Behavioral Scientist* (May-June, 1976), 506.

4.   Franklin D. Margiotta, "A Military Elite in Transition," *Armed Forces and Society* (February, 1976), 155-185.

5.   Ibid., 165.

6.   James Clotfelter and B. Guy Peters, "Profession and Society: Young Military Officers Look Outward," *Journal of Political and Military Sociology* (Spring, 1976), 42.

7.   Ibid., 45.

8.   Richard A. Gabriel and Paul L. Savage, *Crisis in Command* (New York: Hill and Wang, 1978).

9.   Reginald Brown, "The Meaning of Professionalism," *American Behavioral Scientist* (May-June, 1976), 520-522.

10.   Ibid.

11.   Sarkesian and Gannon, 510.

Obedience and Dissent

T he question of obedience pertains to the limits of the military professional's obligation to follow the orders of superiors. The military is understandably sensitive to the issue of the limits of its obedience to civilian authority, so much so that this is rarely addressed in a formal manner. In most instances, the issue is not raised in the curricula of military academies or staff schools. One could be forgiven the impression that the profession assumes that as a practical matter there are no limits to its obligation to obey legitimate civilian authority, and that one way of dealing with this vital question of politics and ethics is to ignore it. It is clear, however, that in a democracy there must be limits to the profession's obligation to obey, and the idea of such limits has been an accepted principle throughout Western military history. It has long been recognized that there are limits to the soldier's obligations to obey superiors. It seems appropriate, therefore, to examine the issues of loyalty, obedience, dissent, and resistance within the profession of arms as legitimate avenues of ethical action open to members when dealing with ethical questions.

The profession's sensitivity to these issues is understandable from the political perspective in that they raise the specter in the minds of the profession's political masters of a rebellious military that could become a threat to the democratic order. But in failing to deal with these important issues adequately, major ethical questions are left unanswered and the ethical principles that could serve as guides for appropriate actions in the event circumstances forced the issue remain unspecified.

There appears no inherent connection between a military profession organized along authoritarian lines whose values are somewhat separate from society and any demonstrable propensity for the profession to become a danger to the democratic civic order. One can point to England, the United States, and Canada as examples of long standing democracies with professional military establishments that have never posed a threat to their political regimes. The tradition is somewhat less strong in France, Germany, and Italy, but then the tradition of democratic rule is also less strong in those societies. The fear that a military profession that establishes clear answers to the questions of when ethical dissent and resistance of its members is permissible will become a danger is groundless. Indeed, the greater danger arises when the military keeps silent in the face of policies with which it seriously disagrees on ethical grounds.

The problem of most concern regarding military establishments is their demonstrated propensity *not* to question civilian authorities even when they pursue policies that run contrary to the best judgment of military professionals. The American military has an unfortunate history of compliance in the face of its own professional assessment that policies it was expected to execute were wrong, failing, or, indeed, unethical. The evidence is fairly strong that much of the senior leadership of the American military was opposed to most of the strategic and tactical policies employed in Vietnam.[1] They simply never spoke up. The recent congressional hearings into the policies being pursued in Iraq reveal one retired senior officer after another testifying that he or she disagreed strongly with the very policies they carried out when on active service without a murmur of dissent. It is the self-imposed silence of high-ranking military professionals far more than the dissent of lower-ranking soldiers that constitutes a potential danger to civilian authority. Officers should not fail to object to orders and policies that run contrary their best military judgment. Examined in this way, when one thinks about dissent, loyalty, and the limits of the soldier's obligations, the central point is this: *Soldiers fail to live up to their oath to serve the nation if they do not speak out when they conclude that civilian authorities or military superiors are carrying out policies that they think are ethically wrong.*

The Limits of Obligation

The individual is always at the centre of ethical responsibility and ethical action. Judgment and choice are central to ethics, and the soldier may never abandon his or her obligation to act ethically to any person or authority without him or herself ceasing to be ethical. *A soldier is never justified in acquiescing in orders he or she judges to be unethical, no matter whether issued by civilian or military authorities.* This is not to say that soldiers may not obey orders of which they are genuinely uncertain, although they will be held responsible for the consequences if, later, the orders turn out to be unethical. *But if a soldier is convinced that an order issued is unethical, he or she may not abandon their ethical obligation to resist or refuse these orders in an appropriate manner.* Thus Lieutenant Watada of the American army in 2007 who, convinced that the war in Iraq was unethical, refused to comply with orders to deploy to Iraq. He refused the military's offer of conscientious objector status on the grounds that he did not oppose all wars, only the war in Iraq. Lieutenant Watada offered to accept an assignment to Afghanistan because "that war is not immoral." The Army refused, and instituted court martial proceedings against him.

The military profession itself is under the same obligation as the individual soldier when it comes to following unethical orders. As a profession dedicated to selfless service to the society, the military establishment, personified by its highest-ranking officers, cannot simply acquiesce without dissent, without protest, and even, perhaps, without public outcry in any order that it concludes is unethical or harmful to the nation. The fact that the order may have been issued by a legitimate civilian authority makes no difference. Here it must be remembered that law has no necessary ethical content. Thus, no one would seriously claim that a soldier ought to follow the order to kill members of a minority group because the court that ordered this was legally constituted. *It is a well-established principle of ethics that human beings cannot abandon their ethical autonomy and judgment to other human beings and thereby escape responsibility for their actions. So, too, soldiers as ethical beings and as members of an ethical profession cannot escape responsibility by acquiescing to unethical orders, even if the orders are legal and issued by a legitimate civilian or military authority.*

In the normal course of things, the military must be loyal to its civilian superiors and soldiers must be loyal to their military superiors in carrying out all orders that are ethically and legally valid. As regards the profession, the obligation is to the nation and society rather than to the transitory occupiers of positions of civilian authority. The military has an obligation to bring its knowledge and expertise to bear in service to the common good. At the extreme, this obligation implies that if civilian authorities issue orders that are harmful to the nation, the military has an obligation to resist. Thus,

> "Faithfulness to one's fellow citizens in terms of the vow to uphold the Constitution means that the effort on the part of any group, even the government itself, to advocate or use violence in an unconstitutional manner is subject to challenge by the highest authorities within the military profession itself."[2]

The Turkish military, for example, has a long tradition of seeing itself as the "guardian of the nation" and has intervened several times in the past decades to prevent civilian authorities from precipitating a civil war. As guardians of the nation, the Turkish military has always reconstituted the civil authority along more peaceful lines, and then withdrawn from the political arena.

Another example arose during the Watergate Crisis of 1973 when some unit commanders, notably those in command of airborne units stationed in the country, feared that President Nixon might order them to take action against Congress or the courts. The unit commanders requested that the Secretary of Defense clarify their legal and ethical options to refuse such an order if it came. The Secretary of Defense, James Schlesinger, made it clear that the president's order would be both unlawful and unethical and could be rightly refused. The illustrative point here is that in both cases military professionals recognized their obligation to the nation as primary to both law and authority on ethical grounds. Hence, there are limits to the obligations the military owes its civilian superiors, and they are drawn very clearly on legal and ethical grounds.

The same principle applies to subordinates and their relationships to their military superiors. A soldier has a legitimate ethical and legal obligation to carry out the orders of his or her superiors providing such orders do not violate the soldier's ethical sense and judgment. When they do, the subordinate has an obligation to question and dissent from those orders and, if need be, to resist their execution in an appropriate manner. *Members of the military profession must recognize that there are limits to their obligations to civilian superiors, and there are limits, too, to the soldier's obligations to military superiors.* These limits are expressed in terms of challenges to the common good and the nation as they make themselves felt in challenges to the ethical sensitivities of soldiers and officers who must decide whether to obey or resist.

While there is no question that civilian authorities properly control the military and that soldiers have an ethical and legal obligation to execute the lawful and ethical orders of their superiors, it is important to understand that this obligation is never open-ended. There is no ethical clause of unlimited liability to obey. When the soldier confronts this obligation, he or she must be prepared not to follow those orders that are unethical or illegal. This counsel of dissent and resistance has a long tradition in the West, beginning with the medieval code of chivalry. The doctrine of limited obligation to unethical and illegal orders is found in the military manuals of most Western military establishments. The American example is found in army manual *FM 27-10 The Law of Land Warfare* and is expressed in the following manner.

> "The fact that the law of war has been violated pursuant to an order of a superior authority, *whether military or civil*, does not deprive the act in question of its character of a war crime, nor does it constitute a defense in the trial of an accused individual, unless he did not know or could not reasonably have been expected to know that the act ordered was unlawful."[3]

It is clear that a soldier who complies with an unethical order may be prosecuted as an accomplice of those who issued orders. Military regulations make it explicit that the soldier must be prepared to question and even disobey or refuse to comply with an order the soldier regards as unethical or illegal. There is no escaping ethical choice or judgment in deciding how one should act. This is true in all aspects of human social behaviour, and it is no less true of the difficult choices soldiers are sometimes forced to make.

The question of the limits of military obligation raises difficulties for most soldiers. Josiah Bunting, himself a professional soldier, points out that members of the military profession seem to have great difficulty recognizing ethical dilemmas and resolving them satisfactorily. Part of the reason is that soldiers usually receive little training in the formal ethical precepts of the military profession and no training at all in the critical intellectual skill of ethical reasoning.[4] Moreover, there are strong institutional pressures to avoid dealing with problems on ethical terms that could put the soldier's superiors at risk of criticism or even legal punishment. These pressures can create serious problems of conscience for the soldier and work directly against his or her ability to frame problems in ethical terms. Bunting notes in this regard:

> "What does the professional soldier do when his conscience troubles him, or even when his intellect alone troubles him, or when the two of them together tell him that the institution of which he is a part is making a very serious mistake? Can he stand up within the institution, make his criticisms forthrightly, dare to hope that they will be scrutinized dispassionately and acted upon in a way which may vindicate his judgement? Can he do this without serious risk to the successful development of his career? Generally

the answer to both questions is no. Even more depressing is the fact that the problem rarely surfaces...Everything in the professional soldier's training runs counter to his even posing the question."[5]

To raise the question of the limits of the soldier's obligations is to levy an enormous burden upon individuals who are already overburdened with obligations. It is necessary to do so nonetheless, for only ethical integrity can guarantee that the democratic processes of a free society remain unchallenged by force from within. Only a truly ethical profession comprised of truly ethical soldiers guarantees that the military will not abandon its ethical responsibility of service to democracy. In this sense the doctrine of limiting the soldier's obligations applies in the same sense that individuals have limits to all other obligations as well. It is this sense of limit that is at the foundation of the expectation that the military will remain loyal to its proper social role as servant of the society, and never its master. It is the failure of the military establishments of new emerging democracies to comprehend these limits that sometimes leads them to strike at their political regimes. Thus, the doctrine of ethical limit is not a threat to democracy at all, and may indeed be the only thing that saves some new democracies from their own military establishments.

The life of the soldier as it relates to the question of limiting obligations presents an intriguing paradox. On the one hand, we have a group of individuals who have willingly undertaken to live a life that demands sacrifice and hardship and the subordination of their own interests to those of the common good. On the other, these individuals who have taken an oath to bear the burden of unlimited liability in combat are very often reticent to speak out against orders they find repugnant or to disagree with their superiors.

> "Perhaps one of the greatest mysteries of the military profession is the fact that so often the officer who is willing to sacrifice his life in combat is hesitant to risk his career to correct an abuse in the system, to suffer the embarrassment by speaking out for justice, or to stand firm on moral grounds when the accepted practice follows a discordant tune. Being a brave combat leader does not guarantee that an officer will have the courage to overcome pressures to behave unethically in a bureaucracy."[6]

The soldier must come to grips with the difficulties attendant to the limits of military obligation, but he or she cannot do so by ignoring the problem. Nor can the difficulty be dealt with by going along with orders he or she regards as unethical. The only manner in which the soldier can deal with the problems of dissent, loyalty, and resistance is to confront the objections openly. *The profession, of course, has the obligation to specify the legitimate ethical alternatives that the soldier has available when dealing with orders he or she comes to believe are unethical. For the most part, military establishments have been less than clear about what these alternatives are and in instructing their soldiers in how they may be applied.*

Two basic questions relate directly to the limits of the soldier's obligation to obey orders. First, what is the ethical responsibility of the soldier when he or she is called upon to execute a policy or order to which they have an ethical objection? In principle, the answer is that no soldier can escape responsibility for his or her acts and their ethical obligations do not bind outside the context in which they must be executed or refused. *Thus, a soldier may not ethically carry out an order to which he or she has a genuine ethical objection.* Second, what are the limits of professional obligations when the soldier is confronted with conflicting ethical imperatives? In principle, when ethical imperatives conflict, a judgment must be made relative to the circumstances in which one finds oneself so that the soldier reaches an ethical decision as to what the proper course of action is. It is from these two principles that the rest of the discussion on dissent, loyalty, obedience, and resistance proceeds.

Legitimate Avenues of Military Protest

We may begin with the obvious fact that not all rules have an ethical content, and not all disagreements involve ethical issues nor are all obligations ethical obligations. The problem of limits, therefore, only addresses important ethical dilemmas and not trivial concerns of disagreement. Important ethical difficulties usually do not arise very often, although within the context of the profession of arms and combat they are probably likely to arise more often than in other professions. This said, a soldier may seriously disagree with an order and even have good reasons for doing so but without the disagreement necessarily involving an ethical conflict. In both policy formulation and execution, the soldier, especially ranking officers, can expect a fair amount of normal disagreement, and soldiers often find themselves carrying out policies with which they may disagree at least to some degree. It is important to avoid the tendency to escalate normal disagreements into ethical problems when there is no good reason to do so. Although grave ethical issues arise only rarely, when they do the soldier must deal with them.

When thinking about the limits of loyalty and obedience and the ethical requirement to resist unethical or illegal orders, the focus falls only upon those orders that involve serious ethical dimensions. When ethical issues of some gravity are not involved, the soldier's obligation to obey is expected to apply. It must also be clear that the soldier is not being counselled to disobey or resist orders *per se*. As we shall see, disobedience and resistance are serious and risky courses of action that can have extremely serious consequences for the soldier involved and ought not to be undertaken lightly. The discussion that follows explores the issue of the ethically acceptable alternatives within the normative precepts of the military profession that the soldier has available when confronted with a grave ethical dilemma.

An awareness of the obligations and the available means of ethical protest makes it easier for the soldier to exercise ethical options in the face of an ethical quandary by providing information on what options the profession itself considers acceptable. One cannot, of course, rely solely upon the soldier's virtue, for even the most virtuous soldier may not be aware of what ethical courses of action are pragmatically available. *The profession bears the important responsibility to clearly specify those courses of action that it considers ethically appropriate and to make certain that the soldier's training is such that the soldier is made fully aware of what legitimate avenues of protest, resistance, and refusal are open to him or her.*

One can be certain, however, that as quickly as the profession attempts to do this the bureaucracy will respond in its own defence so that if the profession creates procedures to allow the expression of dissent and even disobedience, the bureaucracy will move to co-opt these procedures, especially those associated with resignation in protest, and attempt to render them empty of ethical significance. Under these conditions, acts of disobedience and especially resignation in protest may well be reduced to bureaucratic exercises in which the recalcitrant officer is permitted to "go quietly over the side," sometimes even rewarded with a "gangplank promotion" or a medal for meritorious service. The idea, of course, is for the bureaucracy to protect itself by quieting any adverse publicity or public hearings. There is always the risk that the organizational bureaucracy will neutralize procedures for dissent. It is the obligation of the profession's leadership to ensure that the bureaucracy does not permit noble acts of ethical courage to be reduced to paper exercises. In any case, resignation, dissent, protest, or refusal of orders are likely to occur only rarely, making it at least somewhat less likely to sustain the kinds of officious procedures that work to reduce the nobility of ethical acts. The profession itself has an obligation not to permit the importance of an individual's ethical actions to be blunted and nullified by the bureaucracy.

It is often argued that one reason for not "fighting the system" on ethical grounds is that it is pointless to do so, that it does no good to get mired down in such questions to begin with. If a soldier were to resign in protest, refuse an order, or publicly dissent, the results would almost certainly be to ruin his or her career, to isolate them from their peers, to remove them from command, and to withhold promotion. Moreover, the organization would simply find someone else to do its bidding, and the game would go on. The possibility exists that one's replacement would be even less sensitive to ethical concerns. The sad truth of the matter is that all of these consequences might well befall the soldier who chooses to confront the system on ethical grounds.

But even so, the argument completely misconstrues the nature of ethical obligations. *Responsibility for carrying out ethical obligations remains whether or not doing so has the effect of changing policy or stopping the order's being carried out by others. One still has the obligation to try.* No one would seriously argue, for example, that the Ten Commandments should be ignored and not regarded as guides to ethical behaviour because people sometimes violate them. Ethical responsibility remains an obligation regardless of the degree to which it has the desired consequence of stopping or changing behaviour. *If the question is asked, who benefits from an ethical action if others or the organization itself ignores it, then the answer is that it benefits the individual who acted ethically.* The utility of an act cannot be the only criterion for it being judged as ethical. Not all ethical acts always achieve their ends. The point is that sometimes the value of an ethical act resides exclusively within the individuals who observe it, individuals who refuse to ignore wrongdoing because to do so is difficult or costly to themselves. *The obligation to be true to themselves and their ethical code transcends the degree to which it is effective in stopping an unethical order or changing policy.* At Nuremberg, Judge Thomas Dodd used a simple standard to assess the ethical honesty of those Nazi defendants who said that they carried out their orders under duress even though they personally did not wish to do so. He asked them to recount a single instance where they had tried to evade their unethical orders. Not a single defendant could meet the test.

If acts of ethical resistance, protest, and dissent are not likely to change the outcome of events, then where is the value in having soldiers do them? Even if no policy changes occur, the fact that individual soldiers resist policies to which they are ethically opposed or resign in protest or refuse to execute unethical orders breathes life into the values of the profession. Such acts create ethical exemplars, role models, and in some instances, even the stuff of legend to whom young officers and troop leaders can look for future guidance. Examples of ethical courage sustain the meaning and integrity of the profession's code of ethics. *These courageous acts establish precedents which others soldiers can learn from and admire. The fact that an ethical act may or may not "do any good" is not the only relevant criterion upon which to judge its worth.* If one looks to people like Socrates, Thomas Beckett, and Thomas Moore, it is clear that their actions stand by themselves as acts to be admired and imitated, although their actions had no immediate impact on the policies of the organizations they were trying to influence. Yet they remain exemplars whose courageous actions give great meaning to the point of living an ethical life.

The military profession will only be able to encourage its members to follow such examples if it can develop among its members a capacity to balance ethical and career pressures. To do this, the profession must instill within its members a capacity for ethical reasoning and judgment as well as the personal courage and institutional support necessary to exercise ethical options. These capacities are required at all rank levels where soldiers have the responsibility of being in command of other soldiers. *It is imperative, then, that the profession develop a doctrine of ethical protest for its members and that it support the exercise of that doctrine in pragmatic terms. Ethical courage and action must be rewarded in career terms as well as ethical terms.* Of course, this doctrine must be consistent in theory and practice with the values of democratic society and continued civilian control of the military. Any doctrine of protest, dissent, and resistance for soldiers that violated these basic precepts would be unacceptable and dangerous, tending to provide justification for excessive military influence within the democratic civil order. That is never the intention of any honourable soldier serving in a democracy.

What, then, are the ethically permissible avenues of protest for a soldier that are consistent with the democratic values and practices of a free society and continued civilian control of the military? What courses of action may a soldier properly take when faced with being ordered to carry out or acquiesce in policies and orders to which he or she has serious ethical objections? Four legitimate avenues of military protest are available to the soldier in these circumstances: (1) resignation or retirement in public protest, (2) request for relief, (3) appeal of orders to a higher level of command, and (4) direct refusal to carry out the order. None of these courses of action conflict with democratic values, and all are congruent with the Western military tradition. Since none is inherently associated with collective resistance (mutiny), the menace of the coup d'état is not associated with them.

Resignation/Retirement in Public Protest

The most obvious way in which a soldier, especially a senior officer, can demonstrate ethical disagreement with an order or policy is to resign from the profession in a public act of protest. The soldier must leave the profession and seek to influence his or her government from outside as a citizen. This is the soldier-citizen's legal right. Resignation or early retirement as a response to ethical pressures implies that there can be no escape from one's ethical obligations. The obligation continues even after one has left service. If the ethical precepts of the profession are no longer observable because they require the sacrifice of the individual's sense of what is right, or if they run counter to the individual's sense of a higher ethical loyalty or, as is most probably the case when it involves a senior officer, the extant practice runs counter to the profession's own stated code of ethics, the soldier can legitimately resign or retire. The act of resignation puts the soldier beyond the precepts and limits of the profession and the soldier is now free to try and change those policies he or she regards as ethically offensive, but must now do so as a citizen.

Resignation can be accompanied by a public declaration of the reasons compelling the soldier to resign, thus exposing the policy or orders in question to public scrutiny and debate. This is precisely what Colonel Eli Geva of the Israeli Defense Force did when he publicly resigned his position as commander of the lead combat brigade approaching Beirut in 1982. Geva resigned in the middle of a war to bring attention to what he believed was an immoral and illegal war in Lebanon. Resignation in protest is perfectly consistent with democratic values and in no manner challenges civilian control of the military. As a practical matter, resignation or retirement in protest presents evidence to both the military and civilian political establishments, as well as the public at large through the press, that something may be seriously wrong with existing policies. To this extent, public dissent may well increase the rationality of the decision-making process by making available to it more relevant information. The soldier who feels strongly about the ethics of a policy issue or order can satisfy his or her own sense of ethical responsibility by taking this course of action.

Resignation or retirement in public protest is almost always a more effective means of effecting an ethical decision when done by a general officer or other high-ranking military official. Indeed, it is likely to be the most powerful means that a general officer or senior colonel can employ to force a change in policy by focusing attention on the objectionable policy itself. Since a general officer is likely to be closer to decision-makers than his or her subordinates and to possess greater prestige in the eyes of the public, the resignation of a general officer can be expected to have a greater public and press impact than that of a lower-ranking officer. While the substantive impact that follows a high profile resignation in protest is always uncertain, in the main it seems obvious that no unethical policy will be easily changed or challenged from within the bureaucracy if powerful political and military elites have a vested interest in its perpetuation. Thus, we were witness to the American political and military establishments claiming that al-Qaeda had close ties to the Iraqi regime when all the evidence was to the contrary. These elites only tentatively admitted that the claim was untrue years later after leaked intelligence reports forced Congress to hold public hearings. It is an old truism that leaking of classified reports to the public press is often an attempt by an official to bring to public light a policy or practice that he or she has concluded is unethical (secret prisons, torture, forced renditions, cover up of corruption of private contractors, etc. to mention but a few examples that arose during the Iraq war) or harmful to the nation. Faced with the staying power of bureaucratic and political elites, one may legitimately go outside the system to effect changes in ethically dubious policies.

The threat and willingness of military professionals to publicly resign to protest policies they regard as ill-advised, not in the best interests of the nation, or blatantly unethical is a legitimate way of carrying out their ethical obligations to their profession. Being faced with the threat of exposure or caught in the glare of the press may force policy-makers to alter their policies. In this sense, a kind of law of anticipated reactions may operate in that policy-makers, civilian and military, may become more sensitive to some of the harsher aspects of military policy if they know they may be forced to defend them in a public debate provoked by the resignation of a military professional whose stock in trade is his or her expertise in the area of policy being debated. Thus, the soldier or officer who resigns in protest acts as a lightning rod to draw the attention of both his military and civilian superiors, as well as the concerned citizenry and press, to ethically objectionable policies. At the very least, it will force policy-makers to defend their policies. This is exactly what happened when an enlisted army specialist could no longer bear the affront to his own conscience from witnessing the treatment of prisoners at Abu Ghraib prison and reported the situation to his superiors. The result was a public outcry that led ultimately to punishing the offenders.

Pragmatically, of course, the senior colonel or general officer risks little in the way of earned career benefits by his retirement or resignation since in most instances he or she will take their benefits and pension with them. This is not the case with lower-ranking soldiers who are likely to find the price of public protest to be an end to their military careers. Thus, when confronted with an order or policy that he or she finds ethically objectionable, the general officer has the best chance of making these objections felt at comparatively low cost. He or she is likely to have the attention of policy-makers as a result of their high rank and to be identified in the public mind as a figure of some importance. A high-ranking officer who retires in protest relinquishes only terminal career goals. To be sure, he or she is likely to miss the next promotion, but not much more.

The issue of resignation or retirement in protest has more serious repercussions for the soldier than for members of other professions. The soldier has a more serious problem because his or her employer is the state itself, which has a complete monopoly on the employment of the soldier's skills. Unlike physicians and lawyers who may resign from one practice and start another, soldiers have no such opportunity. They may legitimately apply their skills only in the service of the state, and their resignation or retirement places them beyond their profession and there is no going back. To require that military professionals respond to unethical orders by resignation in protest is to place yet another heavy burden on individuals who already carry much heavier ethical responsibilities than their civilian brothers. *Nonetheless, the only alternative is to permit the soldier to escape responsibility for the execution of orders he or she regards as unethical. This alternative is never acceptable in a society that claims to have ethical limits, and it is never tolerable in a profession that claims as its core ethic the obligation of selfless service. So it is that the soldier in one more respect* finds him or herself in a profession that is different from all other occupations and professions. This is why the price of belonging is high. It is also why not all individuals are fit for membership.

It may be argued that high-ranking officers have a greater ethical obligation to protest objectionable policies and orders because their position carries with it a greater obligation to seek the welfare of their subordinates and the country they have sworn to serve. *While all members of the profession of arms bear the same ethical obligations and are responsible for the same actions, the higher one's position in the organizational hierarchy the greater the scope of one's ethical responsibility inasmuch as the damage one can cause by failing to act ethically or by complying with an unethical order is far greater than for those in lower positions.* For example, the horror caused by a single corporal at Haditha, Iraq where an entire family of civilians was slaughtered by a squad of American soldiers pales in comparison to the horror that could be wrought by a brigade or division commander without sufficient ethical restraints. The higher ranks of the profession, those who are directly responsible for advising policy-makers or carrying out orders involving hundreds or even thousands of people, have awesome ethical responsibilities. They must be prepared to defend their professional judgment and ethics by overt acts of dissent when necessary and, perhaps, only as a last resort after attempting to change policies in other ways. If these other attempts fail, senior officers ought to be prepared to make their case through acts of public resignation or retirement in protest.

Resignation or retirement in protest, however, cannot be expected to occur in large numbers among the junior officer and non-commissioned officer (NCO) corps except under very extreme cases. Lower ranking officers, NCOs, and enlisted soldiers cannot realistically be expected to abandon their livelihood and careers except under extreme circumstances. Moreover, the resignation of some obscure captain or color sergeant is likely to have only a marginal impact on the issue at hand, if any at all. The failure of lower ranks, officers and other ranks, to resign in protest, while not an admirable circumstance, is surely understandable. This is precisely why alternatives to resignation in protest consistent with the soldier's ethical responsibilities must be provided. Otherwise, the junior officer corps and enlisted soldiers will have little opportunity to effect ethical choices in the face of unethical orders. What is required are additional ethical options that are pragmatically available to the great majority of soldiers below the senior officer level.

Request for Relief in Protest

To recognize that resignation or retirement in protest will neither be very common nor very effective for lower-ranking soldiers does not imply that they are relieved from their obligation to take action in the face of orders or policies they believe are unethical. As noted earlier, obligations spring from many sources, not the least of which are the values of the society as well as the profession of which the soldier is a part. These obligations exist whether or not the means to carry them out promote career success.

If ethical choices are to be made with any degree of autonomy, however, the soldier must be provided with reasonable options to make them when the circumstances force the soldier to do so. When confronted with "local" policies such as shooting prisoners or civilians, burning dwellings, poisoning wells, or other horrors, the soldier has the legitimate right to formally request of his superiors that he or she be relieved of participating in such actions. The request for relief should detail the facts of the situation as well as the reasons why the soldier believes the policies or orders are unethical or illegal. The soldier may request relief verbally or in writing. If the request is formally filed in writing, it has the effect of immediately engaging the military bureaucracy and creating a formal record of events while bringing the circumstances under question to the attention of higher command and staff authorities. Written requests create formal records that cannot legally be destroyed. Modern technological devices like camera-phones and digital recording devices can capture unethical acts and retain them as part of the record. The Abu Ghraib prison scandal in Iraq came to light when a private soldier slipped a CD containing photographs of prisoners being tortured under his battalion commander's office door.

Filling a formal written or oral request for relief from duties the soldier believes are unethical or illegal provides the soldier with a very practical way to discharge his or her obligation to act ethically in the face of evil. The soldier also observes the obligation to the profession by making improper and unethical conduct known to his superiors. At the very least, this course of action reduces the possibility that superiors can hide behind the notion of "plausible denial" by claiming that they did not know what was happening within their areas of command responsibility. Plausible denial was the implicit basis of the defence proffered by Captain Ernest Medina and Major General Samuel Koster to avoid being implicated in the My Lai massacre of civilians in Vietnam. The commander of the Abu Ghraib prison also argued in her defence that she did not know that prisoners were being tortured. All these people were eventually found culpable and responsible for the atrocities that occurred under their commands.

The plausible denial defence has no standing in ethics or law, and falls easily before the proposition that a "reasonable man" should have known what was going on. It also violates the precedent of *In Re Yamashita* in international law and the traditional responsibilities that have been inescapably linked to commanders throughout history under the doctrine of *respondeat superior.* Thus, Yamashita was hanged not because he ordered the atrocities of the Bataan Death March. The evidence was clear that General Yamashita had little knowledge of the conduct of his forces at the time and even less control. Yamashita was hanged because of the clear implication of the timeworn principle of military ethics that a commander is ultimately responsible for the unethical acts of his command. This principle has long applied to Western military custom and practice, although one can also find examples of such military codes of ethics under Cyrus the Great in Persia, in Arabia under Muhammad, and in India in the fifth century B.C.E.. Thus, the request for relief in protest focuses responsibility upon those command elements responsible for issuing unethical orders, and is a legitimate avenue of ethical action for the soldier confronted with the problem of having to execute orders he or she believes to be unethical or illegal.

To be sure, not all requests for relief will be granted. Yet if the issue raised is one of illegality or unethical acts, the formal request is unlikely to be blocked at the lower levels of command or bureaucracy. Decision-makers at these levels will almost certainly seek to avoid what premises to be a very difficult problem and transmit the request rapidly up the chain of command in classic "pass the buck" fashion. At My Lai, for example, the field reports of the massacre were quickly transmitted up the chain of command until blocked by the division commander to conceal his own complicity. This seems to have also been the case with the field reports dealing with the killings of civilians in Haditha. Here, too, higher-ranking officers with direct command responsibility seem to have attempted to conceal the reports. The point is that a soldier making a request for relief seems to have a reasonable chance that the request will, at some point, come to the attention of authorities higher than the one from whom the soldier is making the request.

A request for relief on the grounds that localized policies or orders are unethical or illegal provides a soldier with a viable and practical means for exercising his or her ethical obligation to the profession's own ethical precepts consistent with the soldier's position within the military hierarchy. There will certainly be costs, especially to the young officer who seeks a further career, and especially so if one's superiors ultimately decide that what the soldier did was incorrect despite the best of his or her intentions. Nonetheless, the obligation to object to unethical policies, orders, and practices remains. The request for relief presents a legitimate way for a member of the military profession within a democratic society to carry out ethical obligations. No one ever said it would be easy, only that it is possible and necessary.

Appeal Orders to Higher Command

The assumption in any military organization in a democratic society is that illegal and unethical orders will not be deliberately issued *as a matter of official policy.* Local commanders may deliberately or inadvertently, overtly or covertly, condone or encourage such policies, but they are held to be decidedly *local* in origin and do not represent the official policy of the military profession or the government it serves. Thus, at Abu Ghraib, local commanders condoned the torture of prisoners even as the official policy of the U.S. government and the military was that torture of prisoners was not permitted. This distinction opens up another course of action available to the soldier confronted with the dilemma of carrying out orders he or she regards as unethical. In these circumstances, the soldier may take the step of "going over the head" of his/her immediate superior as a formal means of protest. The object of this course of action is to bring to the attention of higher authorities the orders and policies that the soldier finds ethically objectionable in the hope that higher authorities will stop or change these policies. Of course, the directed charge is that the immediate ordering commander is exceeding his/her legitimate authority by ordering actions that his/her superiors, both military and civilian, would not permit if they knew about them. *The assumption behind this course of action is that the profession remains a repository of ethical trust and honesty, and that those who hold that trust in their charge can be relied upon to uphold it when evidence that someone is violating it is brought to their attention.*

To some degree, the military provides for this alternative through the office of the inspector general. What is suggested here, however, is that the ethically concerned soldier go to the relevant superior within the immediate chain of command. Conventional military wisdom holds that remedial action can occur more quickly in this way, a fact of some importance if the orders under challenge involve the killing or torturing of civilians or prisoners of war. Moreover, engaging the chain of command makes it clear to all within that chain that something may be seriously amiss, especially so if more than one complaint is brought forward. In some cases, however, one's superiors may not respond, but their silence will be more difficult to purchase even for those who may be involved. There is also the possibility that the propensity for "team playing" may lead to a conspiracy of silence. Even so, a determined soldier still has an avenue of redress if he or she chooses to pay the price. Indeed, one may not legitimately shrink from paying that price without accepting or acquiescing in orders the soldier has already decided are wrong. *Confronted with this Hobson's choice, the direction in which the soldier must proceed is clear: the soldier must refuse to obey and make every effort to bring to the attention of his or her superiors or other appropriate authorities the fact that the soldier is being ordered to do something he or she regards as unethical or illegal.* Even under these difficult circumstances, the soldier who refuses to act in defence of personal and professional ethical precepts betrays the profession and his or her fellow soldiers.

Refusal

The emphasis to this point upon the ease or difficulty with which a given course of ethical action may or may not be implemented should not obscure a fundamental fact: *an ethical obligation not discharged in the face of surmountable practical difficulties remains no less an obligation, and the soldier remains responsible for his or her failure to observe it.* All members of the military will inescapably encounter situations in which they will attempt to change an order or a policy in other ways, or in which the practical cost of carrying out their ethical obligations may be harmful to their careers. As difficult as these circumstances are, the soldier's obligation to professional ethics remains.

In any situation where obligation and obedience are in tension, the ultimate response the soldier can make to orders requiring actions he or she considers unethical is to refuse to carry them out. *Refusal of orders is the last resort and a response to extreme ethical pressures. It must be clear as well that the soldier's refusal requires that he or she be willing to accept the consequences of the refusal if it is later judged to have been wrong.* It is important to understand, however, that the refusal to execute an order is not the end of the process of ethical assessment. Whether in military or civilian life, an act of refusal is judged at a later time as to its acceptability. Thus, the soldier's willingness to "accept the consequences" of the act of refusal is really a statement of the soldier's readiness to justify his or her decision at some future appropriate time. It is *not* an assumption of *a priori* guilt or of a willingness to accept summary justice on the spot.

A code of professional ethics that repudiates disobedience in the general sense must still leave room for the disobedience of orders in particular cases. A soldier faced with conflicting ethical obligations must choose one over the other when he or she cannot do both. Thus, the soldier may sometimes find that disobedience of orders or outright refusal to obey are the only ethical paths open to him or her.

Some might argue that the soldier ought to remain loyal to legitimate superiors regardless of the ethical nature of their orders on the grounds that the soldier is only the technical instrument of the will of the state or nation expressed by duly elected or appointed representatives and authorities. If any one is to be held responsible for the soldier's actions, let it be the civilian or military authorities and let the judgment be rendered by the victor. Like the sense of ethical judgment attendant to the theory of the divine right of kings, only history (or God) may judge man's actions. It is an old argument, and it is ethically flawed.

No attempt to reduce the solider to a mere instrument of another's will can ever be a valid ethical doctrine, at least not within the historical and ethical context of the West. In a serious ethical crisis involving superiors, a subordinate must never confuse his or her loyalty to the profession or the state with loyalty to his or her superiors as persons. General Douglas MacArthur, while himself involved in an ethical crisis concerning his proper role as military subordinate responding to what he perceived to be his higher obligations, expounded a valid ethical position with regard to the loyalty of the soldier trapped in an ethical dilemma.

> "I find in existence a new and heretofore unknown and dangerous concept that the members of our armed forces owe primary allegiance or loyalty to those who temporarily exercise the authority of the executive branch of government rather than to the country and its Constitution which they are sworn to defend. No proposition could be more wrong or more dangerous."[7]

Under certain circumstances, a soldier's ethical obligations transcend and surpass the obligations owed to his or her immediate superiors and even civilian superiors. General George C. Marshall, the epitome of the loyal soldier, was echoing MacArthur's sentiments when he said that "an officer's ultimate commanding loyalty at all times is to his country and not his service or his superiors." In a crisis, the soldier must always treat loyalty as *fides*, that is, "keeping faith" with promises previously made to act in an ethical manner. At times, the crisis can become even more complex and the soldier may be forced to override his/her oath to the profession as well as the state in order to keep faith with his or her humanity. This is precisely what some German officers chose to do when they attempted to assassinate Hitler.

German philosophers have developed a useful distinction in dealing with the question of loyalty to unethical superiors. They distinguish between *Hochverrat* and *Landesverrat*. *Hochverrat* is disloyalty to a superior, which has historically meant disloyalty to the monarch or other governmental officials. *Landesverrat*, by contrast, is disloyalty or betrayal of the nation. Within this distinction there is room for manoeuvre in making an ethical choice. In order to serve the nation, a soldier may sometimes have to be "disloyal" to his governmental or military superiors and refuse to execute their orders. The distinction between the two notions of loyalty throws into relief what every member of the military profession knows to be true, that a soldier's first and most fundamental loyalty is to act ethically and humanely, and in times of crisis he or she must be prepared to observe that higher obligation.

Some would reject this argument on the grounds that it erodes the sense of duty necessary for the military to function effectively. The difficulty with this claim is that it employs the concepts of loyalty and duty far too loosely. When speaking about "doing one's duty," it must be clear that to be dutiful requires a sense of being bound only by what is ethical; duty binds the solider in the context of the ethical precepts of the profession concerning what is acceptable behaviour. As with all ethics, the obligation to do one's duty applies in concrete circumstances. The proper function of duty is to make the soldier sensitive to the relationships and claims made upon the soldier in particular situations so that he or she knows what their duty is, that it arises in a social context, and why the soldier has a duty to obey. To be an ethical soldier, therefore, is to accept one's duty to do what is ethically right and to know why duties bind. *Duty should never be understood to require the soldier to blindly follow orders.*

It is only when duty is tied to an understanding of the *reasons* why one is bound to obey that the soldier can be said to have an ethical obligation to do one's duty. To do one's "duty for duty's sake" is a perversion of its true meaning because it separates the actor from the very reasons why he or she is required to obey. Duty no longer becomes the servant of the ethical claims made upon the soldier by reason of membership in the profession, that is, duty is no longer tied to the obligation to observe the profession's ethical precepts. Instead, duty in this incorrect sense becomes a replacement for these precepts. *This is precisely why to execute unethical orders is never "doing one's duty" in the proper ethical sense of the word. The duty to observe a code of professional ethics is based upon judgments about the ethical applicability of those precepts in a given situational context.* To "do one's duty" when the application of the precepts does not tend to achieve what the code intends to achieve is wrong. It is also no defence for acting unethically. Thus, the claim that soldiers who are allowed to refuse to execute orders they judge to be unethical will not do their duty is based upon an erroneous conception of the notion of duty. *The duty of the military professional is always to do that which is ethically right. The soldier can never have an ethical duty to do that which is wrong. To interpret duty as the requirement of the soldier to carry out all orders simply because they are issued by superiors is to misunderstand the concepts of duty and ethics.*

This aside, the concept of duty is often misunderstood within the military profession itself. Joseph Ellis and Robert Moore discuss this misunderstanding and the difficulties it creates for the soldier. Their analysis is drawn from a study of West Point cadets, but may be extended with equal veracity to most military establishments. Ellis and Moore frame the issue in the following terms.

> "When caught in a moral dilemma, most West Pointers are conditioned to perceive their obedience to lawful superiors as the highest form of duty. Such a perception is regarded as the essence of military professionalism, for it involves putting personal considerations beneath service, duty to oneself. When there is a conflict between what a West Pointer calls duty and honour, then he is likely to have no ethical answers. Or rather, he is trained to answer by equating honor with duty."[8]

This situation represents an ethical failure of the first magnitude as it relates to the soldier's obligation to refuse to carry out orders he or she regards as unethical. It equates obedience with obligation and obligation with honour. Obedience is simply carrying out orders without necessarily comprehending why one must do so. Obedience may even involve an element of duress. Obligations, once again, require the willing execution of legitimate orders for which the soldier comprehends the reason and judges them not to be unethical. The situation described by Ellis and Moore confuses duty with compliance. It suggests that by equating honour with duty the soldier can escape responsibility for his or her actions by submitting to the will of a superior. This view is not only ethically wrong, it is also legally improper within the context of the Western legal tradition. It implies that a soldier can, under some conditions, suspend his or her ethical judgment with impunity. Nothing could be further from the truth. *Ethical responsibility and judgment are conditions of the soldier's very humanity itself, the ethical precepts of the military profession, and the Western tradition of law. As such, they cannot be suspended without penalty.*

Expressed as an ethical problem, the refusal of a soldier to carry out an order which he or she thinks is unethical is more a comment on the nature of the order than on the refusal to execute it, for even the most dedicated proponents of duty would agree that unethical orders ought never to be issued and if they are ought not to be followed. Thus, the principle of refusal on ethical grounds is less an issue than which of the participants in the dilemma, the soldier or the superior, has the right to decide. To suggest that there is an escape from this difficult decision by claiming that the solider can legitimately suspend his or her ethical sense or subordinate it to another person in deference to discipline, the mission, loyalty, duty, or any of a score of other possible rationales is to counsel further unethical action. It is also a claim that erodes the profession's attempts to maintain its ethical centre.

The refusal to carry out an order issued by a legitimate authority is prima facie an illegal act, although not necessarily an unethical one. The refusal to obey is a way to make an immediate ethical choice by the singular act of disobedience, but also has another effect. The refusal to obey an order immediately engages the military's legal conflict resolution process, namely the court martial and its attendant investigation process, in much the same way that a violation of civil law is first necessary to engage the civil courts. The military and civil courts are the mechanisms for having the refused order judged definitively as to its ethical or legal standing. Engaging the court martial process affords the military and the soldier two important opportunities. First, it provides a public forum where the soldier may fully *explain* the ethical reasons which led the soldier to refuse the order. Second, it provides the military with the opportunity to *evaluate* the circumstances of the case relative to the specific order given, and to take appropriate action against either the soldier or the issuing authority. The military court martial is thus a two-way street. Like a civil court, a military court can only hear a justiciable issue, and an issue is only rendered justiciable *after* an order or directive has in fact been challenged by a soldier who refused to carry it out. *Thus, the act of a refusal by a soldier who regards an order as unethical or illegal constitutes an appeal within the military legal system to higher authority for a judgment on the ethical or legal quality of the original order itself.*

Viewed in this way, *the refusal to execute an order on ethical or legal grounds becomes the military equivalent of civil disobedience in the service of a higher cause, namely the ethical sense of the military profession itself. It is not the equivalent of disloyalty or cowardice in any sense.* The important point is that the refusal to execute an order is not the end of the judgmental process. Whether in military or civilian life, the act is judged at a later time as to its acceptability or unacceptability. The willingness of the soldier to accept the consequences of his or her act is a commitment to the soldier's readiness to justify one's actions at some future appropriate time and is by no means a *prima facie* admission of wrongdoing.

Some avenues of ethical protest are more practical than others and all carry with them some risk. Yet, the greater risk for the profession would be a general unwillingness to take ethical risks in its service. All of the avenues of protest discussed to this point are consistent with the fundamental values of the democratic polity that the soldier serves. They are also consistent with the fundamental values of the military profession itself, namely the requirement that soldiers in the performance of their duties still be limited by the boundaries set forth in their code of professional ethics. The fundamental ethical obligation of any soldier is to ensure that his or her conduct as well as that of their superiors is generally consonant with the ethics of the profession.

If it can be assumed for the moment that many of the problems that have been discussed so far are traceable to some extent to the profession's failure to create and use formal mechanisms through which soldiers can make ethical choices when confronted with ethical dilemmas of some magnitude, it must also be said that this failure is only part of the difficulty. The fact is that the *formal* rules of any bureaucracy will influence behaviour only to the degree that they are supported and reinforced by the *informal* rules and values of the institution. *This is why ethical exemplars are so important. They demonstrate for other soldiers to see that the profession is sincere about living up to its ethical values.* In practice, however, behaviour functional to career success, although informally supported, often stands in stark opposition to those precepts which the profession claims it formally supports, so that the soldier's experience runs contrary to the formal expressions of professional values.

This tension between informal norms functional to career advancement and any attempt to develop a formal doctrine of ethical protest can be expected to persist despite the most sincere efforts at reform. The establishment of clear guidelines governing the soldier's right to ethical protest will still require considerable time for the informal norms that support those guidelines in practice to become deeply embedded in the heart of the profession. Over time, the profession's own actions must demonstrate to its members that it truly supports the soldier who is moved by his or her conscience to stand alone against it in defence of the profession's own stated values. If so, over time the profession will demonstrate and come to be believed that the actions of ethical soldiers will also be functional from the point of view of career advancement, thus encouraging their undertaking. Colonel Harry Summers astutely expressed both the challenge to the profession and its solution.

> "We temporize and apologize for those who violate our standards rather than rising up in outrage and indignation and casting them out with the scorn and opprobrium they deserve...The military can, and should, ensure for us lesser mortals that integrity, character, moral convictions, tenacity, and fighting ability pay."[9]

As things now often stand, however, the soldier who goes over his or her commander's head, resigns in protest, or reports an unethical practice is commonly viewed as "disloyal," "untrustworthy," or a "quitter." The military often stresses loyalty to orders and superiors to an exaggerated extent. This tends to neutralize and erode the larger and proper meaning of loyalty that the profession must possess if it is to engender in its members a sense of communal worth. As a practical matter, to the extent that the stress remains upon individual loyalty to superiors and as long as ethical violations are permitted to pay off in terms of career enhancement, it is unlikely that the formal establishment of a doctrine of ethical protest will have much pragmatic effect. Still, the stakes are too high for the profession not to try.

The case for establishing a doctrine of ethical protest for soldiers is not without its opponents, especially as it addresses the twin responsibilities of resignation and refusal to execute orders. The contrary argument suggests that if every commander were required to explain every order or demonstrate that it was not unethical to every soldier and officer in order to gain compliance, the military system of command and execution would become paralyzed and unable to function. The argument is a straw man and not convincing. Questions of serious ethical choice do not arise so frequently as to merit the claim that all or even a significant number of orders would have to be justified to subordinates in advance of their execution. Indeed, if conditions were such as to provoke a substantial number of soldiers and officers to demand such justifications, it would be *prima facie* evidence that the military had already broken down and become paralyzed, the difficulty arising from the obvious unethical nature of the orders themselves far more than from the number of soldiers objecting to them. Under these circumstances, we would be witnessing the symptoms of a disease that in all probability was already terminal.

Resignation as a means of registering ethical protest is further objected to on the grounds that it amounts to "quitting." Why not, the argument goes, stay within the system and work to change it? To the extent that the argument has merit, it is most applicable to general officers who have access to policy-makers and whose advice may be heeded. While the question of future success remains open, the forces arrayed against change in any bureaucracy are formidable. The struggle to change the system from within is likely to be a long and arduous effort. Besides, it does not solve the immediate ethical difficulty that one may have to do something about an unethical policy quickly. A prolonged delay in taking an ethical position risks making one an accomplice. A long career of ignoring or condoning unethical policies, despite the intention to change things once one gets to the top and in a position to do so, may ethically deform a person to the point where he or she becomes incapable of changing things later on. This seems to be what Captain Basil Liddell-Hart of the British Army had in mind when he noted somewhat caustically that his generation of officers knew very well how the system worked. "We all carefully kept our new ideas and brilliance sealed in a bottle," he said. "The trouble was when some of us reached the top, we uncorked the bottle only to discover that the contents had evaporated."

Finally, working within the system while keeping silent deprives the rest of the profession's membership of the opportunity to observe ethical exemplars undertaking courageous acts. In the end, *a decision to defer an ethical judgment on the grounds that the situation may be changed later does not relieve the soldier of his or her ethical responsibility at the moment.* If experience is any guide, it seems probable that the system is more successful at changing the dissenters than the dissenters are at changing the system.

A major consequence of the military's failure to develop a formal doctrine of ethical protest for its officers and soldiers is the tendency for values and practices that are functional to career advancement to take precedence or act as substitutes for ethical judgment in the face of questionable orders and policies. Under these circumstances, careerism can run rampant and no dissent is heard, all of which constitutes a danger to a truly effective military establishment. Under the guises of loyalty and duty, this can lead to a marked failure to question policies and orders that do not work or extract too high an ethical cost. The unethical and brutal behaviour of the French Army in putting down the Algerian insurrection is a case in point. To counter these tendencies, what is needed is for the profession to establish an ethical doctrine that teaches soldiers what the accepted avenues of ethical protest open to them are and encourages the soldier to employ these options when urged to do so by the press of professional ethics and soldierly virtue.

We must, of course, always take care to ensure that the pathways of ethical protest for the solider and the profession remain consistent with the democratic values and practices of the civil polity and that they are never permitted to become an excuse for coordinated action by the profession against properly constituted civilian authority. However, we have far less to fear from a military establishment of ethical soldiers than we do from one full of careerist values and self-seeking entrepreneurs. *A military establishment unaccustomed to making ethical judgments risks disaster for both the civil order and itself, not through design, but through incompetence manifested in its increasing inability to challenge policies that run contrary to its best professional judgment.* The inability of a soldier to act ethically, to dissent, resign, or refuse to be part of unethical or harmful policies, is a serious failure of ethics.

Endnotes

1. Douglas Kinnard, *The War Managers* (Hanover, NH: University Press of New England, 1977).

2. Arthur Dyck, "Ethical Bases of the Military Profession," *Parameters*, no. 1 (March, 1980), 43.

3. Quoted in James Toner, "Sisyphus as a Soldier: Ethics, Exigencies, and the American Military," *Parameters*, no. 4 (1977), 6.

4. Josiah Bunting, "The Conscience of a Soldier," *World View* 16, no. 12 (December, 1973), 6-11.

5. Ibid., 10.

6. Francis A. Galligan, *Military Professionalism and Ethics* (Newport, RI: Naval War College, 1979), 78.

7. Zeb B. Bradford, Jr. "Duty, Honor, Country vs. Moral Conviction," *Army* (September, 1968), 43.

8. Joseph Ellis and Robert Moore, *School for Soldiers: West Point and the Profession of Arms* (New York: Oxford University Press, 1974), 180.

9. Quoted in a book review by Colonel Harry G. Summers, *Military Review.*

The Soldier's Character

O ne of the main purposes of a code of military ethics aside from ennobling the profession and specifying its obligations is to establish points of reference that can be used in the character development of the soldier. A code of professional ethics is central to the processes within the profession that are designed to build good character among the members. A treatise on military ethics must of necessity discuss those qualities of personal character that are expected of the soldiery in general and the officer corps in particular.

Ethics and Virtue

Western societies have been generally hesitant to set ethical standards in formal ways that apply to social groups, preferring instead to rely upon law. This approach is bolstered by the claim that the need for ethical codes can be avoided by encouraging the development of certain character traits or virtues among members of the society. Thus, citizens of good character who join the military will be soldiers of good character. The assumption is that persons, in this case soldiers, who manifest certain character traits will automatically have their actions governed by these traits. While character-building of the individual soldier by the profession is a valid and valuable exercise, it in no way guarantees that the soldier will act ethically. Virtue or character defines what an individual *is*. Ethics, on the other hand, has to do with how an individual *acts*. While ethics and virtue are closely related, they are also quite distinct qualities of a human being.

To understand the role of military virtues in building the character of the soldier requires an understanding of the distinction between ethics and character. Character encompasses an individual's personal qualities as a human being. In the military, for example, a good officer should be loyal, honest, trustworthy, and courageous. These qualities are not only good in themselves, but are also desirable *in any person* as well as the soldier. *But virtues or character traits are not ethics.* Virtues are not innate and must be acquired by teaching and practice. Virtues are traits of character rather than traits of personality, and are stable and not the transitory feelings a person displays at certain times. Virtues involve deep dispositions to act in certain ways, but they are not the equivalent of the actions themselves. Nor are they skills or abilities. Virtues are predispositions to act in some ways and not in others.

Those who maintain that the possession of certain character traits by members of the military will ensure ethical actions are not correct, for ethical actions are comprised of more than traits of character. As Immanuel Kant noted, "I am inclined to think that principles without traits are impotent and traits without principles are blind."[1] To understand the tension between ethics and virtue one must understand a fundamental distinction: virtues are predispositions to act in certain ways which humans tend to affirm as good. Ethics, on the other hand, are precepts about how humans ought to act that specify what individuals ought to do if their acts are to be judged as ethical. One might distinguish, then, between an *ethics of virtue* and an *ethics of duty*.

An ethics of virtue addresses what a good person *ought to be* while an ethics of duty addresses how a good person *ought to act*. An ethics of virtue refers to those traits of character that are regarded as predisposing a person toward ethical action while an ethics of duty refers to the way one actually behaves in observing specified obligations. The role of virtue in an ethics of duty is not to tell a person how he or she ought to act, for the ethics of duty already specifies that, but to ensure that one does what one ought to do willingly and conscientiously by enabling one's predisposition to act ethically, a predisposition that is, however, conceptually and empirically distinct from the act itself. Virtues, therefore, are *ways of being* rather than *ways of doing*, although the two are closely intertwined whenever ethical choices are involved.

But will the person who has certain desirable character traits always act ethically? Probably not, although the chances that a person will act ethically are likely to be higher among persons of good character than those of bad. Virtues do not reveal what a person ought to do. From this perspective one can examine the SS officer, the terrorist, the assassin, or any other such individual who are likely to share certain character traits with the military professional. Thus, these disreputable types and a good soldier might all possess virtues of loyalty, dedication, self-sacrifice, courage, and righteousness. Yet, no one would argue that the SS officer who possessed all these traits of character and still carried out the execution of civilians was acting ethically. Nor would we judge the jihadist who possessed similar personal qualities as acting ethically when he planted a bomb in a crowded market square. But if soldiers do not possess the character traits usually associated with ethical actions, they cannot reasonably be expected to act ethically at all, for virtues are predispositions to actions. On the other hand, the mere presence of these virtues does not guarantee that the soldier will act ethically. *Thus, without some virtues ethical acts are difficult if not impossible. But the inculcation of character traits in and of itself will not produce ethical soldiers.* The paradox is that people of good character are quite capable of committing grievously immoral acts.

The inculcation of virtue is necessary to the soldier's development as a person whose ethics and character are in concert. While humans have an innate sense of sociability that gives them a general awareness that there are limits to personal behaviour in human relations, virtues, like ethics, must be taught, and this teaching most often occurs within social and organizational settings. Character traits facilitate ethical action and are a legitimate concern of the military profession in deciding who is to be allowed membership and to remain in good standing. Persons of bad character may be prohibited from belonging or may be expelled.

This said, there is a general tendency to equate character with ethics, ethical training, and even ethical acts. If in its training of the soldier the profession focuses only on the inculcation of character without significant consideration for ethical codes, the effort is likely to fail. Wrong, too, are those who suggest that if only those persons of highest virtue are selected from the populace to serve in or lead the military, they will necessarily be persons of the highest ethics. It is incorrect to assume that virtue is ethics or that one results *necessarily* from the other. Nor can the military abandon its responsibility to establish standards of character by suggesting that those who enter the profession already bring with them a developed sense of virtue and that, accordingly, the military must accept individuals pretty much as it finds them. This is to imply that the profession cannot teach ethics or virtue, and that it need not do so anyway. It is also to deny that the profession can separate itself in any meaningful way from the larger society by its level of ethical behaviour or the character of its members. *Character development remains an important part of the profession's responsibility toward its members and the profession itself.*

In a discussion of virtue as it applies to the military, the notion of *perfect virtue* needs to be explained since it is often the cause of much confusion in comprehending the role that virtue plays in human behaviour. Originating with the Greek philosophers of the Classical period in ancient Greece (550-350 B.C.E.) and further developed by Medieval thinkers, perfect virtue is defined as a state of being in which the predisposition to act in a virtuous manner results almost automatically from the presence within the person of the virtue itself. Thus, a recovering alcoholic may find it difficult to resist the desire to drink at first. But as he or she succeeds in resisting that desire, it becomes easier to resist the next time until, over time, the alcoholic needs neither will nor conscious decision to resist taking the drink. The exercise of abstinence itself produces habitual good behaviour that no longer requires special effort.

Virtues refer to a person's state of being, and for our purposes they imply that a soldier ought to be a certain kind of person. But no human being can in any meaningful sense attain all the virtues perfectly. To suggest otherwise seems only a possibility of philosophical conceptualization that flies in the face of experience. If ethics requires that ought implies can, then there is every reason to apply the same standard to the development of virtue. People being what they are, they will sometimes succeed at virtue and sometimes fail. So, too, in the inculcation of virtue. Some will become virtuous and some will not. Goethe made this point clearly when he said, "If you treat a man as he is he will remain as he is. If you treat him as if he were what he could be, he will become what he could be." Virtues can be said to be an idealized sense of what the character of the good soldier ought to be. But it is not in the possession of virtue in the perfect sense that one becomes virtuous and capable of always acting ethically as much as in the *attempt* to develop those virtues in a perfect sense. There is a Greek philosophical sense in which virtues can be seen as constituting a set of *idealized predispositions* of which humans are capable that, in the striving to attain them, ennobles the individual who becomes virtuous even though the person never attains the virtues in their ideal state. It is in striving to become virtuous that one is often said to be virtuous.

If ethics is more than conformity to internalized rules and requires the observance of obligations that are externally imposed, then it is clear that some traits of character are more desirable than others insofar as they predispose, but do not cause, the soldier to act in an ethical manner. Thus, ethical choice and character are separate but intertwined qualities of moral action. Those who suggest that ethical codes alone will suffice in the absence of character virtues are bound to be disappointed, as are those who suggest that character alone is sufficient to produce an ethical soldier. Both are important and necessary, but neither guarantees an inevitably ethical result.

The Character of the Soldier

The following discussion addresses those virtues that have historically been associated with the character of a good soldier giving almost equal space to each of them even though it is clear that some virtues are more important than others. The order in which they are treated does not imply the order in which they ought to be preferred or taught within any system of military education. This said, let us now examine those military virtues which centuries of war and military experience have revealed as being vital qualities of the soldier's character.

Judgment and Integrity

Judgment and integrity can be said to be more important than other virtues insofar as they serve to integrate other dimensions of the soldier's character into an integrated whole. Judgment is more concerned with ethical action than is integrity, which seems more related to character. Judgment indicates an ethic of duty while integrity indicates an ethic of virtue. In the absence of judgment, no ethical code would have much chance of being carried out. At the same time, without integrity any sense of becoming a person of character apart from one's actions could not develop.

Judgment is defined as "the action of mentally apprehending the relationship between two objects of thought; predication as in the mind; the critical faculty in the formation of personal or individual opinion as opposed to acceptance of doctrine or authority." Soldiers must be able to judge not only what obligations take precedence over others under given circumstances, but also why one obligation takes precedence. Judgment cannot be taught without permitting some attempt at its exercise. The best way to provide the soldier with the opportunity to act ethically is to provide him or her with the opportunity to act unethically and watch the soldier choose. A soldier who possesses judgment must be able to discern the connections between events as they occur in the empirical world, discern the connections between his or her actions and their consequences, and choose among them. But the act of choice follows upon the soldier's ability to develop a "discernment of mind" as to what courses of action are open. *The quality of judgment is, therefore, central to observing an ethical code since judgment rests at the centre of making ethical choices. Judgment is the means by which a soldier chooses among obligations, and it is a primary military virtue that should be developed to the extent possible within every soldier.*

An equally important military virtue is integrity. The word is derived from the Latin *integer*, meaning wholeness, entireness, or completeness. Integrity is "the condition of having no part or element wanting; the soundness of moral principles; the character of uncorrupted virtue especially in relation to truth or falsity." Integrity provides an overall perspective as to where other virtues fit in an individual's ethical character. Without it, without a sense that a person must be an integrated moral whole if he or she is to be an ethical person, the teaching of ethics and virtue must always fail. Any attempt by the military profession to instill virtues must inevitably aim at developing the whole person in the humanistic sense that the soldier understands that what he or she is asked to do by the profession is only one facet of his or her whole ethical being. The soldier must comprehend that all these facets are bound together, and that there will be times when conflicts among them will arise. *The integral soldier understands that there is no escape in a false compartmentalization of ethical responsibilities, that virtues and ethics are closely bound insofar as the presence or absence of both defines what kind of human being the soldier is.*

Duty, Honour, Country

Duty may be defined as "an action or act that is due by reason of legal or moral obligation; that which one ought to do or is bound to do as an obligation." Duty consists essentially in living up to one's professional obligations, but within ethically acceptable limits. A soldier is not doing his or her duty if they become like the SS officer who executes civilians because he is following orders. As Arthur Dyck notes, "to educate the military professional is precisely to increase the extent to which morally appropriate options in difficult contexts are identified and understood."[2] Duty does not consist only of carrying out the orders of one's lawful superiors or the state or, for that matter, even the profession. Duty consists of fulfilling the obligations of one's profession against the background of a genuine moral sensitivity, realizing that the obligations of the soldier are not the total obligations of a complete moral person. Thus, in some cases an obligation to disobey may well arise. It is the realization that ethics consists of recognizing and making difficult choices that constitutes the background against which the virtue of duty should be taught and practiced. *Duty never involves complete obedience. It is only the obligation to obey those lawful orders that are judged by the soldier not to be ethically wrong.*

Failure to understand this can lead the soldier to act unethically on the grounds that he or she is fulfilling the obligation to be loyal to the profession. A good soldier can be generally said to be one who is loyal to the country and who keeps faith with fellow citizens in terms of the oath taken to uphold the lawful (and ethical) dictates of the state. The soldier's oath to the civic-legal order implies that an effort on the part of any group, even the government itself, to use violence or force in an illegal, unconstitutional, or unethical manner is subject to challenge by the highest authorities of the military profession itself. The soldier must understand that the profession serves the country and the legally constituted civic order. *The soldier's oath is not an excuse for blind patriotism, nor is it an excuse for executing the orders of civilian authority, no matter how stupid or criminal those orders may be, because they are issued by a civilian authority.*

The fundamental idea of loyalty to one's country rests in understanding that the military's obligations to its civilian authorities extend beyond defending the country against external threats to include loyalty to the larger concept of the society, the nation, and the people. The soldier must be aware that there are times when appropriate legal authority may order actions that he or she regards as harmful to the nation. In such circumstances, the soldier will find him or herself confronted with an extremely serious ethical dilemma that will require a choice among competing ethical obligations. Faithfulness to one's fellow citizens and to the country imply the ability and willingness to look beyond the short run policies of particular civil administrations and to understand that one's loyalty as a soldier is to the larger value of the nation. Loyalty to one's country ought never to be allowed to degenerate into blind and total obedience to superior authority and policies that the soldier regards as unethical or detrimental to the nation itself.

Honour, among its many meanings, has much to do with moral sensitivity. Honour is the ability to recognize ethical dilemmas and to have the integrity and strength of character to act upon's one's beliefs.[3] It is an integrating trait of the soldier's character, and it prevents the application of the soldier's technical skills from becoming an exercise in horror. Honour, like integrity, as a perspective of ethical sensitivity, gives meaning to other character traits. The soldier must be aware that he or she will be asked to carry out tasks that involve grave ethical issues. The soldier must be aware that his or her sense of integrity and sense of ethical balance, honour, is all that stands between them and immorality in the practice of their profession. The soldier's acts have an influence that reaches beyond him or herself and affects the ethical tenor of fellow soldiers and the profession itself. Honour ultimately rests in the soldier's sense of ethical sensitivity, of being aware of the multiplicity of ethical dimensions that surround the soldier's task and actions and being able to resolve them in a manner that preserves the soldier's ethical balance and integrity.

In one sense, the motto "Duty, Honour, Country" made famous by West Point and adopted in various forms by other military establishments has the virtues it proclaims out of order of importance. In its present form it implies that the soldier's first loyalty is to him or herself as a military professional when, in fact, it is to him or herself as an ethical human being. Duty to one's country is no longer a duty if the soldier is asked to carry out immoral acts. The motto might be more properly expressed as "Honour, Country, Duty" to emphasize its true meaning within the context of instilling military ethics in the soldier.

Honour, as the first trait, implies an ethical awareness and sensitivity that gives meaning and direction to other military virtues. Country, the second loyalty, affirms that the ethical goals of the profession transcend duty understood as rigid adherence to orders. Duty is understood as the soldier's obligation to carry out orders only when the order is understood and judged not to be unethical. Arranged in this fashion, the motto places the responsibility for ethical judgment squarely upon the individual soldier as ethical agent. It emphasizes the important point that the commands of duty are valid only within an ethical context. Understood in this way, the motto serves to mitigate any tendency toward blind obedience. Whatever the order of importance, however, there is no doubt that duty, honour, and country express well the central values of the profession of arms. They also express the core of the soldier's character.

Loyalty, Honesty, Sacrifice

Every ethical soldier must possess the virtues of loyalty, honesty, and a recognition of the requirement to sacrifice as central to his or her character. Loyalty can be defined as "the faithful adherence to one's promise, oath or word of honour." The term itself derives from the medieval concept of fealty, that is, carrying out obligations to one's superiors assumed freely by oath. The soldier's loyalty is ultimately rooted in the oath he or she takes upon entering the profession to preserve and protect the legitimate civic order. In this sense, loyalty ought never to be confused with *obsequium*, a perverted obedience to persons that can confuse one's higher loyalties to the nation. Loyalty to superiors ought never to be interpreted so as to interfere with the soldier's higher loyalties to nation and profession. Loyalty, therefore, as a virtue, rests in the soldier's adherence to his or her promises or oaths. In the context of military ethics loyalty is extended to faithfully and ethically carrying out those obligations one has sworn to uphold as a member of the profession, and requires that the profession's code of ethics be observed as the basis for the soldier's actions.

The confusion of the soldier's loyalty to oath, ethics, and profession is all too often equated with loyalty to his or her superiors and with terrible consequences. This confusion distorts both loyalty and ethics, and puts the soldier at great risk of committing unethical acts by following unethical orders. This confusion was amply demonstrated at West Point when the commandant was forced to resign for his complicity in the slaughter of Vietnamese civilians by American soldiers at My Lai.

> "West Point cadets cheered their Commandant, Major General Koster, when he announced his resignation from the Academy citing the charges against him as the commander of the division involved at My Lai. Many doubtless cheered in affirmation of their loyalty to the Point at a time when it seemed under attack. But those who read or heard of the event could legitimately raise serious questions about the moral discrimination of young men chosen for military leadership"[4]

Understanding loyalty as a military virtue requires one to recognize that loyalty is never a substitute for ethical judgment, nor can it be used to refuse to ethically discriminate among events, or as a defence for failing to render ethical judgment. Loyalty properly understood does not imply that the soldier may abandon his or her ethical autonomy on the grounds that superiors know best what the soldier must do. *Loyalty is part of the soldier's ethical autonomy, not a replacement for it. Loyalty expressed in following orders or failing to make ethical judgments is never an excuse for the soldier not to observe his or her higher ethical obligations to the profession and the nation.*

Another military virtue crucial to the success of the military profession is honesty, for its absence creates the possibility of drastic miscalculation wherein the lives of soldiers can be spent needlessly. Honesty is defined as "uprightness of disposition and conduct; the quality as opposed to lying, cheating, and stealing. Honesty is honour gained by action or conduct." A soldier who is not honest is a liability to the unit and can become a grave danger to himself and his colleagues.

It can be argued that honesty is even more important to today's soldier than to warriors of the past because of the vast destructive power of modern weapons. The number of lives that could be lost on the modern battlefield and the consequences to oneself and one's comrades that could result from a failure to tell the truth are potentially enormous. Samuel Hayes puts it right when he said that "lives, careers, battles, and the fate of nations have hung on the ability of military leaders to state all the true facts to the best of their knowledge regardless of what effect these facts may have on themselves or others."[5] Honesty is crucially important to the development of a good soldier, for if the soldier cannot be relied upon to tell the truth and to be honest in is dealing with his fellow soldiers, superiors, and subordinates, then the bond between leaders and led is destroyed and the practical and ethical consequences can be devastating. *A dishonest soldier, especially a dishonest officer or NCO, has no professional worth.*

The virtue of sacrifice rests at the very foundations of military professionalism. The military is sworn to serve the state and society. This inevitably means that at some point the members of the profession will have to serve the interests of their client instead of their own, especially so on the battlefield. As noted earlier, the obligation of sacrifice is clearly reflected in the clause of unlimited liability to which all soldiers are subject. As harsh (or idealistic) as it sounds, the truth is that the soldier may legitimately be required to make the ultimate sacrifice of his or her own life in observance of professional obligations. This said, it must be kept in mind that sacrifice is a virtue when it is done for values that are worthwhile. *There is no virtue in pointless sacrifice.* If it is understood that the nature of the military profession is to render service and to act ethically in rendering that service, then the sacrifice of the soldier's life for trivialities or in pursuit of unethical policies is not only pointless but also wrong in itself. Consider, for example, the Nazi regime wherein the lives of thousands of conscript soldiers were sacrificed in service to a gang of thugs who themselves had no ethics. Or as a young naval officer returning from Vietnam asked before Congress in 1974, "How do you ask a soldier to be the last one to die for a mistake?" To suffer and die for unethical or stupid policies is a perversion of the virtue of military sacrifice.

Those who enter the military profession must, therefore, be willing to accept the possibility that their lives will be sacrificed to a higher cause, although the giving of one's life is not always or even usually involved. At the minimum, however, the notion of sacrifice requires that the soldier be prepared to forego his or her own self-interests in the service of the higher good of the profession and the nation. This said, *the soldier must understand that if circumstances warrant, the contract of unlimited liability may come due and when it does the soldier will be expected to pay in full.* This sense of virtuous self-sacrifice is not easily developed or sustained, nor indeed is it developed without an unambiguous understanding as to what it implies in terms of the price the soldier may have to pay. It seems dishonest, for example, for the military to entice recruits to service with promises of cash bonuses and future educational benefits while implying that the recruit will "not have to go to Iraq." *Members of the profession of arms who willingly accept the risk of death and wounding and who succeed in remaining faithful to their promise when the circumstances turn dangerous deserve to be regarded as among the most noble of their fellow soldiers.* Soldiers themselves know this, and that is why the soldier who has seen battle or been wounded is accorded great respect in their eyes. They are called heroes.

Patriotism

Patriotism is defined as "the quality of disinterestedly or self-sacrificingly exerting oneself to promote the well being of one's country; one who maintains and defends his country's freedom or rights." Life in the military extracts far more in the way of responsibilities than it returns in the way of benefits. Soldiers are expected to be *true* patriots, giving service to their country willingly out of affection for it at costs that are largely absent from occupations or professions in civil society. Patriotism implies a love of one's country founded on clear notions of ethics, not a blind and unconditional loyalty to the state regardless of its values or conduct. Thus, the soldier is obligated and prepared to serve the nation in pursuit of those tasks and policies that have some ethical foundation or at least are not fundamentally unethical. In this sense patriotism cannot be, as Samuel Johnson suggested, "the last refuge of scoundrels." *Soldiers who do the bidding of an unethical political order or carry out policies that are unethical are not patriots. They are accomplices.* Patriotism is no refuge at all. It is the first place where honourable soldiers, members of a special profession, are found willing to sacrifice in defence of a nation whose policies and objectives are ethical.

Obedience

A distinction was made earlier between obligation and obedience. Obligation, it will be recalled, is defined as observing those precepts that one understands and willingly agrees to observe for the reason that they ought to be observed given the context in which they arise. Obedience, on the other hand, means complying with the will of another even if one does not completely understand the reasons why certain instructions have been given. The concepts of obligation and obedience are two of the basic distinctions in ethics that are most often confused, so much so that some contend that encouraging a proper sense of obligation, based upon an understanding of the ethics involved, risks producing a tendency for the soldier to be disobedient. The argument misses the point.

Not every sincere disagreement, different point of view, or different perspective surrounding a question, issue, or problem raises an ethical question. Nor, indeed, are all obligations ethical ones. The obligation that a good soldier ought to ensure that the tanks are painted every month is not an ethical obligation in the normal sense of the term, although it could perhaps become one in the extreme as when the tanks painted dark green are then shipped to a desert environment. The obligation to paint the tanks is not an ethical obligation since it involves no ethical content or serious choices to be made among competing obligations. It is simply an obligation to follow legitimate orders.

Obedience involves executing *legitimate* orders, even those the soldier disagrees with or does not understand completely, as long as they do not raise serious ethical concerns in the minds of those who are expected to obey. To be obedient to the will of one's legitimate and lawful superior, even in the face of disagreement, does not necessarily involve an ethical conflict since many of the orders to be executed do not involve ethical questions and may have no ethical content at all. Expressed in an analogy, a quarterback may call for a play with which the halfback disagrees, but which requires that the halfback execute the play anyway. In these conditions, it is rightly expected that the halfback will obey and attempt to carry out his instructions to the best of his ability. Only when the quarterback orders the halfback to throw the game does a simple question of obedience to the orders of a legitimate superior become transformed into an ethical dilemma requiring the halfback to make a clear distinction between obedience and obligation.

A line must be drawn between orders involving ethical obligations and those requiring obedience. A good soldier is an obedient soldier who executes the orders of his/her superiors even if he/she does not like them or fully understand the reasons behind them. Superiors, after all, cannot be expected to explain their orders to every soldier all the time. However, the soldier's virtue of obedience can never be taken to mean that it condones or allows him or her to abandon their ethical obligations in any sense whatsoever. *The soldier's ethical autonomy and responsibility always remain primary. When the orders of a superior raise ethical questions in the mind of the soldier, the soldier is obliged to resolve the ethical dilemma before carrying out the orders. The soldier's solution to the ethical quandary may require that he or she refuse to carry out the order.* This is the very crux of ethical responsibility and the soldier may not rightly avoid it by ceding his or her ethical autonomy to the superior. If the soldier does that, he or she will still be held ethically and legally responsible for the consequences of their action. *Obedience to orders, then, is never a substitute for ethical judgment.* At the same time, however, the requirement of obedience does not always bring to the fore questions of ethical obligations or judgments, and when it doesn't of course the soldier must obey.

Dissent

Not every directive or order involves ethical issues, but when they do the soldier has certain basic obligations. Among these is what a former commandant of the U.S. Naval Academy called "the will to dissent."[6] A good soldier is courageous enough to disagree with his superiors when he or she thinks that the issue involved is of some importance. In these circumstances the soldier should make his or her objections known. Dissent is the opposite of the "CYA (Cover Your Ass) Syndrome" in which officers "go on record" as having "taken a position" so that if things go wrong they can refer to their file of "memoranda for record" to escape responsibility for the consequences of failure. The CYA Syndrome is a corruption of the virtue of dissent.

The willingness of the soldier to dissent implies a willingness to explore with his or her superiors the rationale behind the controversial directive and to point out the difficulties the soldier sees as being associated with it. The object of dissent is to bring to the attention of superiors information the soldier feels may not have been given sufficient weight or even considered at all. The idea is to help one's superiors make the best possible decision under the circumstances. There is, of course, no question of the soldier's willingness to execute the order once given by the superior unless the soldier judges that some issue of ethical gravity is involved. All soldiers, particularly troop leaders and mission planners, should be encouraged to develop "the will to dissent."

Admiral Lord Nelson was famous for his willingness to dissent and question the plans and orders of his superiors, and he encouraged his own officers to do likewise. Before battle, the admiral would assemble his officers in the wardroom and ask them what they thought he ought to do. He always required his junior officers to answer first so they would not be cowed or have their views influenced by their seniors. Nelson felt strongly that a good officer should be willing to offer a contrary point of view without fear. Nelson's practice had a profound influence on the famous Japanese Admiral of the Second World War, Admiral Isoroko Yamamoto, who required the same practice of his officers. Of course, dissent should never be permitted to degenerate into carping or bureaucratic self-defence, tactics designed to reduce the soldier's responsibility, not enhance it. Dissent requires that one take responsibility for one's views. A good soldier is obedient yet willing to dissent when he or she feels it is required to do so. "Yes men" rarely make good soldiers or officers. Once more the judgment when to dissent rests with the individual soldier. A military professional must also learn to assess when dissent is appropriate.

The dangers sometimes associated with dissent in the military environment are often exaggerated. It is highly unlikely that dissent within the military would result in large-scale emotional debate paralyzing the military into inaction. One imagines that this might have happened in the United States on the eve of the Civil War or to the Yugoslav national army once Serbia broke free of the national union. By far the greater danger lies not in too much dissent, but in not enough dissent. *The danger in a profession as bureaucratic, hierarchical, and authoritarian as the military is that a lack of dissent will permit the perpetuation of failed or even unethical policies if only because the military professionals, those able to offer the most expert advice on military questions, simply remain silent.* One cannot but point out that not a single senior officer publicly criticized or resigned in the face of ten years of failed war policies in Vietnam. The military strategy in Iraq has been failing for more than two years and no serving officer has publicly dissented before Congress. Indeed, the officer who presided over that failed policy for the last year and a half has been promoted to Chief of Staff of the Army! It may be surmised that an officer who is unwilling to dissent is an officer who is uncertain of his or her own competence and, perhaps, even his or her ethical moorings.

Ability to Listen

A good leader must be a good listener. He or she must be willing to explore all areas and facets of a question and consider all available information by listening to others before finalizing their decisions. *The enemy of innovation and discovery is not ignorance, but the presumption of knowledge.* This presumption leads to one becoming closed-minded to new ideas on the assumption that one already has the answer. A leader must be willing to change his or her views if any new information is presented that sheds doubt on the initial decision. In a society and profession that emphasizes expertise and specialization, the tendency is to defer excessively to expertise. This deference should never become a substitute for independent judgment or for a willingness to listen to and consider dissenting views. Nor should the soldier allow expertise to blunt questioning of a decision. To prevent this, the soldier must be able to grasp the subtleties of the arguments of others not simply to rebut them, but to understand them and the role they are playing in the decision. The imperative to learn by listening to others is no less important for the soldier than for anyone else.

Intellectual Curiosity

Soldiers and leaders must be thinkers infected with an intellectual curiosity. *The basis of all creativity is curiosity.* A person who is not curious will never discover anything new for he or she lacks the impetus to ask why things are as they are. Action, of course, is required of all soldiers, but actions without thought and plan can produce disasters. Thought rests behind ethical judgment since it depends upon a willingness to explore all aspects of the circumstances. A good soldier must be able to improvise as circumstances demand, and that requires that he or she think about those circumstances in a disciplined manner. It is simply not true that discipline is the enemy of thought, that the thinking soldier puts himself in danger through hesitation. True discipline is the steady application of a course of action carefully thought out. Thus soldiers, and especially officers and non-commissioned troop leaders, must develop intellectual curiosity and a willingness to explore areas that are unfamiliar to them. This is known as "thinking outside the box" or "non-paradigmatic analysis." By whatever name it is called, a soldier must acquire a genuine desire to know and to learn about new things. *A good soldier must be willing to exercise his or her mind, to think the unthinkable, and to trust his or her judgment. On the field of battle, only the mentally aware are likely to survive.*

Ethical Reasoning

To suggest that the soldier be a thinker and a good listener and possess the willingness to dissent implies that he or she must also possess the virtue of ethical reasoning. If the essence of ethical choice is the ability to choose one obligation over another and to know the reasons that underlie one's choice, then ethical reasoning rests at the centre of ethical action for any moral agent, including the soldier. One of the shortcomings of most military education is a tendency to avoid serious instruction in ethical reasoning, relying only upon case study presentations which emphasize selecting the correct answer by choosing among rules. Ethical reasoning is developed more like an art. Learning to think systematically to reach a prudential judgment is far more than choosing among applicable rules. It is also true that for the most part soldiers do not enter military service already equipped with a sharpened ability to reason ethically and, therefore, must be taught. *Ethical reasoning occupies an important place in the soldier's character and it is a primary task of the profession to inculcate and develop this ability in each and every soldier to the extent possible.*

Responsibility

If one were forced to choose one virtue that the soldier must demonstrate above all other military virtues, many would choose responsibility. Responsibility involves understanding that the individual is an autonomous ethical agent responsible for his or her actions. To accept responsibility means being willing to accept the burden of ethical decisions and the consequences of those decisions. Responsibility also implies that the soldier recognize that to be human is to be obligated and that to make difficult choices among less than ideal options is an unavoidable task of every soldier trying to act ethically. The soldier begins to be responsible by recognizing the special obligations he or she is required to observe. Without a comprehension of these obligations, the soldier will not develop the ethical sense required to be responsible. Thus, the soldier who tries to avoid responsibility is acting more like the manager or bureaucrat, and is not likely to contribute to the moral development of either the person or the profession. A soldier who will not bear responsibility is not a true military professional.

Humanism

To be a humanist, the soldier must understand that what he or she does cannot be isolated from its impact upon other human beings, even the enemy. The soldier must understand that while the acts of a good solider might be approvable in a narrow professional sense, there are times when to be a good soldier is likely to mean that one is a less good human being. Killing, as David Grossman has pointed out, seems to have a terrible impact upon the soldier's sense of being human and often leads to despair. This despair complements Aristotle's assertion that "man is a social animal," and it is this realization that leads us to feel that "each man's death diminishes us all." The soldier must possess an ethical awareness that transcends a narrow professionalism and incorporates the realization that the application of his skills can have terrifying effects on other humans. In this the soldier must also bear a sense of *social* responsibility. He or she must understand that no man is an island, that what one does affects not only him or herself but other human beings inside and outside the profession as well. High-ranking officers must be especially aware of the responsibilities they have to a larger humanity, for upon their recommendations or orders whole societies can be sentenced to death. The awareness that the military carries out its tasks within a larger social and human environment that often suffers the consequences of the military's actions is a virtue that all soldiers must never lose at risk of diminishing their own humanity.

Compassion

The soldier, aware that he or she deals in life and death and that their decisions may unleash terrible violence upon fellow human beings, must develop compassion for human suffering and relieve the suffering of others when he or she can. The doctrine, noted earlier, of a minimal application of force is ethically appropriate to guide the soldier's actions in war. Violence is central to the profession of arms, but the soldier ought never to revel in its effects upon other human beings, even enemies. To do so is to diminish oneself. This is not to say that the soldier cannot be a proud professional in applying his or her skills. It is only to say that the soldier must always be aware that the destruction of human life, often necessarily so, is a less than ideal means to sometimes good ends. *The soldier must feel some genuine regret at the willing destruction of other human beings and he or she must not do it too readily or enjoy it too much. It is the soldier's ethical responsibility to stay the hand of the sword when it is possible to do so.*

Realism

A soldier must be capable of making an honest and impartial assessment of the application of rules for him or herself, their men, and even the enemy. *A good soldier is starkly realistic and understands that in an imperfect world only imperfect solutions are usually available for serious problems.* The soldier must develop a sense of realism that helps him or her realize their own limits and understand that humans are limited in their ability to grasp even the consequences of their own actions completely, to say nothing of the consequences of the acts of large-scale organizations dedicated to the application of systematic violence. Being a realist means resisting the application to become a narrow professional, to resist the pull of exaggerated self-interest, and to resist the tendency "to get ahead" at any cost. *Realistic soldiers understand that they cannot do it all, that they cannot be perfect, and that the real world is almost never fair and seldom lends itself to easy solutions to most problems.* Yet, a sense of realism ought never to lead to despair, but to a careful balancing of means and ends, and to the selection of goals that are possible to attain. Even in an imperfect world it is possible to try to achieve objectives that are in themselves worthwhile. An officer who is unrealistic in his or her choice of goals or in the manner in which means to ends are chosen will not be of much help to his or her superiors or the soldiers they lead. Thus, a realistic soldier must balance a concern with humanity, social responsibility, compassion, fairness, and justice — all noble things in themselves—with a concern for what is possible in an imperfect world.

Vocation

A sense of special obligation is required if the profession of arms is to manifest the aura of a vocation. The soldier must realize that what he does is categorically different from what other men and women do in other occupations, and that the obligations soldiers undertake are also different and special in their scope and level of responsibility. A soldier who enters the military only to further career goals will quickly discover in the carnage of the battlefield how disjointed these priorities are. No sane or well-balanced human being can be expected to endure the terrors of battle and the responsibility of sending others to their deaths and inflicting death upon other human beings simply in pursuit of his or her own power, prestige, income, and career status. These factors may indeed motivate people in civilian life, but are quickly proven by experience to be insufficient to motivate soldiers. *One of the main means for preventing soldiers from degenerating into hired killers or armed thugs is their awareness of their special obligations to others, obligations that rest at the centre of military professionalism and make the profession a true vocation or calling.*

What is required among soldiers is a sense of brotherhood, of understanding that one's fellow soldiers share the same obligations, risks, costs, burdens, and, one would hope, virtues. Members of the profession are bound together by their willingness to assume and pay the price of belonging as members of a special group of individuals. In this regard, the calling to serve in the military is not that different from a calling to serve others in any other vocation.

Introspection

If we expect soldiers to feel a sense of dedication and to support that with a sense of brotherhood, we had best be prepared to require of them the virtue of introspection. It is no accident that monastic orders require their members to reserve a certain period of every day for introspection. Introspection should also be a an essential part of the mental training of the soldier, a regular period of stopping and thinking in an effort to "make sense of it all." When the German Army adopted the general staff system in the mid-nineteenth century, it institutionalized the concept of introspection in the practice of a tactical walk. It often sent their staff officers away from the army to a completely different assignment in a completely different place or even on an extended leave of absence for study. During this time, officers were required to think about solutions to novel problems to which they had not previously been exposed. Others pursued courses of study, often music, philosophy, and literature, that were completely unrelated to military matters at all.

Introspection is necessary because the solider can easily be lured by the prestige of rank and status and become completely wrapped up in his or her job or career thus losing the ability to think independently or in other than familiar terms. These are the military versions of the narrow workaholics found in business corporations. *A reduction in the soldier's ability to think independently and to reason through the unfamiliar threatens the sense of special calling required by the profession and ultimately threatens its ethics and virtues.* In reacting exclusively to external and familiar conditions almost as if by rote, the soldier risks responding to these conditions as if they were fixed circumstances of all environments. The soldier will develop what Balzac called "a nostalgia for the familiar," and see change as a threat. The soldier who cannot respond to the unfamiliar is at great risk and necessarily puts others at risk as well.

It is introspection that permits soldiers to maintain their ethical balance and the sense of special obligation that make them true professionals. If the soldier starts to lose this sense, introspection can lead the soldier back to the right path. The military virtue of introspection is the application of an old monastic principle to the modern military profession. It is, perhaps, even more valuable in the modern age because it is more rare.

Dedication

Soldiers who share a special sense of obligation as in a brotherhood must also be dedicated to its welfare. They must demonstrate the virtue of dedication, a term from the Latin, *dedicare*, meaning "to proclaim or to devote or to consecrate." When a soldier is said to be dedicated, he or she is said to possess a sense of being set apart. This is the sense in which the soldier must be willing to devote much of his or her life to a purpose beyond self. The commitment or dedication to the brotherhood and its special obligations transcends the soldier's personal interests. *The soldier becomes a dedicated professional when he or she understands, recognizes, and assumes the special tasks, burdens, responsibilities, and obligations of the profession in which membership is professed.* Dedication to one's career and personal advancement are not the same thing. Dedication means "a devotion to a sacred purpose with solemn rites," and implies a devotion to something beyond oneself, to the community, the nation, and the profession. One has only to attend a military funeral to see such dedication on full display.

Imagination

Imagination does not readily come to mind as an important quality of the soldier. This is because to those who are not soldiers, the soldier is stereotyped as a person immersed in a large organization governed by rigid rules and orders that permit no deviation. Yet, military people themselves always rank imagination very highly as a personal attribute of a good soldier. The soldier requires imagination if he or she is to survive and be effective on the battlefield. As General Graf von Moltke was fond of pointing out, no matter how brilliantly conceived, no battle plan survived more than twelve hours contact with the enemy. A good soldier uses his or her intellect to conceive courses of action and opportunity not covered by regulations, plans, standing orders, and even training rituals. Thus, the constant need to "innovate, endure, and overcome." Conditions of virtue are essentially conditions of the mind, and the quality of imagination is a vital one in any soldier. Nothing could be more false than the belief that an ideal soldier is a person addicted to following only the proven path. *A soldier who does not think imaginatively is likely to be quickly killed. And a soldier who does not think imaginatively will quickly find him or herself in ethical difficulty.* The best soldiers, and certainly the best leaders, are those who "make their own tracks" as one armour commander put it. Moreover, without imagination many of the other qualities of the good soldier can be pointlessly squandered in doing what everyone else has already done.

Confidence

A soldier's virtues and technical skills will count for little if he or she does not possess the confidence to execute responsibilities boldly. Without confidence of self and purpose, the soldier will not be given to risk or daring or any of the other qualities so important to survival and success in battle. *Worse, lack of confidence is contagious. Leaders who do not radiate confidence and calm will quickly find that their troops will lose confidence in them and their decisions.* The soldier's confidence must be publicly on display so that others, too, may take example from it and stay the difficult course. In the end, the Special Boat Service has it right: "Who Dares, Wins."

Courage

Physical courage in the face of fire and hardship is, of course, required of the good soldier, especially so in positions of leadership. The difficulty is that it is almost impossible to predict which soldiers will be capable of courageous action and which will choose the path of caution. That is why those who are capable of it are called heroes. But most soldiers will not spend much of their careers under fire. Still their daily activities will require courage, but courage of another kind, ethical courage. *Ethical courage requires a willingness to confront difficult situations without fear, to accept the risks and responsibilities of position, and, if need be, to be willing to bear the costs of a course of action that one believes is right.* Without physical courage, a soldier cannot be an effective combat leader. Without ethical courage, the soldier cannot be effective during times of peace or war.

Battlefield Virtues

Military professionals writing about military virtues tend to divide considerations of these virtues into those that are most important on the field of battle and those most appropriate to the non-combat environment. More often than not the division is unconscious, although it remains a constant theme of military writing. In biographies and memoirs, soldiers most often cite the following virtues as those most desirable in troops and officers they command in war: aggressiveness, willingness to attack, daring, risk-taking, initiative, endurance, and flexibility. Moulding these qualities together is the virtue of perspective, an ability to assess risks as they relate to initiative and daring so as not to endanger or squander one's troops meaninglessly in pursuit of personal bravery and glory, but to be aware of mission requirements relative to human costs. A brave soldier must remember that the soldiers he or she commands are not always equally fearless.

An important battlefield virtue is discipline. To be disciplined is to be dedicated to a course of action that is beneficial to attaining the goals of one's life or profession. The discipline of a leader is important to maintaining the discipline of his or her troops, and disciplined troops are vitally important to good leadership and military effectiveness. But discipline has another dimension, an ethical one. Discipline is also required if soldiers are to act ethically in war, to minimize the damage and killing. Only when the mind is properly disciplined can it think and make choices essential to the proper conduct of military ethics.

Bearing

The physical and ethical bearing of a soldier establishes a point of reference between himself and the ethical code of the profession expressed in terms of what the soldier ought to do as a good soldier. Equally important, bearing establishes a reference point between a soldier and his or her fellow soldiers and even more crucially with the soldiers he or she commands. A leader serves as the ethical reference point for his or her troops by providing an example for them to emulate or, at the minimum, to follow. *A leader sets the example of ethical behaviour for his or her troops, and must convince them that he or she is very serious about the ethical limitations of combat.* The leader must ensure that his or her soldiers observe these limits

Decisiveness

A soldier must always be willing to decide. *A leader can be forgiven making the wrong decision, but will not be forgiven the failure to decide.* At the centre of military leadership is the ability and willingness to make decisions and accept responsibility for them. This is the essence of command. It would seem that military life requires that decisions be made more frequently than in civilian life and, of course, these decisions are likely to be more important as well. Many of these decisions deal with material things, but all too often they involve the lives and deaths of other human beings and have to be made with incomplete information and very quickly. There is, of course, the additional element that the soldier's decisions often place his or her own life at risk, a circumstance not usually found in other professions or occupations. Thus, a soldier who will not or cannot decide is useless. *A good leader must be able to decide and to make his or her decision felt with a sense of confidence and aggressiveness if he or she expects troops to follow.*

Dignity

A soldier must possess dignity of character. The term dignity is derived from the Latin *dignus*, meaning worth. A soldier, then, must have self-worth and must demonstrate this characteristic of his or her personality to subordinates, superiors, and peers. Like the Medieval knights of the West and the Muslim religious warriors of the East of the same period, there is a sense in which to be a soldier is to be different. An essential part of this difference is that the soldier ought to be the personification of a set of special virtues, values, and ethics that come to constitute his or her personal *raison d'être*. The way of the warrior is demonstrably different and separate from the larger society, and the soldier's possession of a sense of this difference is expressed in his or her self-worth. Leaders must be able to transmit this sense of dignity to the soldiers they lead. But even as an individual standing alone on a desert plain the soldier must retain his dignity, the sense that even here, alone, he or she stands above the normal daily marginal concerns of human existence. The soldier's bearing and dignity reflect the worth of the profession of which he or she is a special member. *Dignity is what you think of yourself when no one is looking.*

Technical Competence

The ability to demonstrate an acceptable level of technical competence is an asset that is required frequently in modern armies as they become more complex and specialized. The imperatives of the organization itself tend to press officers into narrow areas of technical competence rather than into broader areas of general experience. The artilleryman, for example, may not know how to disassemble and clean a rifle, while the rifleman may have no concept of the applications of armour or artillery. The United States Marine Corps attempts to broaden the experience of its officers by ensuring that every one, even their pilots, experiences infantry basic training and has spent time in command of an infantry platoon. Fortunately, most military establishments recognize the dangers of overspecialization and have made significant efforts to create within the profession a general sense of the importance of broad general competence as an antidote to the narrowness attendant to specialization. Thus, most officers who have attained senior rank reflect career patterns that forced them to circulate through a series of different assignments in an attempt to generalize their experience and to psychologically wean them away from narrow technical specialization. This often leads platoon and company combat commanders to decry the fact that their seniors have not "smelled a soldier in years" and have forgotten the essence of command. It is a charge without merit. Technical competence implies not only competence in the skills one is most likely to use in any given assignment, but also the ability to comprehend how those skills fit together at all levels of command to ensure that the military as a whole is combat ready and competent. The future still belongs to the generalist.

Power

Military effectiveness is only partially related to technical competence in the sense of troops possessing adequate military skills. Rather, combat effectiveness seems to be more closely tied to unit cohesion. *Units without a high level of social attachment of soldiers to one another are unlikely to fight well regardless of the quality of their weaponry or even the degree of their training.* Unit cohesion, the social glue that holds human beings together under stress, is a function of the interpersonal relationships that develop among soldiers, and between leaders and led. *Military effectiveness, then, depends heavily upon the degree to which leaders are capable of creating, developing, and sustaining those interpersonal skills that permit the leader to create strong bonds with his or her troops.* Without these bonds, combat units will not likely withstand the stress of the modern battlefield.

Thus, the soldier who holds a position of command also holds a position of power, and he or she must never forget that effective leadership is closely bound up with the application of this power in fostering unit cohesion. A leader must understand that he or she is directly responsible for developing his or her own social skills that permit the leader to establish and foster the bonds of unit cohesion that make military units function well under fire.

Conclusion

The list of military virtues presented here reflects the connection between the special responsibilities of the military and the character required of the soldier in order to bear them. No one realistically can expect soldiers to demonstrate all of these qualities all the time. The notion of perfect virtue is not attainable in the imperfect empirical world in which the soldier finds him or herself. These virtues constitute a list of ideal traits of character worth striving for. They serve as guideposts for assessing the soldier's humanity and actions as a military professional.

Virtues in themselves are not equivalent to ethics or ethical acts. All too often military academies and staff colleges have tended to suggest that the inculcation of personal virtue, that is, character, will provide the soldier with adequate guides for acting ethically. The soldier cannot be expected to act ethically in the absence of these virtues, for virtues represent dispositions to actions. But they are not ethical actions themselves, and are not specific in their applications of what one ought to *do*, especially for the soldier in the unique and challenging circumstances he or she is likely to confront. Only a code of ethics applicable to the challenges of the profession of arms can provide specific ethical precepts as requirements of action. Yet, a code of ethics is likely to be rendered meaningless for a soldiery that did not possess some military virtues, if only because none of the predispositions to ethical action would be present. *A code of military ethics and the education and training of the soldier in military virtue go together in producing an ethical soldier.*

Soldiers who lack virtue and ethics can never be adequate servants of the society and the profession they are sworn to serve. As S.L.A. Marshal pointed out, "To the extent that military men lose their faith in virtue and become amenable to ill-considered reforms simply to appease the public [or their superiors!], they relinquish the power to protect their society." To reaffirm once again, the way of the warrior is different from the life of the civilian, as are the requirements for virtue and ethics. Those called to the profession of arms are required to bear heavier and qualitatively different ethical burdens from those of their fellow citizens, and it is in willingly assuming those burdens that the soldier becomes truly ennobled.

Unless military professionals do their job well, no one in the larger society can expect to benefit from the advantages of a peaceful society. *It is a curious irony that the pursuit of self-interest can only be made possible when a group of special men and women are willing to forego that pursuit and instead serve and protect the society so that others may engage in it.* The survival of society and its quality of life depends upon the existence of a dedicated military profession attending to the society's defence. The profession depends upon a corps of virtuous professionals who are willing to live by a code of ethics that sets them apart from their fellow citizens while placing themselves at their service.

Endnotes

1.   Kant's dictum is quoted in William K. Frankena, *Ethics* (Englewood Cliffs, NJ: Prentice-Hall, 1973), 65.

2.   Arthur J. Dyck, "Ethical Bases of the Military Profession," *Parameters* (March, 1980), 44.

3.   Ibid.

4.   John H. Moellering, "The Army Turns Inward," *Military Review* (July, 1973), 68.

5.   Samuel H. Hayes and William N. Thomas, *Taking Command* (Harrisburg, PA: Stackpole Books, 1967), 51.

6.   Kenneth H. Wenker, "Professional Military Ethics: An Attempt at Definition," *Air Force Journal of Professional Military Ethics* (April, 1980), 25.

An Ethical Code

A number of arguments can be raised in opposition to the establishment of a formal ethical code for the military profession. All of these, in my view, misunderstand the nature of ethics *per se* and the role played by ethical judgment in bringing about ethical decisions and actions. Some of these misunderstandings have already been addressed in the preceding chapters. Nonetheless, it is worth examining in detail the question of whether or not a code of ethics for the military profession ought to be devised, disseminated, and enforced as a means for meeting the challenges of the future and to resist the erosion of the profession's identity as a unique social institution.

Advantages of a Code

One of the American army's most highly-regarded senior officers, General Maxwell Taylor, had long been a proponent of an ethical code for the U.S. military when he wrote:

> "There may be justification, or even a definite need, to restate in strong and clear terms those principles of conduct which retain an unchallengeable relevance to the necessity of the military profession and to which the officer corps will be expected to conform regardless of behavioral practices elsewhere."[1]

General Taylor correctly emphasized that the code would be used to govern only the *professional* values and actions of the soldier, and "would not presume to serve as a universal ethic for all men at all times or even for officers in fulfilling obligations unrelated to the military."[2] In this, General Taylor shows an awareness of the proper role of professional ethics as pertaining only to the obligations of the profession and not to some universal ethical standard.

Lewis Sorley has noted another advantage of a code. Ethical conduct lies at the core of the trust between civilian society and the profession of arms. If the civil society is not convinced that the military governs its conduct by a clear set of ethical standards against which it will be held responsible, the trust between civilian society and the military profession is weakened and in extreme cases breaks down altogether. Sorely notes that, "during the long history of the profession of arms, strict adherence to professional, ethical, and moral codes has been essential if the power and influence of military organizations were to be an effective servant, rather than the arbitrary master of the state."[3] A breakdown in trust between the civilian populace and the military establishments of the emerging democracies presents a real problem for the new democratic civic orders that can be mitigated to a significant degree if their military establishments can be convinced to observe a code of professional ethics that recognizes the elected establishment as the final arbiter of civil-military disputes. *The formulation of a clear code of ethics for the military serves as the foundation for a special trust between the profession and the civil society and its elected representatives that the military has sworn to preserve and protect.*

Other advantages of a formal ethical code are evident. A code would unify the profession in a shared respect for its common ideals and values and would help create a sense of community by specifying the "cost of belonging" to that community in terms of the obligations that members of the profession are expected to observe. Without a common ethical centre, there can be no true profession. The creation of a community within the profession requires the recognition that membership is a special calling to service that should be formalized in a code of special ethics for all to witness. At the same time, a code of military ethics would aid the profession in developing social pressures toward shaping the soldier's character. A code would set standards of socialization for the new recruit by establishing the ideals toward which the recruit would be expected to strive. Of course, ethical ideals are not attainable without great effort. It is the striving itself that ennobles. *A code would contribute to setting standards of character development with which the profession could socialize its members.*

A code of military ethics would demonstrate to the civilian populace that the profession possesses a special sense of obligation. It would demonstrate in unequivocal terms the pledge of the soldier and the profession to uphold certain core ideals. The promulgation of a clear ethical code would likely help solidify public support for the military. One of the primary reasons why the military profession usually scores highly in public opinion polls that measure the support, trust, and confidence of the general populace is precisely because the general populace of most democracies in the West recognize that the military is different from other players in the game of representative government. *A clear statement of that difference expressed in a formal ethical code that delineates the special obligations and values of the profession will further strengthen that support.*

High-ranking military officers are often required to interact with their civilian overseers at the highest levels of government where they serve as key advisers on policy matters. The fact is that many of these officials have no first-hand military experience and are often unaware of the special nature and burdens of the life of the military professional. The establishment of a code of military ethics stating these special obligations and burdens may help the profession's civilian superiors realize the special nature of the military way as well as to understand better the background ambience necessary to sustain it. *An ethical code can facilitate understanding between military professionals and their civilian superiors and aid the civilian leadership in carrying out their responsibilities with regard to the military.*

If the military requires special obligations and expects to attract and retain good men and women to carry them out, it must understand that the way of the warrior cannot be for everyone. By clearly stating the responsibilities expected of the soldier and the special sense of dedication and sacrifice required for soldiers to serve honourably within the profession, a formal code of ethics will help attract those individuals who are willing to live up to these ideals and obligations. The code can also be used to weed out those who will not or cannot meet the required standards. *By stating clearly what the military profession is and what it expects of its members, a code of ethics can be a powerful force in attracting to the profession the very best in society, namely, those who are willing to accept the special challenge of military service with all its hardships, sacrifice, and responsibilities.*

For all these reasons, the formal establishment of a code of military ethics aids the profession in retaining its sense of uniqueness. *The code of the warrior proclaims to the world what the military profession stands for and by what standards it accepts judgment of its own actions.* In this sense, a code of military ethics is strongly analogous to a code of monastic rules that specifies the special nature of the profession, the obligations required of its members, its core values, the price of belonging, and the penalty of expulsion for those who fail to observe the creed. As with monastic rules, the ethical imperatives of the profession ought to be phrased in unambiguous language. Some degree of linguistic obfuscation and lack of clarity may serve the law well, but it produces no benefits for a code of ethics. Whatever else, a code for the way of the warrior must be clear.

Objections to a Code

Not everyone agrees that a code of ethics for the military would be a good thing or make much difference. It is important to examine the most common arguments for this view. An analysis of these arguments ought to demonstrate the need for a formalized ethical code by removing the most common objections to it.[4]

1. An ethical code for the military would be meaningless since one cannot teach ethics to begin with; one acquires ethics as a consequence of one's total life experiences. By the time the recruit enters the military, his or her ethics are already fully formed and are unlikely to change. In response, it must be noted that the claim that one cannot teach ethics is nonsense. Moreover, if professional ethics is defined as those obligations pertaining to what the soldier ought to do as a member of the military profession, then clearly no one acquires any knowledge of professional obligations through life experience any more than one acquires a knowledge of physics that way. *All ethics, and surely the ethics of a specific profession, must be taught in the same manner as any knowledge attendant to any discipline. All virtues must be learned as well.* On the face of it, then, the question is not can ethics be taught, for the answer is yes because there is no other way to acquire ethics. The real question is how best to teach ethics.

    Even though soldiers acquire much of their general ethical sense before they enter the military, they are likely to have learned almost nothing about *the rules of ethical actions specific to the military profession.* Of course some general ethical precepts may be similar, but the specific ethical requirements of a profession can only be learned *after* one has applied for and gained membership in it. A profession's use of its ethical code to teach the obligations attendant to the profession is accomplished by the profession itself and not some outside agency. Even a good person who makes ethical judgments outside his or her profession and demonstrates certain values may still have to learn new ethical obligations and new values when he or she becomes a member of a special profession like the military. No tool is more useful to this task than the specification of a formal code of professional ethics.

    The idea that a profession cannot change an individual's ethics acquired prior to entering a profession is false and misses the point. The fact is that no one has any ethical sense of a profession until he or she becomes a member and is made specifically aware of its ethical requirements. No one, for example, would expect a physician to know and observe the ethical obligations of the medical profession until he or she became a physician. So, too, with the lawyer or the priest. Why should it be different for members of the profession of arms?

A good person *outside* the profession may not be a good person *within* it. A range of ethical values and habits acquired outside the profession may be good for those circumstances that are likely to arise *outside* the profession but may be very poor guides for actions that are required *within* the profession. Thus, a Christian pacifist may be an ethical person in many ways, but he or she is likely to make a poor military professional. Or a person who makes a habit of being empathetic to the suffering of others may make an excellent clergyman but is unlikely to make a good psychiatrist, a profession in which excessive empathy is regarded as dangerous to the practitioner himself. One ought not to confuse the possession of virtues with ethics nor assume that all ethical precepts possessed by an individual are of singular relevance to any given profession. *The professional ethics of different professions are quite different.*

To put the matter another way, some obligations and responsibilities are more relevant to some professions than to others. If by ethics is meant a series of obligations that specify what one ought to do as a member of that profession, to include the capacity for ethical reasoning, then both can be learned only *after* the individual becomes a member of the profession that can impart this knowledge to him or her. This seems especially so if the capacity for ethical reasoning is to be relevant to the ethical judgments that are likely to be required of the soldier as a member of the profession. Thus, to claim that one ought not to develop a code of ethics because one cannot teach ethics is to fail to understand the nature of ethics and how one acquires ethics. *Ethics cannot be plausibly taught without first specifying the necessary obligations, and there seems no clearer way to specify those obligations than to enshrine them in a formal code.*

2.   Codes are useless because ethics cannot be enforced from outside the individual but must come from within. There is no doubt that ethical codes bind more strongly when their precepts have been internalized

and that, indeed, is the goal of professional ethical instruction. But whether or not a formal ethical code is internalized, it can still provide a standard of judgment against which to measure the actions of the profession's membership. Without a code of ethics, one can at least claim that it will be more difficult to internalize the ethical precepts of the profession because the precepts themselves and their meaning and application are less clear. If internalization of professional ethical precepts is the goal, it must first be clear to the soldier what precepts are to be internalized. The best way to do this is to employ a formal code which clearly states what the precepts are. It is not suggested that a code *per se* compels ethical acts. *What a code can do is specify those obligations that the military professional is required to observe.*

Studies have demonstrated that the mere existence of a formal ethical code within an organizational setting by itself raises the level of ethical behaviour, if for no other reason than that the code clarifies what is expected of people in the way of ethical conduct.[5] In order to internalize norms and values, one must first identify them by stating the precepts of the code. The statement of values by itself seems to influence conduct and is likely to contribute to the internalization process. To suggest that extant internalized values somehow negate the influence of a formal code is to misunderstand the process by which individual's internalize values. One cannot internalize values of which one is unaware, and one can be made aware of professional obligations very quickly by formally stating what they are in a code of ethics.

3.   A code might become a substitute for ethical judgment. It has been pointed out that minimal ethical standards have a way of becoming maximal. A code of military ethics might come to be perceived as constituting the total sum of the ethical obligations that the members of the military profession are required to observe. Under these circumstances individuals would live up to only a minimum code of ethical obligations which they might then regard as the sum of their ethical responsibilities. In short, the soldier might come to conclude that to be a good soldier is just to be a minimally good human being.

Members of the profession must understand that *a code of military ethics constitutes only the most important of their professional obligations and that the professional code does not constitute the complete sum of the soldier's ethical responsibilities.* The obligations of the professional code may at times be brought into conflict with the soldier's other obligations derived from the other promises he or she has made to others. In these circumstances, the soldier must choose which of the obligations to observe. Moreover, the tendency to reduce ethical codes to a book of rules distorts what they are supposed to do. Mal Wakin has cogently pointed out that "the immature or unsophisticated frequently narrow their ethical sights to the behaviour specifically delineated in the code so that what may have originally been intended as a minimum listing becomes treated as an exhaustive guide for ethical action."[6] Any tendency to regard a code of military ethics as an exhaustive list of the soldier's ethical obligations is simply wrong.

To say that humans can misapply or misunderstand ethical codes does not seem a convincing argument against their existence *per se*. Ethical codes usually delineate obligations in general terms. It is the function of ethical reasoning and judgment to determine what obligation is to be observed under what circumstances and how that obligation is to be carried out. To claim that codes can be misapplied is not an argument against their proper use in the first place. This said, it may be conceded that the existence of a code *per se* will achieve little unless the soldier is also educated in ethical reasoning.

4. A code would state ethical obligations in an ideal form and many of the ideals would be empirically unattainable. Accordingly, there is no point in stating ideals that cannot be attained; such codes are useless in a practical sense. This claim misses the point of ethics and what ethical codes can be expected to accomplish. As noted earlier, a basic philosophical premise for understanding ethics is the notion that "ought implies can." An ethical code that established precepts and values that were unattainable in an empirical sense would not be legitimate since no one can be held ethically responsible for obligations that do not have a realistic chance of being carried out.

On the other hand, the ethical precepts of a code should be stated in such a way that they are difficult to live up to. *For a code to be useful in engendering ethical actions and aiding character development there must be some gap or separation between the ideal and the real, between aspiration and attainment. A minimal code of ethics that everyone could observe all the time without significant effort is not a proper code at all.* This separation produces a "creative tension" so that striving for the ideals makes the soldier a better person because of the striving itself. This notion derives from Aristotle's concept of virtue, which suggests that the striving for ideals tends to ennoble the individual in the process of striving regardless of whether or not the individual actually succeeds in attaining them. Seen in this way, it can be said that the failure to live up to a code is not a criticism of the code as long as the precepts within it are attainable, though not always attained by any given individual. On the other hand, if the gap between aspiration and attainment is so wide that no one ever succeeds, at some point individuals will stop trying and begin to pay only lip service to ideals they cannot realistically achieve.

5. It is impossible to construct a code of ethics because the range of circumstances and alternatives it would have to encompass would be impossibly large. Codification would also require the impossible task of soldiers having to learn how the code's precepts apply in all circumstances. Under these conditions, enforcement of such an extensive code would be impossible. The argument suggests that a code of military ethics would have to be so specific as to address in advance all the possible instances and circumstances under which any included ethical precept might apply. It is a task that is simply not possible. The argument is overly legalistic and confuses a code of ethics with a body of law.

Ethical codes are not the same thing as legal codices. Ethical codes specify in general terms what soldiers ought to do and permit the individual to choose which obligations he or she will observe when they cannot observe all relevant ones. The centrepiece of a code of ethics, then, is the necessity for choice in rendering ethical decisions. Law, on the other hand, makes no allowance for choice and denies the legitimacy of individual choice in obeying its stated obligations. The very specificity of law is intended to remove choice and substitute obedience for obligation. In addition, there is no necessary connection between a law and any specific ethical content, and most laws do not address ethical elements at all. Speeding laws, for example, do not involve ethical conditions as a rule nor do zoning codes. Ethical codes, by contrast, are designed to specify ethical imperatives and require ethical content by definition.

If one accepts the legalistic argument, the codification of ethical precepts indeed becomes an impossible task for it would have to specify how every precept applied in all possible combinations of circumstances and would transform a code of ethics into a codex of laws or rules. The confusion of ethics and law is a common one that leads to the false assumption that one can solve ethical problems with legal remedies. This identification of ethics with laws leads to a situation where the measure of the integrity of military and public officials comes to be judged by the fact that they have kept within the letter of the law. *The distinction between ethics and law is among the oldest in the philosophical tradition of Western culture, and the soldier would be wise always to keep it in mind.* The point is that a code of ethics is not a code of law and it cannot be expected to function as one. A code of ethics is stated in more general terms than law, its application cannot be specified as precisely as law rather requiring individual judgment to determine proper application, and its enforcement depends more on social sanctions than legal ones. Thus, to argue that a code of ethics for the military is impossible or useless because it does not meet the requirements of a code of law is to miss the point of both ethics and law.

The confusion of ethics with law leads to the fear that an ethical code would not be sufficiently specific to allow for the assessment of legalistic penalties and protections, or that it would allow for penalties for ethical transgressions in circumstances that would be far less clear than those required by a court of law. As one of my colleagues at the U.S. Army War College put it, he had no objection to a code of ethics as long as it wasn't written down! He feared that it would become the basis for judging the actions of members of the profession in ways that were less than clear in legal terms. One might easily admit that the fear has some merit, but it is the nature of ethical prudential judgments to be somewhat uncertain and subject to final assessment only after the fact. Once more, it is not proper to expect an ethical code to function as a body of law.

6. Under certain circumstances, the precepts of an ethical code may conflict. The ethical precepts of a code may indeed conflict in the circumstances in which the soldier may be forced to apply them, but the soldier must still choose among the conflicting obligations of the code when he or she cannot observe both. This is not, however, the same thing as saying that the precepts of the code conflict in an *a priori* sense, that is as precepts *per se* rather than precepts as they must be applied in certain circumstances. This lack of *a priori* conflict is what makes it possible to claim that all precepts of the code bind equally. It

is only the circumstances in which the soldier must apply the code's precepts that confer a sense that one obligation is more important than another, and it is in this situation that the soldier must render ethical judgment as to which one binds more than the other. *The fact that the precepts of a code may be made to conflict by the circumstances in which they must be applied is not an argument for failing to establish a code in the first place. It is merely to describe the nature of ethical dilemmas in an empirical world.*

Others suggest that while a code of ethics may establish ethical goals and ideals for the profession, it could not determine the degree of value any soldier might attach to different precepts in given circumstances. Because individual members of the profession will place greater value on some precepts than others, the argument goes, the value of an ethical code is rendered worthless. This argument, like most of the previous ones, reflects a failure to understand the nature of ethical codes.

It is certainly true that some soldiers may choose to observe different obligations of the code even in similar circumstances. But this is the very nature of making ethical choices. The reason why a soldier chooses one obligation over another is because the soldier judges that one obligation in a given set of circumstances ought to take precedence over another precisely because he or she deems it to be more valuable. Nonetheless, all postulates of the code are *prima facie* binding. It is the circumstances in which the precepts have to be applied that force the soldier to render a judgment that one precept has greater worth than the other and must be observed first. But as precepts *per se*, they are all equally ethically imperative insofar as they require the obligations to be observed *if the circumstances permit*. They are also equally imperative in the sense that they can be raised by the principle of universality so that if all soldiers carried out all the precepts *per se*, we would judge their actions as ethical. *The fact that one soldier may value one obligation over another in a different set of circumstances than another soldier does not negate the value of the code in stating what obligations ought to be observed in the first place.*

7. All codes are futile because they can be misapplied. The existence of a code does not guarantee compliance with it. No one seriously claims that the promulgation of an ethical code for the military will guarantee its observance. On the other hand, codes are statements of what soldiers ought

to do, and it is unlikely that one can establish ethical standards without codes, nor can one expect soldiers to carry out their obligations until they know what their obligations are. The same is true of enforcement. One cannot correct or judge ethical lapses without some idea of what the standards of ethical action are. A good code says nothing about bad practice or lax enforcement. The promulgation of a code will specify those ethical precepts against which ethical actions or lack of them can be measured. Without an ethical standard, judgments about ethics become very difficult indeed, especially so when the profession attempts to render a communal judgment about the actions of one of its members.

8.   A formal code of military ethics could actually come to constitute a danger to the men and women of the military profession. Soldiers might come to perceive obedience to the code as relieving them of all other obligations for ethical choice by simply obeying the code. Under these circumstances, obedience would become a substitute for ethical judgment. The argument is based upon a misconception of the notion of obedience. Following the obligations of an ethical code presupposes that the soldier knows *why* an obligation ought to be observed. *Blind obedience to a code of ethics that is not understood is not ethical action at all; it is merely obedience.* This said, to the degree that the ethical precepts of the code are legitimate, a soldier who attempts to apply them in concrete circumstances without knowing the reasons why the precepts ought to bind may well commit an unethical act.

Obedience to a code, however, does not remove the individual's ethical responsibility. Observing an ethical precept without regard for the circumstances in which it must be applied can easily become an unethical act because the circumstances are such that the soldier should have followed another precept of the code. *The soldier cannot escape ethical responsibility by simply following the precepts of a code any more than he or she can escape ethical responsibility by following the precepts of the law or the orders of superiors.* Ethical acts require that soldiers be aware of their obligations and the circumstances in which they have to be applied. Failure to take due cognizance of the latter can lead to grave ethical lapses. This is what seems to have happened to a company of Dutch soldiers in Bosnia charged with protecting civilians in a refugee camp. Surrounded by Serbian troops, the Dutch commander chose to save his men by surrendering their arms. In saving his troops, he rendered his command powerless to protect the civilians who were then massacred by the Serbians. Ethical acts never occur in a circumstantial vacuum. Ethical obligations require their observance to be applied with an understanding of their consequences in light of the circumstances in which the soldier finds him or herself.

9. An ethical code is unnecessary for the profession of arms. An ethical code would be needed only if one believes that soldiers are inherently bad and cannot be relied upon to do what is right on their own. Those who argue for a code seem to be saying that human beings are inherently corrupt. If this is so, then the provision of an ethical code will make no difference. Again, the argument is misplaced. Codes provide statements of the obligations that soldiers ought to observe and which they must live up to if they are to be permitted to become and remain members of the military profession. By attempting to live up to the code, soldiers are ennobled in the very acts of striving. Yet even corrupt individuals are not corrupt all the time, and the profession's ethical guidance as to what soldiers ought to do seems to be a good first step in convincing them to do it. Ethical codes are brought into existence not because individuals are corrupt, but because individuals are capable of being made good through instruction and example. *The purpose of the code is to show soldiers how to do good. It is only a secondary function of an ethical code to discern unethical acts. Its primary purpose is to inspire ethical actions.*

10. Three related arguments against the creation and use of a formal code of military ethics are contained in the following argument made by the Superintendent of the United States Military Academy, General Andrew J. Goodpaster. At a speech before the Association of American Colleges, General Goodpaster said:

> "It may be, however, that we should make the point more sharply and strongly. Military service does require a certain basic pattern of ethical commitment in ethical beliefs. But...it is not possible to prescribe in advance and in detail for every situation. An unthinking acceptance of a set of ethics prefabricated by others seems to us to have little promise for military officers."[7]

General Goodpaster's argument implies three objections to a code. First, a code would be unworkable because "it is not possible to prescribe in advance and in detail for every situation" the manner in which a code would apply. But, as we have seen, there is no need to prescribe in advance the manner in which an ethical precept will apply in given circumstances. To suggest that such prescription is a requirement for an ethical code is to confuse ethics with law once again. Ethics requires *judgments* about what and how obligations will apply in given circumstances. To remove the responsibility for making ethical judgments from the soldier on the grounds that we cannot realistically tell him or her what to do in advance is to remove the central responsibility for making ethical choices that is necessary to all ethics.

A second argument implied by the Superintendent's statement is that because one cannot specify in detail how ethical obligations will apply, one ought not to formally require and state the obligations in the first place. But if the obligations are not delineated somewhere in some fashion, how are they to be taught to the soldier in the first place? One is left only with the hope that somehow and in some fashion the soldier will acquire the proper ethical obligations from his or her experience. The argument implies that good ethical standards are not taught so much as they are "caught" by being a member of the military community and osmotically absorbing the ethical lessons and precepts that emerge from the ambience of the profession itself. This is an act of faith for which there seems to be little support.

In place of a formal code of professional ethics, the soldier is forced to rely upon what he or she can infer informally through their experience. The difficulty is that in an entrepreneurial democratic society it is the ethics of the marketplace that inevitably become the basis for these informal norms. In the absence of a formal code of competing values, the soldier is likely to be unable to distinguish personal ethics from professional ethics and self-interest will likely become the most important element in the soldier's personal ethics as it is in the society at large. Under these conditions, the values attendant to a corporate ethical system are made moribund. Self-interest is of necessity an *individual* concern when the true measure of a professionally oriented soldiery is the extent to which individual actions serve *communal* concerns. While informal norms are important insofar as they reinforce communal values and precepts, they are unlikely to do so in the absence of a professional code because they are derived from an environment characterized by entrepreneurial self-interest. Precisely because they are informal, one suspects that such norms are not likely to be derived from any higher ethical notion of the good soldier, namely, the soldier's ability and willingness to live by a code of ethics congruent with his or her own sense of ethical integrity and that of the profession.

The fact of the matter is that the profession abandons its ethical responsibility toward its members if it simply assumes that sound ethical sense will be absorbed through a kind of social osmotic process. *If the soldier is to be aware of his or her ethical obligations, then the profession must teach them to the soldier, and one way to do this is for the profession to state them formally in a code.* To assume otherwise is too great a leap of faith for a profession whose stock in trade is death and destruction.

The third objection contained in the Superintendent's argument is that "a set of ethics prefabricated by others seems to have little promise for military officers." But who is more qualified than the keepers of the profession's ethical flame, its most senior officers, to establish a code of professional ethics for the military? If not they, who else has the knowledge, experience, and standing to "prefabricate" a code for soldiers? All professions have codes of professional ethics that have been created by the profession long before the present membership was permitted entry. All professional codes are "prefabricated" in the sense that they exist before an individual qualifies to gain entry into the profession. It is only then that the individual is made aware of and becomes responsible for observing the obligations of the profession. Why these circumstances do not apply to soldiers as well is not clear from the Superintendent's argument. The Superintendent is wrong when he asserts that ethics cannot be formulated in a useful way and that ethical obligations cannot be taught to soldiers. To do exactly this is a primary ethical responsibility of the profession and to deny that it is to deny that the military is a profession, for it will have no statement of values and obligations that its members profess which distinguishes it from other professions or mere occupations and business enterprises.

A Code of Military Ethics

What follows is an attempt to show what a code of professional military ethics might look like when made consistent with the arguments and propositions put forth so far in this treatise. No claim is offered that the code is definitive, and it is to be expected that any effort by national military establishments to create their own professional codes will likely differ in some details. On balance, however, the core values represented in this example seem to me to strike the main value themes that almost any code of military ethics should consider including. The example offered here does not attempt to state the sum of the soldier's ethical obligations, but only those that are most directly relevant to the soldier's role as a military professional. It assumes the task of delineating the soldier's ethical obligations against the general background of a profession dedicated to the ethics and values attendant to *command* and *combat* and the *responsibilities* and *obligations* derived reasonably from them by a profession whose primary task involves the risk to and the taking of human lives. The code seeks to govern the ethical actions of a profession that is unlike any other profession or occupation in that the centre of its responsibilities involves the unlimited liability of its members and the responsibility for sending other members of the profession to their deaths in carrying out its responsibilities. We take as our ethical ideal the leader, commissioned and enlisted, performing his or her duties in the highest test of the profession, leadership of soldiers in combat.

The code presented here seeks to develop and sustain the values, habits, and practices traditionally associated with the profession of arms as a special community of brethren bound together by special virtues, ethics, and responsibilities. As such, the code itself is able to contribute to establishing and reinforcing a community by engendering a sense of belonging to a special group of human beings committed to certain virtues and ethics which, in themselves, come to define membership in the professional community. In this sense, a code of professional ethics for the military is not unlike the ethical code of a monastic community. Let us now examine the precepts of the code.

> *"The nature of command and military service is an ethical charge that places each soldier at the centre of unavoidable ethical responsibility."*

The code affirms that command is an "ethical charge" that places the soldier at the centre of ethical responsibility and a matrix of professional obligations. The responsibilities of command apply at all levels of leadership, from squad leader to general officer, where soldiers have direct responsibility over others and where, as in combat, this may involve sending fellow soldiers into harm's way and even to their deaths. Command, therefore, is the central responsibility of military life. Whatever prerogatives it conveys are greatly outweighed by the responsibilities for the fate of others that it levies, so that bearing these responsibilities in a correct manner comes to define the ethical soldier. It will avail a military establishment little if its staff and support elements are in order but it finds itself incapable of producing competent combat field commanders and high level leaders. War is the art of conflict and command is the expression of that art in human terms. Command *responsibilities* assume an almost mystical place in the litany of military values and occupy a central place on the altar of military ethics. The failure to emphasize command as the centre of the profession's ethical responsibilities and to require that the soldier bear this responsibility in an ethical manner is to deny that there is any difference between the profession of arms and other professions and occupations.

> *"A soldier's ethical integrity is at the centre of his or her effectiveness as a soldier and leader. To violate one's sense of honour and integrity is never justified. The soldier must always be true to his or her own ethical self."*

The claim that ethical integrity is at the centre of a leader's effectiveness is premised on the pragmatic truth that a leader's compromise of ethical standards cannot usually be hidden from his or her fellow leaders or, indeed, in most instances from the soldiers under one's command. Under these circumstances, the trust between leader and led and leader and peers is eroded, often beyond repair, and effective leadership becomes impossible. The concept is simple: some things are not done. There is a line beyond which a truly ethical soldier will not go, and in the profession of arms that line is often drawn very clearly for all to see. The notion that one "has to go along to get along" is rejected as the first step down a path leading to ever-greater compromises of ethical standards. Effective leaders cannot compromise their ethics and remain either good soldiers or good leaders.

> *"Every soldier holds a special position of trust and responsibility. The soldier will not violate that trust or avoid his or her responsibility, no matter the personal cost."*

The precept affirms that to be a soldier is to occupy a special position of trust and confidence and that this trust, which goes hand-in-glove with the virtue of integrity, must never be violated or relinquished because of the press of events or expectations of career advancement. There will almost certainly come a time in the life of every soldier when he or she will be forced to choose between going along with something the soldier regards as wrong or being true to him or herself and the values of the profession. At times, the rewards for betraying one's personal values can be significant. The code establishes the simple standard that the soldier's personal integrity and position within the profession are inseparable; to violate one is to violate the other. The soldier must never betray his position of trust for to do so is to betray his fellow soldiers, his profession and him or herself.

It might be objected that this precept of the code is too individualistic, that it emphasizes too strongly the role of individual conscience and that could lead to disobedience. In response, it should be understood that only individuals are truly capable of ethical actions. To say that the "profession" did this or the "organization" did that is, in a strict sense, to speak in linguistic fictions. Ultimately, only individuals are capable of ethical actions and only individuals can be held responsible for the consequences of their acts. The focus of ethical decision-making remains squarely upon the individual soldier. The code is not too individualistic and does not stress individual conscience at the expense of authority. It merely recognizes that a soldier acting within an organizational setting may be subject to severe ethical cross pressures. Even so, the soldier cannot abandon his or her conscience or their ethical responsibilities. All ethical acts remain the acts of individuals, and no less so because these acts occur within the context of the profession.

> *"In faithfully executing lawful orders of his or her superiors, a soldier's loyalty is to the welfare of the nation, soldiers, and mission. While striving to follow orders, the soldier will never permit his/her command or fellow soldiers to be misused in any manner."*

The precept that a soldier's obligation is to the men and women he or she leads ought not be interpreted to imply that a commander should be fearful of putting them in harm's way. Indeed not, for it is the very essence of the military profession that it engage in combat when ordered to do so. It may also appear that there is a tension within this precept in that it states a soldier's loyalty is to his or her troops whereas the emphasis should really be placed upon the loyalty to his superiors and mission. Loyalty to one's command has relevance in the context of loyalty to the mission which must be accomplished. In the event of a conflict between looking after the welfare of one's troops and following the orders of an incompetent superior, the soldier must have another ethical anchor to guide his or her actions besides the dictum to follow orders. The tension is, therefore, deliberately expressed in the code in order to demonstrate the requirement for making ethical choices. A commander's concern and loyalty for his or her troops in no way implies that he or she should not be prepared to execute the mission assigned. It only implies that in carrying out the mission the commander is responsible for the consequences that result and remains the focus of ethical responsibility. As General Matthew Ridgeway noted, "a commander has a deep duty to the men whose lives he is temporarily entrusted with as they have to him—and part of that duty is to see that those lives are not needlessly squandered."

A soldier in a position of leadership at all levels of command must never permit his or her troops to be used in a manner that is not directly related to the true ethical purposes of command. Danger is central to battle; the object is to expose one's soldiers to that danger only in pursuit of legitimate military objectives and goals. What constitutes a legitimate objective or order is a determination that commanders may have to make when they find themselves in a situation that makes them doubt the wisdom or competence of a superior in ordering certain actions. There is no doubt, of course, that part of that determination will involve ethical considerations as well as practical ones. Commanders must be prepared in defence of their oath and ethics to question superiors and, if they deem it necessary in defence of the ethical precepts of the profession, to refuse to expose soldiers to great risks to achieve doubtful or unethical objectives. No soldier may permit him or herself, nor the troops entrusted to his or her care, to become mere tools in the service of unethical ends by superiors of doubtful competence.

> "Soldiers will never permit their subordinates to endure hardships or suffer dangers to which they are unwilling to expose themselves. Every soldier who leads others must share the burden of risk and sacrifice to which comrades are exposed. In this, a soldier is first and foremost a leader and must lead by personal example. Leaders must always set the standard for personal bravery, courage, and ethical actions."

When in a position of leadership, a soldier must be willing to share the risks and dangers of combat to which his or her subordinates are exposed and to be willing to suffer the ultimate sacrifice if conditions warrant. It is this physical and ethical burden that differentiates the military profession from all other professions and occupations. To be an effective commander, the soldier must be seen on the field of battle. A good soldier understands that subordinates will follow his or her judgment if they are convinced by example that their commander has as much to lose as they have and that he or she is willing to share the risks of death and injury with them. It is impossible to manage troops to their deaths; they must be led. If the soldier is to be an effective leader he or she must accept the risk of exposing themselves to the dangers to which their followers are exposed and, if necessary, to fulfill the obligation of unlimited liability with them.

> *"A soldier will never carry out an order he or she regards as unethical, and will report all such orders, policies, and actions of which he or she is aware to appropriate authority."*

One of the most important and controversial precepts of the code affirms that a soldier cannot escape responsibility for his or her actions before the law, peers, ethical precepts of the profession itself, and his or her conscience. The problem of following orders with which they disagree is faced somewhat regularly by soldiers outside of any zone of combat. The injunction that a soldier will never execute any order regarded as ethically wrong goes far beyond the bounds of action that the soldier is likely to encounter in combat. It addresses as well the activities that often permeate a highly bureaucratized military establishment. The directed ethical responsibility is that a soldier is in violation of his or her professional responsibilities—in betrayal of his or her special trust and obligations—if they have knowledge of unethical occurrences and acquiesce in or fail to report them.

It could be argued that an ethical code that requires a soldier never to execute an order he or she regards as unethical wrongly invites disobedience. This is not the case. The precept merely restates the commonly agreed upon ethical principle that no soldier can escape responsibility for his or her actions, and that following unethical orders is never an excuse for doing so. The object of ethical training is to give soldiers the ability to recognize ethical dilemmas and to work their way through them by making sound ethical choices. The responsibility remains with the soldier, and it is not the intention of the code to invite disobedience by suggesting that lawful orders ought not to be carried out. The code's precept only points out that instances are likely to arise where a soldier perceives serious difficulties between what he or she is ordered to do and what he or she thinks is ethically permissible. In these instances it is no ethical or legal defence or excuse to abandon one's primary ethical responsibility to follow the ethics of the profession and one's conscience in order to obey the order. We return to a fundamental ethical principle: only human beings are capable of ethical acts. As such, it is the human being, in this case the soldier, who must remain the focus of ethical responsibility.

> *"A soldier will not willfully conceal an act of his superiors, subordinates, or peers that violates his or her sense of ethics. A soldier cannot avoid making ethical judgments and must assume responsibility for those judgments."*

Among the most corrosive norms which some military establishments have borrowed from the business world are those that reward the soldier for "getting on board" and being "a team player." These norms require of the soldier, as they do of the business executive, that as subordinates soldiers ought to be "loyal" to their superiors, following their policies unquestionably because to challenge them places the individual in the position of "fighting the problem" and not "trusting in his betters." In this view, subordinates are expected to be "part of the team" and always to be loyal to superiors.

But what does it mean for a subordinate to be loyal to his or her superior? Surely whatever loyalty is legitimately owed to superiors cannot ethically be construed to include a requirement to conceal the superior's ethical failings and operational shortcomings, especially when they may have a bearing on the ability of a unit to function or when soldiers may be put unnecessarily in grave physical and legal danger. There must, therefore, be a higher loyalty and that is to the soldiers, the profession and its code of ethics, and the nation. Loyalty can never be correctly taken to mean that policies or orders that are unethical or detrimental to the profession, mission, or nation ought to be tolerated by subordinates without due protest. *Loyalty to one's superiors is never anything but a conditional relationship predicated upon the soldier's continued conviction that one's superiors are acting ethically in the conduct of their professional responsibilities.* If superiors act otherwise, that relationship is dissolved and the obligation to make appropriate higher authorities aware of existing circumstances or to refuse to obey takes ethical precedence.

> *"A soldier will not punish, nor permit the punishment of, or in any way discriminate against a peer or subordinate for telling the truth."*

No profession can adequately respond to the problems that may develop within it, including problems of unethical behaviour, unless it has adequate information upon which to take corrective action. There is, then, an organizational as well as an ethical imperative for soldiers to be truthful with their superiors, leaders, and others who occupy positions of authority within the profession. Members of the profession will only feel at liberty to be honest with peers and superiors if they can be reasonably certain that telling the truth will not be regarded as punishable disloyalty or trouble-making. The profession ought never to strike at a soldier for exposing even the most embarrassing shortcomings of the profession, and certainly not for revealing unethical or criminal actions. The greater harm would be to hide the truth, not only because to do so would be unethical, but because concealment could have devastating practical consequences on military capabilities and operations. It may well be an open question whether the truth will make one free in any given instance, but clearly falsehoods never do. If the soldier is made to be responsible for observing the higher code of the profession in a way similar to the way members of a monastic community or church are responsible for doing so, then there can be no justifiable punishment for revealing the truth.

> *"Soldiers are responsible for the actions of their comrades. The unethical and dishonourable acts of one diminish us all. The honour of the military profession and military service is maintained by the actions of its members, and these actions must always be ethical."*

Soldiers ought never to lose sight of the fact that the profession of arms is in many respects not unlike a church or religious brotherhood or any other corporative community that shares and upholds, that is, professes, unique values and ethics. Soldiers of the profession are brethren, brothers and sisters, in the same sense that monastics or members of a church community of believers are brethren. This means that the dishonourable acts of one soldier besmirch and diminish all members of the community. *Responsibility becomes collective in that the community is unwilling to tolerate or permit in their midst any soldier who fails to observe the community's common ethical standards and code.* It is in this sense that every soldier becomes responsible for his or her comrades, and in this way all soldiers share the responsibility for ensuring that other soldiers remain true to the profession's ethical standards.

The profession must be prepared to enforce its own ethical standards upon the membership and to dismiss or seek the correction of those whose actions are unbecoming to their station within the profession or who testify by their actions to their inability or unwillingness to pay the price of remaining within the ethical community of military peers. *The responsibility for this enforcement falls most heavily upon the senior ranks, the guardians of the profession, who have the power and authority to enforce the ethical code.* Unwillingness to remove those who fail to profess proper actions, or any hint of the existence of a "protective association" operating within the profession, or any evidence of hypocrisy on the part of the profession's senior guardians will diminish the compelling power of the ethical code. With rank goes power, and with that power goes the responsibility of insuring that the ethical code of the military profession is enforced at all levels of command.

Even the most trusting observers of military organizations know that the promulgation of an ethical code by itself will not ensure its effectiveness. Yet one cannot resist pointing out that it is difficult to expect the soldier to learn and practice professional ethics unless the profession itself teaches him or her what that code entails. The code offered here is but one example of what a code of professional ethics for the military might entail. Such codes might differ in detail among the military establishments of different countries and cultures as each reacts to its own history and development by emphasizing those ethical precepts which each considers to be most important for its soldiers. Still, one might reasonably expect that the core beliefs of all these codes—a belief in conscience and the personal ethical responsibility of the soldier to the nation or people—is likely to be found in some form or another. In modern democracies of some long standing, the time is past when the profession of arms can rely upon the ethics of the civilian marketplace to proffer proper ethical standards for its soldiers. The values and ethos of the entrepreneur work against the establishment of a sense of social community by offering no basis beyond material self-interest upon which to develop personal ties among soldiers. But without these strong interpersonal bonds, combat effectiveness as a function of unit cohesion erodes. For this very practical reason, if for no other, the profession ought to establish a code of military ethics.

In a broadly human sense, military ethics is the only thing that can make the horrors of war bearable for those who experience them. Without the psychological fortification that results from the soldier being part of a larger community in a profession and unit upon which he or she can rely for succour and support, the soldier might fall into the trap of becoming a value-free technician plying his or her trade in unethical ways because they were just following orders. Without communal ethics to govern the soldier's actions in war, there is the attendant danger that he or she will become like the entrepreneur and "destroy the village in order to save it," that is consider only the goals of one's action with little or no consideration of ethically proportional means. Without the ethical community to surround the soldier and to guide his or her actions, the soldier confronted with an ethical crisis will find him or herself very much alone.

War is a *human* activity. If it will not go away of its own accord, then the ethical task is to limit its individual and collective horrors. It is the ethical precepts of the professional military code that create and sustain a sense of ethical community and offer the soldier the possibility of bringing a human and humane dimension to the terrible task of war with its awesome responsibilities. We dare not fight without it, for in doing so we might yet win the battle, but the fruits of victory will be ashes in our mouth. The cost of victory will be the loss of our humanity.

Endnotes

1.   Maxwell Taylor, "A Professional Ethic," *Army* (May, 1978), 18.

2.   Ibid.

3.   Lewis Sorley, "Duty, Honor, Country: Practice and Precept," *American Behavioral Scientist* 19, no. 5 (May-June, 1976), 638.

4.   I am deeply indebted to my old friend Major Steve Brodsky of the Canadian Forces for his help in sharpening my understanding of the arguments against a formal code of ethics for the military.

5.   Steven Brenner and Earl Molander, "Is the Ethics of Business Changing?," *Harvard Business Review* (January-February, 1977), 66.

6.   Malham M. Wakin, "The Ethics of Leadership," *American Behavioral Scientist* 19, no. 5 (May-June, 1976), 573.

7.   From a speech by General Andrew J. Goodpaster before the Association of American Colleges entitled, "Moral Choices: Ethics and Values in the 80's," in Washington, DC (February 4, 1979).

Establishing Professional Ethics

T he problem of establishing a code of professional ethics within the life and rubric of the military profession resolves itself into the question of how the code can be instilled in its membership. To make an ethical code effective in governing the actions of the soldier, the profession must make a serious effort to inculcate its core ethical precepts. If the profession does not, it risks ceasing to be a profession, for there will be no formal statement of the norms, values, and obligations that the soldier is required to profess. The profession risks becoming a caricature of itself where its members lack a sense of special obligation and purpose, pursuing whatever values serve their interests. The responsibility for establishing an ethical code and inculcating its values within the profession's membership rests with the profession itself and not with the civilian society or political establishment.

The task of establishing military ethics can be approached from three perspectives: (1) the difficulties involved in teaching military ethics as a proper subject of military education; (2) the institutional forces that would have to be put in place to support the ethical code and its application on a day-to-day basis; and (3) the enforcement mechanisms required to ensure that those who do not live up to the code are not permitted to remain within the profession. Employing these three perspectives as an organizational schema, the means for establishing a code of professional ethics within the military can be examined.

Teaching Ethics

To teach ethics successfully requires that basic assumptions about the nature of professional ethics be understood. The military is a profession and not another occupation like those found in the civilian society. The values it maintains are separate and different from those of the civilian sector. As a profession, the military has at its professional core a sense of vocational calling that demands special obligations and sacrifices from its members. Membership in the profession, therefore, is defined precisely in terms of the members' willingness to observe these obligations and bear these sacrifices. Those unwilling to do so must leave or not be permitted to enter in the first place. The first task in teaching military ethics is for the profession to clearly delineate the ethical obligations of membership. Thus, there is a requirement that a formal code of professional ethics be created.

The first step in creating an ethical code for a profession is to clarify its principles and commit them to writing. From the times of the ancient Egyptians when the command of the Pharaoh was "so let it be done, so let it be written," until the present, those who would establish ethical codes have always found it necessary to formalize them. To instill ethical principles into the military profession requires that they be clearly espoused in a written code. Without a written code for all to see, it will be very difficult to teach military ethics effectively.

Once a formal code has been established, the next task is to create courses of instruction that are appropriate to teaching the code to members of the profession. Perhaps the first place to begin is at the military academies and colleges that are the primary schools for creating military professionals. Institutions such as West Point, RMC, Sandhurst, and Saint Cyr have adequate time in the academic year to design and test courses in military ethics. These courses could then serve as models for wider use throughout the profession. Shorter versions could also be used in basic training and officer candidate schools.

The service academies should institute four new courses specifically designed to teach the profession's ethical code and train the soldier in ethical reasoning. While other parts of the curriculum might support the courses in ethics, the courses proposed here would be specifically designed *to create within the professional curriculum an independent field of study dealing with military ethics. Ethics has too long been regarded as an appendage to other areas of military education, and it is time for it to have its own place in the education of soldiers in light of its importance to the profession.*

The first of these new courses should focus on the *History of Ethical Thought* and present the full range of developed ethical theories drawn from a history of philosophy. The course would not be much different from existing introductory survey courses in philosophy, but would emphasize the ethical perspectives of the different ethical theories. The goal is to provide the members of the profession with a common philosophical background, informational base, terminology, and conceptual schematic relative to the kinds of questions and difficulties that have concerned ethicists through the ages. The course would focus on *descriptive ethics,* that is, presenting a range of ethical theories while making no attempt to suggest that any one is preferable to another. This course might closely parallel courses already found in some military academies and require only a change in emphasis.

A second course should provide instruction in *Ethical Reasoning*. Training in the processes of argument and ethical reasoning equips the soldier with the intellectual skills to think through ethical issues in light of the various ethical theories taught in the previous course. The soldier must not only be aware of the precepts of an ethical code, but also know *why* these precepts ought to govern his or her actions. Instruction in ethical reasoning ultimately equips the soldier to explore the reasons underlying the code's precepts. Since a soldier cannot avoid ethical judgments, understanding the ethical arguments behind the code's precepts is vital to the soldier's ability to reason his or her way through ethical problems. *It is impossible to successfully inculcate military ethics in the soldier without training in ethical reasoning.* Ethical reasoning, by itself, does not ensure that the soldier will *act* ethically. But has Derek Bok as noted, "formal education will rarely improve the character of a scoundrel. But many individuals who are disposed to act morally will often fail to do so because they are simply unaware of the ethical problems that lie hidden in the situations they confront."[1] At the very least, then, we might expect that a soldier with some training in ethical thinking will be more likely to recognize and sort through ethical dilemmas in the first place than one who has not been educated to think in ethical terms.

The third course in a military ethical curriculum should be a course in *Professional Ethics* in which the precepts of the profession's ethical code are taught as constituting its ethical centre that all soldiers are required to understand and observe. The course would examine the code in detail, explain its value to the profession and to the soldier, and explore the reasons why its precepts ought to be obeyed. The course in professional ethics would constitute the centrepiece of the curriculum of ethical instruction. Soldiers would take the course only after they had already been exposed to the previous courses. This would prevent the ethics course from degenerating into a discussion of case studies and "war stories." The course in Professional Ethics provides the profession with an opportunity to state and examine the ethical obligations it expects its members to observe.

The profession's ethical code is not to be offered as just one more ethical theory that the soldier may accept or reject. Rather, it ought to be presented as constituting the ethical core of the military profession. The examination and presentation of the code would take on a quality of *normative indoctrination*, especially when taught at the staff schools and in basic training in shorter versions. Soldiers must be made to see that the ethics of the profession are necessary to its proper functioning and the ethical behaviour of the soldier. No soldier should be permitted to remain in the profession who cannot agree with the precepts of the code or who is unable to comprehend the reasons for it. *As the ethical centre of the profession, acceptance of the code and willingness to abide by it define the conditions of membership in the profession of arms.* Any soldier who seriously disagrees with the profession's ethical precepts cannot remain a soldier any more than one would tolerate within a monastery a monk who kept a harem. One simply cannot at one and the same time be a legitimate member of the profession and reject or be uncertain about its core ethical precepts.

The Professional Ethics course would provide intellectual education, a demonstration of the ethical and practical value of the code, normative reinforcement, and would aim at convincing the soldier that the specific ethical precepts that constitute the centre of the profession do so for very good reasons. *A code that fails to affirm that it is preferable to other codes and has special applicability to the professional tasks the soldier will encounter will convince no one of its worth.* If the profession is not prepared to affirm to its members that those who do not believe and observe the code must leave, that its code is better than others, and that freedom of ethical choice does not extend to the ability to select and observe values contrary to those expressed in the profession, and if it is not prepared to enforce its precepts, it will have no success in teaching ethics.

The final element in the curriculum of professional ethical instruction ought to be a course in *Ethical Dialectics* in which members of the profession employ the seminar and Socratic approach to solve ethical dilemmas presented in case studies. The emphasis is placed upon the intellectual process of devising solutions and determining the reasons for accepting certain solutions over others. The goal of instruction in ethical dialectics is to sharpen the soldier's ethical reasoning skills in a context where the cases used are drawn expressly as applications of the code under various circumstances. The problems, examples, and solutions should be related as much as possible to the kinds of ethical dilemmas, combat and non-combat associated, the soldier is most likely to encounter. A heavy dose of realism and honesty is required. *It ought not to be forgotten that the education of the soldier in military ethics should as much as possible be specifically appropriate to the ethical problems the soldier is likely to confront.*

Besides the service academies and colleges, courses in ethics, perhaps in shortened versions to accommodate academic schedules, should be included in the curricula of the various staff schools and war colleges. Clement and Ayers study of the ethics curricula in military staff schools found that "students lack conceptual understanding of professional ethics to address issues substantively, and they also lack a common vernacular to communicate on the substantive issues." They also observed that even when ethics courses are offered, they are offered as electives instead of requirements. Discussions of ethical issues often degenerate into telling "war stories" in which superiors are often blamed for ethical lapses while "the underlying ethical issues are left unaddressed."[2] While Clement and Ayers studied these conditions only in the United States, it is likely that the circumstances they describe can be found elsewhere.

Exposing young soldiers and officer cadets to courses in military ethics at the beginning of their careers and letting it go at that will not be sufficient for the profession and its soldiers to sustain their ethical skills over time. All of the service staff schools as well as the higher-level war colleges should require *mandatory refresher courses* designed to keep a soldier's ethical awareness and thinking sharp and functioning. The higher one ascends in rank and responsibility, the more likely the soldier can expect to face new ethical challenges. It is a good idea to ensure that the examples used in these refresher courses address the kinds of dilemmas that soldiers at these higher rank levels can expect to confront. These higher-level refresher courses should stress ethical dialectics with a review section at the beginning on the subject of the profession's ethical code. *Requiring courses in ethics at virtually all levels of military instruction would signal to those within and outside the profession that professional ethics is to be taken very seriously.*

To make ethics effective on a day-to-day basis, one might also consider an additional instructional program. It is important to create and enforce conditions that support the observance of what has been taught in the classroom. The American Army has some practical experience with the institutionalization of ethical codes that might offer a valuable example to other military establishments. In 1953, largely in reaction to the poor performance of American POWs held during the Korean War, President Eisenhower ordered the creation of the Code of Conduct of the American

Soldier. The Code stated in ten short sentences the military profession's expectations of how POWs ought to conduct themselves while in enemy custody. The military itself was tasked with the formulation of the code. This done, they set out to teach it to every soldier in military service.

The military devised pocket-sized cards on which the precepts of the code were printed and distributed them to every soldier. Soldiers were required to carry a copy of the code with them at all times. The military devised larger posters of the code that were prominently displayed in every office, barracks, and other prominent places throughout every military installation of every service. Appropriate plaques and other documents, some printed on formal parchment, enshrining the code were produced. The military then provided all soldiers with several hours of ethical instruction in the meaning and intention of the code's precepts. Interestingly, the stress was placed upon the soldier understanding why the precepts were useful in captivity along with their ethical value. Soldiers in basic training were required to memorize the code, and the ability of the soldier to recite the code when ordered to do so by a superior became a fixture of military inspections, bringing into being a new American military ritual, this one centred around ethics.

Judging from the behaviour of American prisoners of war held during the Vietnam War, the Code of Conduct seems to have worked well. Except for a very small number, the behaviour of American prisoners was exemplary bordering upon valour. Unlike the Korean War experience, large numbers of prisoners did not become informers, sign statements, or make propaganda broadcasts as they had done during the Korean captivity despite the fact that most prisoners in Vietnam were held far longer than in Korea. It is likely that this improvement in ethical behaviour can be attributed to some degree to the education and belief in the proper ethical courses of action encouraged by the Code of Conduct.

There is no good reason why a code of professional ethics cannot be similarly promulgated and printed in the form of cards, posters, and plaques to be displayed throughout the military establishment. It is, after all, not unusual to see codes of professional ethics prominently displayed in the offices of physicians, lawyers, and other professionals. Why should the military's code not be similarly displayed? There is also no good reason why several hours of instruction regarding the code, its meaning, and its obligations cannot be easily accomplished for new recruits in basic training. Nor is there any good reason why soldiers should not be required to carry the code with them, to memorize it, and be held responsible for carrying it out. There is at least some evidence from the American example that the establishment and promulgation of a code of ethical conduct can produce beneficial results.

If one is going to articulate a professional military ethic and invest it with unique value in the eyes of the soldier so that he or she can internalize its values, then there is no other way to do it effectively, if at all, except to teach the ethic to the soldier. Accordingly, a code must be formulated, mechanisms of teaching instruction created, and an emphasis placed upon teaching the soldier to think in ethical terms by educating him or her as to why the precepts of the code ought to be observed. The level of sophistication and length of this instruction will vary as one moves from the basic enlisted level, through the NCO corps, to the officer corps. It ought not be difficult for the military to set such a program of instruction in place. But it must first be willing to do so. That raises the question of the kinds of institutional forces that must be overcome within the military bureaucracy before the code can be successfully established.

Institutional Forces

How are new ethical values to be established within the military and how are they to be enforced? In addressing this question, it must be remembered that the military establishment is more of a *corporative* than an entrepreneurial entity, although strains of the latter are clearly evident within it. It is a profession with all that implies in terms of the characteristics and limits upon individual behaviour that have already been discussed. Military bureaucracies are, strictly speaking, *institutions* that are "value-infused" and are not mere instrumentalities for the marshalling of human energies to the accomplishment of tasks. *The institution has meaning in itself as well as a utilitarian instrumental mechanism for accomplishing objectives.* As an institution, the bureaucracy has a "history" defined in terms of its investment in existing practices and values. Any proposed change in these values and practices, such as a new code of ethics that runs contrary to the history of the institution, will not easily garner support, especially from those senior leaders whose positions derive from the support of the old values.

In this regard, it is important to understand the distinction between latent and cognate values. Latent values are those that already enjoy the *public* support of the bureaucracy, even though they may not be very effective in compelling individual or organizational behaviour. Cognate values are those that can be directly deduced or implied from existing values. There is likely to be greater institutional resistance to completely new values than to either latent or cognate values. In the case of cognate values, it may only be a mater of making already acceptable values operative to stimulate the required organizational changes.

Most of the values offered in the code as ethical precepts throughout this treatise are not new to the military, and generally fall into the category of latent or cognate values. They already enjoy widespread *public* support within the profession, but mostly in terms of the formal lip-service paid to them. The problem is that these values are not very effective in compelling the behaviour of the membership. They have no *community* impetus to compel, which is why a formal code is needed. Nonetheless, *the task is made somewhat easier if the values one seeks to implement are essentially the ones the profession publicly claims it already espouses. It will be easier to convince the military bureaucracy to reassert its latent values than to get it to adopt and assimilate entirely new ones.* Given these few preliminary distinctions, we may now ask, what institutional forces play a role in convincing the military bureaucracy to adopt a code of professional ethics?

One of the most important factors in the change process is the degree to which the profession can marshal the open, formal, and forceful support for these values from the elites positioned at the highest level of the profession, that is, the senior commandatura who are expected to be the guardians of the profession itself. These guardians must lend the new values the force of their authority and prestige. The Ayers and Clements study of leadership models of organizational ethics demonstrated that *subordinates look crucially to their superiors as role models, especially with regard to ethical thinking and example.*[3] A number of studies of civilian and military bureaucracies have found that *the conduct of one's superiors is among the most important variables in convincing the membership of any group to adopt and assimilate new ethical values.* A study of civilian managers found that the conduct of superiors ranked second only to formal ethical codes as the most influential factor in engendering ethical actions among subordinate executives. *The study also revealed that poor ethical example ranked first as a factor in promoting unethical conduct among subordinates.*[4]

If the profession's guardians fail to support the establishment of an ethical code, the membership will remain unclear as to what their superiors require of them. There must be no gap between what the code requires and what the leadership of the profession actually supports by their public statements and personal actions. The leaders' support helps clarify changes in policy and values, removing much of the ambiguity as to what actions are expected of subordinates and what values the profession is expected to uphold. *Those who occupy the highest levels of command and staff are charged with initiating and overseeing the establishment of the new code's values and precepts, and must share and live them themselves.* The senior officers of the profession must support the new code by their actions, and they can be certain that their actions will be closely observed by their subordinates, who are searching for clues as to how to behave themselves.

But how is the elite of the profession to be converted to a new code of professional ethics when by their positions within the professions they have demonstrated an ability to succeed without such a code? *Without elite support, the effort to establish the code and new values will likely fail.* Two solutions are possible, neither of which are ideal. First, pressures from outside the military establishment can be brought to bear by the chief political executive or the national legislature to convince the profession's guardians that a formal ethical code is required. One characteristic of a military bureaucracy is that it can respond rapidly to clear political directives. This was exactly the case when President Eisenhower ordered the military to create and teach a code of conduct for American soldiers. It was also the manner in which President Clinton ordered a new policy regarding gays to be taught and implemented.

A second solution is to remove those senior officers who resist the new code and to replace them with officers who support it. This practice of "circulation of elites" is not new. Often, promotion to general officer or to preferred assignments is done on the basis that the candidate is a supporter of the "right" policy. Permitting officers to retire who are not in accord with political directives occurs regularly in military establishments, as the resignation of General Abizaid and the replacement of General Casey in Iraq shows. Both were opponents of a "surge" of combat troops in Iraq. General Casey's replacement, General Petraeus, was a strong public supporter of a surge. The "accelerated circulation of elites" is more common in country's with parliamentary political systems, and has its counterpart in the American military's practice of "deep selecting" officers for promotion ahead of their more senior contemporaries precisely on the grounds that these officers are advocates of a favoured policy. With regard to professional ethics, this practice is likely to have the effect of reinforcing the belief that the profession is sincere about enforcing the new code. There is, of course, no clearer indication of the profession's sincerity than the removal of those at the top who refuse to cooperate in the code's establishment and implementation.

Another factor in the process of establishing a code of professional ethics in a military bureaucracy is the employment of value indoctrination programs at all levels that teach, explain, and reinforce the new values and delineate the proper ethical actions that are expected. This is precisely how the American military informed its ranks and enforced President Clinton's policy concerning gays in the armed forces. These programs must be particularly strong at the entrance level, for it is the young officers and soldiers who will be expected to carry the profession's new ethics throughout their careers as part of their personal and professional system of values. This approach is not different from that used by other professions in conducting ethics programs. The idea is to create a sort of "missionary corps" of young officers and NCOs imbued with a code of ethics to "leaven" the profession over time. The future of the profession, after all, belongs to the young.

Middle and upper rank officers and NCOs could be required to participate in a series of seminars focused on the new ethical code taught at the various schools and colleges. Exposure of junior officers and new soldiers at the entrance level places functional limits on the actions of higher ranks who do not observe the new ethical precepts. Faced with a junior officer and NCO corps indoctrinated in the new code, higher-ranking opponents will not be able to violate the new code without risk of protest or exposure. In short, failure to adapt to the new precepts would be a "career killer."

No policy of value change is likely to succeed without the support of *informal groups* within the profession. Peer support is needed at all rank levels for the new values and actions to take institutional root. This support will take time to develop, but should be based upon the common experience of the membership and its exposure to the code, courses of instruction in professional ethics, and the realization that observing the new ethics is the best way to succeed in one's career. The profession must demonstrate in practical terms that soldiers acting in a manner consistent with the code will be rewarded for their honour and integrity. The soldier must believe that his or her own interests in career advancement are tied to observance of the new ethics. Here, however, the career interests of the soldier cannot be permitted to be defined exclusively in terms of careerism, entrepreneurialism, and managerial self-advancement. The assumption is that a range of rewards and goals relevant to and supported by the profession work to satisfy the soldier. It is a mistake to reduce the soldier's interests only to "hard" benefits like pay, leave, and promotion. While such things are not unimportant, they are hardly sufficient to motivate the soldier over the long run. *What is required is a larger sense of psychological meaning, of belonging to something larger than oneself, of doing something not everyone can do, to motivate the soldier for career service.* Thus, a large part of the soldier's career interests must be redefined and expressed in terms of communal obligations and values. Observance of the ethical code is an important element in establishing the soldier's feeling of uniqueness by belonging to a unique community. The soldier must come to perceive that in observing the new ethical precepts he or she will be recognized as a good soldier in a special profession entitled to all the rights, privileges, and honours due loyal members.

It ought to be evident, then, that the enforcement of new value codes must consistently demonstrate to the members of the profession that the values and their expected actions strengthen communal and integrative links among peers, subordinates, and superiors. It is by rewarding and honouring those who honour and live by its ethical precepts that the profession can signal to its members that it is sincere and honest about selecting for advancement not only the most technically competent of its members, but also those who are most heavily imbued with its values, actions, and spirit. *If official support for the new ethical values is not forthcoming, the code will become a latent or cognate value and will have only a minimal influence upon the soldier's behaviour.* The initial formulation of a new code of professional ethics ought properly to come from the profession itself as an overt indication of its serious commitment. Once drafted, the military may request that the code be publicly recognized by an act of the national legislature or as a directive from the chief executive of the government.

Among the most important factors involved in grafting new ethical values on to the military bureaucracy is time. The transformation of an organization into an institution takes time. The transformation is, among other things, a function of the adjustments that the organization makes over time to its own experiences. Out of these experiences and adjustments it constructs a history, which in turn greatly affects the manner in which its members perceive the world. It is elements of this history that have to be overcome if the introduction of new ethical values is to succeed. Moreover, a profession's history can be modified only when the experiences that result from its adoption and application of new values are such as to provide a positive experiential base for the development of a new history. *The new ethical code must have positive consequences for the bureaucracy in order to reduce the latter's resistance. A critical element in this development is the passage of sufficient time for that experience to accrue.* Thus, any attempt to reform the profession's values system will require a strategy that can deal with the institutional forces identified herein.

Enforcing the Ethical Code

Institutionalizing military ethics requires that the ethical code be taught throughout the profession and that certain institutional changes in support of the new values be brought about. A third element in the equation is enforcement. Enforcement involves the ability of the profession to reward those who observe the code and punish those who do not. At the same time, however, the military cannot spend all its time punishing ethical transgressions nor should it try to develop enforcement mechanisms that are overly legalistic and omit the judgment of the membership, substituting for it a sterile legalism. The profession must, therefore, involve the profession's membership in the process of judgment and levy admonitions in its name. The concept is like that of pre-medieval Germanic law in which membership in the community implied that one was willing to observe the laws and participate in their enforcement. When members of the community broke the law, their own actions placed them beyond the community, its law, and its protection. They became in the original sense of the term "outside the law" or, more commonly, "outlaws" from the community.[5] Superiors and peers were responsible for enforcement, and any admonition, punishment, or expulsion was ordered in the name of the community.

One of the more appropriate mechanisms for enforcing the profession's ethical code is the honour court. It is a mechanism designed to bring peer and community pressure to bear upon the transgressor short of activating the formal enforcement processes associated with the legal court system. *The honour court is not a substitute for the legal adjudication mechanisms already in place. Rather, it addresses offences to the honour, ethics, and professional spirit of the community without invoking the military court system.*

What is to be done with a soldier whose actions have discredited the profession but who has committed no legal violation of civil or military law?

As things now stand, the military may use the formal court system for which there may be scant legal grounds, or do nothing. A procedure that offers an alternative between these two extremes is needed. This alternative mechanism should ensure that the basis of its action be violations of the profession's code of ethics as observed within the community. In other professions, boards of professional review comprised of the profession's senior members hear cases in which no legal issues are involved, but which involve questions of professional ethics. The result is often a "finding" sometimes followed by a "reprimand" and a report filed with the profession as to the officer's status or "punishment." Extreme cases can result in expulsion or the suspension of the offender's license to practice for a specified period or even permanently. The honour court is the military equivalent of professional boards of review that are used by other professions.

The military honour court has a long history. It can be found in warrior societies of the eighth and ninth century Germanic tribes. It is also found, at least as it reflects the absence of legalisms and the employment of communal peer judgments, in the Mongol Empire of the fourteenth century. The Mongol military code, the *Yasak*, was enforced by boards of senior officers. The brotherhood of medieval knights reserved to themselves the right to judge the actions of their peers, even when such actions were not technical violations of civil law. More recent examples include the German Army. The reforms of von Scharnhorst in the 1820s established military honour courts throughout the German military establishment where they continued in use throughout the Second World War. The British Army had an equivalent system in which a board of regimental officers could be convened to deal with ethical violations short of legal sanctions. One punishment was expulsion from the regiment. The Japanese Army from 1860 to 1945 also had honour courts. The use of honour courts within the military profession is not a new idea, and has much to recommend it as a means for enforcing an ethical code.

In 1956, the Soviet Army created a system of honour courts called the Officer Comrade's Courts of Honour specifically designed to instill and enforce a sense of proper Socialist values and behaviour for the Soviet officer. It is ironic in a totalitarian society whose political control extended to all aspects of life that the Soviet regime should insist that the military be responsible for insuring its own proper behaviour and honour. The Soviet honour court investigated offences that "discredit the rank and reputation of the military profession, that violate military honour, and that are inconsistent with the Soviet view of civic morality." The court did not hear criminal offences, did not replace existing regulations or criminal codes, and did not serve as a means for dealing with violations of discipline. The court was convened to investigate an officer's "moral conduct" upon request of the commander under whose sanction the court had been established, and then only with the approval of the offender's immediate superiors. These honour courts were established at regimental and division levels.[6]

The manner in which the Soviet courts operated followed the tradition of honour courts in other countries. *These courts were not legal instruments of the state. They were instead instruments of social and peer pressure based on the proposition that the military ought to be the guardian of its own conduct.* The courts were comprised of officers elected at the level at which the court had jurisdiction. Separate courts existed for junior officers up to the rank of captain, with other courts for field grade officers and above. Hearings were conducted in public in order to facilitate peer pressure and to advertise the nature of the offence to the accused's peers. Attendance was regulated by rank; no one below the rank of the accused was permitted to attend. No permanent documentation was kept. The idea was to use professional peer pressure as an informal mechanism for bringing the ethical sense of the professional community to bear in judging offences against professional ethics that, although not technically illegal, discredited the profession.

The Soviet honour courts did not levy criminal penalties and had no ability to enforce the recommendations they make. The court is rather an institutional expression of the fact that not all violations of the profession's ethical code are violations of law or military regulations. Accordingly, the court does not levy criminal penalties. What it does is formally draft findings and recommendations, make them public, and send them on to the next higher authority or the offender's commanding officer who may take appropriate action. Here the offending soldier may be publicly reprimanded, passed over for promotion, or reduced in rank. The court can recommend that the soldier be transferred to the reserves, to another unit, sent for counselling, medical treatment in the case of alcohol or drug abuse, or separated from the profession entirely. The recommendations are made publicly by a board of officers and peers acting in judgment of the conduct of one of their comrades for the rest of the profession to witness.

The Soviet system of honour courts seemed to work to discourage improper behaviour through the threat of public disclosure and reprimand, and represents one way of institutionalizing and enforcing the profession's core ethic. The honour court offered the profession a pragmatic mechanism for interpreting and applying the code to its membership. The fact that the Soviets used it for more than thirty years might be good reason for the profession to examine it more closely. The fact that the honour court has been used in the West throughout history suggests that it ought to be seriously explored as a means for dealing with those members of the profession who are unable or unwilling to live up to the special obligations that constitute the ethical heart of the profession of arms.

Summary

To institutionalize a code of professional ethics, the military must reject any characterization of itself as equivalent to a mere occupation. If service in the military were only another job, there would be no need to levy upon it the burden of a special calling. But for the military to claim that it is a profession requires an ability to clearly state those precepts that comprise its core ethic. One way of doing this is to establish a formal code of professional ethics. It is nonsense to affirm that the military is a profession with a required sense of special obligation and then plead inability to formulate a code of values and actions that rests at the centre of this sense of obligation. Until the profession clarifies its own role, it will remain uncertain of its ethics, and until it develops a code of professional ethics for its members, it will be difficult to institutionalize a sense of its own ethical worth.

If the military is to institutionalize a code of ethics, it must also establish a course of study in ethics to which the membership must be exposed. Soldiers cannot reasonably be held responsible for what they ought to do unless they are told what ought to be done and why. If the military is required to remain separate from the larger society, novices must be informed of the special obligations required of them. There is a clear need to teach ethics to new recruits as well as to continually reinforce the soldier's professional ethical values through the use of appropriate rituals and symbols. The promulgation of a code of military ethics along the lines of the American Code of Conduct might be further supported by requiring every soldier to reaffirm his or her oath at least once a year in some appropriate ceremony, perhaps on the birthday of the respective services. *Symbolism and ritual are powerful psychological mechanisms for reinforcing and sustaining values, especially in the military where they are directly associated with the most potent of anthropological forces, life and death.*

If the military is to succeed at establishing and institutionalizing an ethical code, it must be prepared to reform the existing bureaucratic apparatus so as to weaken those institutional forces capable of resisting the new values. There is need to restructure the organizational apparatus so as to develop institutional mechanisms for promulgating, sustaining, and enforcing a code of professional ethics. Without these organizational reforms, the new values will not be easily adopted.

Finally, adequate enforcement mechanisms are crucial. A code of ethics is not a body of law and its enforcement mechanisms are not the equivalent of courts of law. Mechanisms for enforcing ethical codes should consist of formal procedures for bringing the ethical consensus of the profession to bear on the judgment of the action of the membership. To this end, the honour court as a historical means of doing this ought to be considered. To make the court work effectively, however, requires a sense of communal trust among the membership to enforce the code with judgment and justice. *If the profession cannot trust its own members to judge each other, to enforce ethical discipline, and its officers to act ethically in assessing the ethical quality of the actions of their peers, then no amount of legal guarantees or lawyers will be able to do so either.* The profession of arms, like other professions, must be the guardian of its own honour and integrity. In this sense, the military profession is starkly similar to the Germanic warrior tribe, the *communitas militaris* of the medieval knights, and the communal brotherhood of the monastery.

The responsibility for achieving these goals rests most clearly with the highest-ranking leaders of the profession, its guardians. Unless they are willing to provide the institutional support and the ethical example to move the profession in the direction of establishing a formal ethical code, little is likely to be achieved. The ability to set standards which will ennoble the soldier in striving to attain them represents one instance of the greatest qualities of human character. It is this quality that the guardians of the profession must bring to bear as they seek to establish an ethical code for the profession. It is the responsibility of the profession itself to profess high ethical standards by which the soldier must live, for it is only in living up to these high ethical standards that the sacrifice we require of the soldier can be justified.

Endnotes

1.   Derek C. Bok, "Can Ethics Be Taught," *Change* (October, 1976), 28.

2.   Stephen D. Clement and Donna B. Ayers, *A Matrix of Organizational Leadership Dimensions* (For Benjamin Harrison, IN: U.S. Army Administration Centre, 1976), 21.

3.   Ibid.

4.   Steven N. Brenner and Earl A. Molander, "Is the Ethics of Business Changing?," *Harvard Business Review* (January-February, 1977), 64.

5.   Fritz Kern, *Kingship and Law in the Middle Ages* (Oxford: Basil Blackwell, 1968), Part II.

6.   "Soviet Army Discipline," *Military Review* (November, 1975), 46.

CHAPTER 14

Final Thoughts

T he one constant that emerges from the long history of war is human nature. Technology, weaponry, strategy, and tactics all change from period to period, but the soldiers who employ them have not. The soldiers who fought at Marathon and Thermopylae in ancient Greece were no different from those who fought at Waterloo, the Somme, Bastogne, Khe Sanh, and Fallujah. Their hopes, fears, and desire to live were the same, as were their expectations of themselves, their peers, and their officers. In the 150,000 or so years that *homo sapiens* has walked this earth, human nature has not changed in any important way. Nor, indeed, have humans often foregone one of that nature's most common manifestations, war.

The technology of modern war raises questions about its devastating impact upon the human beings who fight it. That technology will increase the lethality of the battlefield seems certain. That technology, as had been hoped in the past, will prevent wars or remove the psychological forces that soldiers need to sustain themselves in the crucible of combat and the horror of collective destruction is unlikely. But technology will count for little if the soldiers behind the weapons lack the human qualities of courage, determination, skill, and composure in the heat of battle that soldiers armed with simpler weapons in earlier times possessed. The long prophesied "push-button battlefield" has yet to arrive, and the technology of war still requires brave soldiers to utilize it effectively. Technology has never been a substitute for courage and determination.

As we look to the battlefields of the future, it seems certain that the rate at which human lives will be consumed by the macabre dance of death will increase as will the number of those driven insane by the sheer horror of the occurrence. The lethality of weaponry will increase the level of stress that combat troops will be expected to bear, and the amount of time soldiers will be able to endure this stress before becoming psychologically numbed will shrink dramatically. The number of psychiatric casualties will rise exponentially. The rate of psychiatric casualties suffered by American troops in Iraq is already more than double that seen during the Vietnam War and one in every three soldiers today is suffering from some form of psychiatric condition as a result of exposure to combat. In future wars, the need for unit cohesion will increase or the social and psychological shield between the soldier and the battle environment will disappear and whole units will be unable to function. And still the battle must be joined.

Ethics is crucial to the ability of soldiers to bond to one another and to their units. There must be a strong faith among soldiers in battle that their peers and superiors will live up to their responsibilities if soldiers are to be expected to live up to theirs. In an environment of common horror, a belief in the values of the profession and one's fellow soldiers is critical to psychological survival. It is these beliefs that give meaning to life and death. Without a sense of ethics at the centre of the profession to define and enforce obligations and responsibilities, soldiers will find it very difficult to withstand the rigours of war.

War is a terrifying experience and at the same time a very human act. Perhaps the tendency toward war is sown in our genes. Certainly no society in history has been able to do without the soldier. While the work to eradicate war must proceed, it seems unlikely to succeed in the near future. But as long as war is a characteristic of human affairs, its excesses can only be limited if those who fight war bring to it a belief that it ought to be limited. This awareness and observance of military ethics affords the profession of arms great import beyond the ability to destroy, and only a sense of professional ethics can limit the human destruction by establishing a proper concert between means and ends in war. A soldier without ethics will be destroyed by the terrors of the battlefield. Without ethics, the humane quality so necessary to ethical human beings will die. *Only the ethics of the military profession, the primary practitioners of war, can place the destruction of war in a human and humane perspective and prohibit soldiers from inflicting violence beyond reason or purpose. Without professional ethics, the evil of war becomes even worse.*

As long as soldiers remain human there will be a need for professional ethics to sustain that humanity, to give meaning to actions that otherwise would be regarded as terrible, and to place limits upon the destructive capabilities of the soldier. This is especially true for the military establishments of democratic societies whose reason for being is the pursuit of ideals and values based in human worth, ideals that separate them from the naked power upon which non-democratic regimes are based. For the military to fail to develop, teach, and practice a code of ethics is to ignore the crucial obligation to its members to make them good in the exercise of a profession that directly confronts the face of evil. *If we do battle without ethics at the centre of the profession, the chances are great that we will destroy that which we seek to preserve by our efforts and by our sacrifice— the recognition of a common humanity shared by all human beings.*

In an age of increased complexity, specialization, and bureaucracy the propensity to limit the solider's judgment or confine it to narrow tunnels of experience and expertise or to try to do away with it altogether by subordinating it to prearranged rules or to direction by electronic communications on the battlefield raises the danger that the soldier will lose sight of the purpose and reasons for all the risk and sacrifice. Trapped in a web of systems of control, there is the real possibility that soldiers will willingly accede to an escape from freedom and permit their judgment to be suspended and replaced by the dictates of superiors. Under these circumstances, the soldier risks becoming expert in the application of violence, plying his or her trade in the service of the state with little regard for the ethical concerns that might be involved. *As the exercise of ethical judgment becomes more difficult, the temptation to abandon ethical judgment altogether may prove overwhelming.* If this is permitted to happen, the profession will bear witness to its own ethical demise and the cooperation with evil will not be far behind.

The profession of arms by its nature is concerned with special ethical responsibilities. A profession that deals with the lives and deaths of human beings on such a large scale carries with it heavy ethical burdens, more so in an age where whole societies may be destroyed in a single stroke. Only a sense of ethics, of right and wrong, of limit and proportion, and of special service can forestall the degeneration of a noble profession into a senseless purveyor of violence and suppression. It will avail a free society little if in the effort to protect its freedoms it allows the emergence within it of a military establishment whose actions are not governed by clear ethical perspectives in assessing ends and means. Over time such a force will become increasingly out of step with the values of the society it serves, becoming one more self-interested pressure group within it and, inevitably, a threat to it, if not by overt action then by poor example.

We cannot, therefore, permit the erosion of the way of the warrior by allowing the profession to be drawn away from its traditional norms and values to see them replaced by the corrosive values of managerialism and careerism. We cannot abide the transformation of the military from a profession into a mere occupation. To do so is to make one of the most ethically difficult acts, the taking of human life, into an ordinary job. This takes those who, in the service of something noble lived up to their oath of unlimited liability and gave their lives, and turns their sacrifice into a mockery of economics. *It is unacceptable that we should count the sacrifice of brave men and women in the service of ideals as merely the "cost of doing business."* But that is all we are left with if we permit the profession to become a mere occupation. If we are to stop the erosion of our ideals and protect the profession, if we are to steel the psyche of the soldier against the horrors of battle, if we are to give meaning to the sacrifice of those who have gone before, and if we are to expect those now in service to follow their example even unto death, we must constitute the profession along ethical lines.

This means that we must be the keepers of our own flame. It rests with us, the members of the profession, to bear the burden of sending our fellow citizens to their deaths and having to live with their ghosts. This terrible burden will become unbearable unless we are reasonably certain that what we did is right and that the ethical standards for knowing this are clearly present in our code of professional ethics. Without an ethical code we will fight on, but as hollow men and women uncertain of our own humanity.

Abbott, Andrew, "The Army and the Theory of Professions." in Lloyd Mathews (ed.), *The Future of the Army Profession.* New York: McGraw-Hill, 2002.

Aitken, R.I. "The Canadian Officer Corps: The Ethical Aspects of Professionalism." Canadian Forces Staff School (unpublished paper, April, 1979).

Acquinas, Thomas. *On Law, Morality, and Politics.* Edited by William P. Baumgarth and Richard J. Regan. Indianapolis, IN: Hackett Publishing Company, 2003.

Aristotle, *Nichomachean Ethics.* Translated by Terrence Irwin. Indianapolis, IN.: Hackett Publishing Company, 2000.

Baarda, Thomas A. *Military Ethics: The Dutch Approach.* Leiden: Martinus Nijhoff, 2006.

Bellene, Stephen. *Individual Responsibility In War.* Thesis, University Of Virginia, 1982.

Bentley, William. *Professional Ideology and the Profession of Arms in Canada.* Toronto: Canadian Institute of Strategic Studies, 2005.

Brennan, Joseph G. *Foundations of Moral Obligation.* Newport, RI.: Naval War College Press, 1992.

Buckingham, David. W. *The Warrior Ethos.* Newport, R.I.: Naval War College, 1999.

Caforio, Giuseppe. "The Military Profession: Theories of Change." *Armed Forces and Society*, vol. 15, no. 1, Fall, 1988.

Capstick, Mike. *Canada's Soldiers: Military Ethos and Canadian Values.* Ottawa: Land Personnel Concepts and Policy. 2005.

Challans, Tim. *Meditations on Moral Autonomy and the Military.* Thesis, Johns Hopkins University, 2001.

Challans, Timothy. *Awakening Warrior: The Revolution in the Ethics of Warfare.* Albany, NY: State University of New York Press, 2007.

Cook, Martin L. *The Moral Warrior: Ethics and Service in the U.S. Military.* Albany, NY: SUNY Press, 2004.

Cook, Martin. *Why Serve The State?: Moral Foundations of Military Leadership.* Colorado Springs, CO: U.S. Air Force Academy, 1994.

Cotton, Charles. "Canada's Professional Military: The Limits of Civilianization." *Armed Forces and Society.* March, 1978.

Bibliography

Cotton, Charles. "A Canadian Military Ethos." *Canadian Defence Quarterly*, 12, no. 3 (Winter, 1982/83).

Denton, Edgar. *Limits of Loyalty*. Waterloo, Ont. Wilfrid Laurier University Press, 1980.

Donovan, Aine. *Ethics for Military Leaders*. Needham, MA: Simon & Schuster, 1998.

Dyck, Arthur J. "Ethical Bases of the Military Profession." *Parameters* no. 1 (March, 1980), 39-46.

English, Alan. *Understanding Military Culture: A Canadian Perspective*. Montreal: McGill-Queen's Press, 2004.

English, John. *Lament For An Army: The Decline of Canadian Military Professionalism*. Concord, ON: Irwin, 1998.

Ethics in the Canadian Forces: Making Tough Choices. Toronto: Canadian Forces Leadership Institute. 2006.

Ethics in Practice: Proceedings of the Conference on Ethics in Canadian Defence. Ottawa: 1997.

Ficarrotta, Carl J. *The Leader's Imperative: Ethics, Integrity, and Responsibility*. West Lafayette, Ind.: Purdue University Press, 2001.

Frazier, Joseph J. *The Military Profession: What Happens When Values Collide*. Carlisle Barracks, PA: U.S. Army War College, 2006.

Gabriel, Richard A. "Legitimate Avenues of Military Protest in a Democratic Society." *Journal of Professional Military Ethics* (April, 1980), 2-9.

Gabriel, Richard A. *To Serve With Honor: A Treatise on Military Ethics and the Way of the Soldier*. Westport, CT: Greenwood Press, 1982.

Gabriel, Richard A. "Military Structures and Combat Cohesion: Lessons for the Canadian Regimental System." *Royal Canadian Military Institute Yearbook*. (Winter, 1979).

Hill, Thomas E. *Conscience and Authority*. Colorado Springs, CO: U.S. Air Force Academy, 1996.

Jensen, Arthur F. *Virtue Ethics and the Professional Formation of Army Officers*. Thesis, Catholic University of America, 1990.

Kant, Immanuel. *Grounding For The Metaphysics of Morals*. 3rd. Ed. Translated by James W. Ellington. Indianapolis, IN: Hackett Publishing Company, 1993.

Keijzer, Nico. *The Military Duty to Obey*. Amsterdam: Vrije Univeriteit, 1977.

Kolly, Timothy S. *Democracies and Dirty Wars: Hard Cases in Military Ethics*. Chicago, Ill.: McCormick Tribune Foundation, 2003.

Krupnick, Charles and Richard S. Workman. *Foundations of the Military Profession*. New York: American Heritage Custom Publishing, 1997.

Kultgen, John. *Ethics and Professionalism*. Philadelphia: University of Pennsylvania Press, 1988.

Lee, Min-Soo. *Military Virtues and Superior Orders*. Thesis, University of Tennessee, Knoxville, 1992.

Lucas, George R. and Paul Eugene Roush. *Ethics for Military Leaders*. Boston, MA: Pearson Custom Publishers, 2001.

Mattoon, Ernest Ray. *Morality and Military Necessity*. Thesis, University Of California at Berkeley, 1995.

Micwski, Edwin R. and Hubert Annen. *Military Ethics in Professional Military Education*. New York: Peter Lang, 2005.

Mileham, P.J.R. *Ethos: British Army Officership*. Camberley, Surrey: Strategic and Combat Studies Institute, 1996.

Mill, John Stuart. *Utilitarianism*. 2nd. Ed. Indianapolis, IN: Hackett Publishing Company, 2002.

Montor, Karel. *Ethics for the Junior Officer*. Annapolis, MD: Naval Institute Press, 2001.

Muskopf, James A. *Integrity Failures: A Strategic Leader Problem*. Carlisle Barracks, PA: U.S. Army War College, 2006.

Plato, *The Trial and Death of Socrates*. 3rd. Ed. Translated by G.M.A. Grube. Indianapolis, IN: Hackett Publishing Company, 2001.

Rawls, John. *Justice As Fairness*. Cambridge, MA: Harvard University Press, 2001.

Rubel, W. and George R. Lucas. *Case Studies in Military Ethics*. Boston, MA: Pearson Longman, 2005.

Sandin, Robert T. *The Rehabilitation of Virtue: Foundations of Moral Education*. New York: Praeger, 1992.

Schafer, Arthur. *The Buck Stops Here: Reflections on Moral Responsibility, Democratic Accountability, and Military Values*. Ottawa: The Commission, 1997.

Bibliography

Sommers, Christinia Hoff. "Teaching the Virtues." *The Public Interest*, no. 111 (Spring,1993), 3-13.

Toner, James H. "Teaching Military Ethics." *Military Review*, (May, 1993), 33-40.

Torrance, Iain R. and S.J.L. Roberts. *Ethics and the Military Community.* Camberely, Surrey: Strategic and Combat Studies Institute, 1998.

Tucker, David. *Teaching Military Values and Ethics.* Thesis, Seattle University, 1983.

Wakin, Malham M and Kenneth H. Wenker. *Military Ethics: Refections on Principles.* Washington, DC: National Defense University Press, 1987.

Wakin, Malham H. *War, Morality, and the Military Profession.* Boulder, CO: Westview Press, 1979.

Wenker, Kenneth H. *The Morality of Obedience to Military Authority.* Thesis, Ohio State University, 1978.

Wentz, Walter E. *The Foundation of a Soldier's Obligation.* Carlisle Barracks, PA: U.S. Army War College, 1996.

Wilson, James Q. *The Moral Sense.* New York: Three Press, 1993.

Woodgate, John R. *Analysis of the Canadian Defence Ethics Program.* Fort Leavenworth, KS: U.S. Army Command and General Staff College, 2004.

Zwygart, Ulrich F. *How Much Obedience Does an Officer Need?.* Fort Leavenworth,KS: Combat Studies Institute, 1993.

INDEX

Brenner, Steven **183, 201** *notes*

Britain 48, 51, 97

Brodsky, Major Steve **183** *notes*

Brown, Reginald 102, **105** *notes*

Bunting, Josiah 111, **133** *notes*

bureaucracy 28, 29, 55, 83, 93, 94, **96** *notes*, 112, 114, 115, 118, 121, 122, 129, 131, 191-196, 205

business corporation 4, 48, 50-53, 91

business techniques 50, 51, 54

Canada ix, 48, 51, 52, 107

career pressures 116

Casey, General 193

categorical imperative 38

character 9, 17-19, 35, 40, 59, 69, 111, 130, 135-142, 150, 157, 159, 162, 167, 187, 200

character development 135, 137, 162, 167

chemical weapons 17

choice 4, 15, 20-23, 25, 26, 32-34, 39, 57, 60, 62, 63, 66, 80, 90, 99, 104, 108, 111, 124, 126, 128, 131, 138, 139, 141, 150, 152, 168, 171, 188

Christian pacifist 165

circulation of elites 193

circumstances 5, 8, 9, 12, 14, 15, 16, 18, 19, 21, 23, 24, 25, 29-43, 45, 46, 48, 53, 55, 57-60, 62-65, 84-89, 91, 93, 107, 113, 117, 120, 121, 123, 124, 126, 129, 131, 132, 139, 141, 145, 147, 149, 153, 159, 165-174, 176, 180, 188, 189, 205

civil courts 128

civil disobedience 129

Civil War 48, 110, 148

civilian values 2, 98, 99, 100

clause of unlimited liability 52, 75, 110, 144

Clement, Stephen D. **42** *notes*, 189, **201** *notes*

Clinton, President 193, 194

Clotfelter, James 101, **105** *notes*

code of chivalry 110

Code of Conduct of the American Soldier 189

code of ethics 2, 16, 28, 29, 31, 34, 41, 42, 44, 48, 72, 93, 95, 103, 104, 116, 117, 143, 159-171, 174, 180, **183** *notes*, 191, 194, 197, 199, 200, 204

code of professional ethics 7, 34, 37, 72, 125, 127, 129, 135, 162, 164, 173-175, 182, 185, 186, 190, 192-195, 199, 200, 206

INDEX

INDEX

obedience 2, 4, 20, 21, 26, 31, 32, 77, 104, 107, 113, 114, 124, 127, 128, 140-143, 146, 147, 168, 171

obligations xi, 1, 2, 5, 7-10, 15, 16, 19-31, 33-35, 37-40, 42-44, 49, 52, 53, 64, 66, 69-74, 76, 79, 80, 84, 85, 87, 88, 98, 100, 103-105, 107, 108, 110, 112-115, 117, 118, 120, 121, 123-126, 128, 135, 136, 138-144, 146, 147, 150, 152-154, 161-166

obsequium 143

occupation 4, 44, 48, 71, 80, 89-91, 175, 185, 199, 205, 206

occupationalism 83, 89, 90, 96, 102

Officer Comade's Courts of Honour 197

officer as entrepreneur 54

officer corps 48, 52, **55** *notes*, 80, **81** *notes*, 92, 95, 120, 135, 161, 191

"only following orders" 14

Operation Rolling Thunder 61

Operation Desert Storm 60

"ought implies can" 10, 19, 138, 167

oughts 12-14

pacifist 21, 33, 165

patriotism 50, 97, 141, 145

peer support 194

people's army 102

perfect virtue 137, 138, 159

personal responsibility ix, 74

personnel management 91

Peters, B. Guy 101, **105** *notes*

plausible denial 121, 122

post-industrial age 89

post-industrial societies 8, 70-72

power 13, 21, 51, 55, 66, 89, 118, 144, 152, 158, 159, 162, 182, 204

praetorianism 31, 81

"pre-modern" organization 83

prescriptive ethics 14

President DeGaulle 48

President Nixon 110

prima facie duties 32, 33, 37

principle of universality 37, 170

prisoners of war 124, 190

profession vi, ix, xi, 1-5, 7-10, 14-16, 20, 22-31, 33-35, 37-39, 41-49, 52-55, 58, 60, 64-66, 69-73

INDEX

U.S. Naval Academy 27, 147

unit cohesion 49, 50, 52, 69, 70, 92, 93, 99, 158, 182, 203

United States 26, 47, 48, 51, 97, 101, 107, 148, 158, 172, 189

United States Marine Corps 158

universal precepts 31

Upton, Colonel Henry 97

urban combat 46

value-free technician 7, 183

Viet Cong 61

Vietnam xi, 29, 45, 47, 50, 59, 61, 70, 92, 93, 108, 121, 144, 148, 190, 203

Vietnam War 50, 61, 70, 93, 190, 203

virtue 2, 43, 58, 70, 114, 132, 135-140, 143, 144, 147, 150, 151, 153, 154, 156, 159, 168, 176

vocation 71, 90, 92, 152, 153

voluntary actions 19

Waffen SS 29

Wakin, Mal 167, **183** *notes*

war ii, xi, 5, 11, 15, 22, 24-26, 45-48, 50, 51, **55, 56** *notes*, 60-62, 64-67, 69, 70, 80, **81** *notes*, 84, 93, 97, 101, 108-111, 117, 118, 124, **132, 133** *notes*, 139, 148, 151, 155, 156, 169, 176, 182, 183, 187, 189, 190, 197, 203, 204

war of all against all 25

war stories 5, 187, 189

warrior ethos 93

Watada, Lieutenant 108, 109

Watergate Crisis 110

Waterloo 69, 203

way of the warrior 157, 159, 163, 205

ways of being 136

ways of doing 136

Weber, Max 29

Weigley, Russell F. 97, **105** *notes*

Weimar Republic 48

Wenker, Kenneth H. 160

West Point 48, 127, **133** *notes*, 142, 143, 186

Western legal tradition 128

Western military tradition 117

working ethics 14